D1348878

JUDGING SOCIAL SECURITY

JUDGING
SOCIAL SECURITY

*The Adjudication of Claims
for Benefit in Britain*

John.Baldwin, Nicholas Wikeley,
and Richard Young

CLARENDON PRESS · OXFORD
1992

Oxford University Press, Walton Street, Oxford OX2 6DP

Oxford New York Toronto
Delhi Bombay Calcutta Madras Karachi
Petaling Jaya Singapore Hong Kong Tokyo
Nairobi Dar es Salaam Cape Town
Melbourne Auckland

and associated companies in
Berlin Ibadan

Oxford is a trade mark of Oxford University Press

Published in the Untied States
by Oxford University Press, New York

British Library Cataloguing in Publication Data
Data available

Library of Congress Cataloging in Publication Data
Baldwin, John, 1945–
Judging social security: the adjudication of claims for benefit
in Britain/John Baldwin, Nicholas Wikeley, and Richard Young.
Includes bibliographical references and index.
1. Social security courts—Great Britain. 2. Judicial process—Great Britain.
I. Wikeley, Nicholas. II. Young, Richard. III. Title
KD3199.B35   1992   344.41'02'0269—dc20   [344.10420269]   91–47630
ISBN 0–19–825720–1

Typeset by BP Integraphics Ltd., Bath, Avon
Printed in Great Britain by
Bookcraft Ltd,
Midsomer Norton,
Avon

Acknowledgements

In conducting the research reported in this book, we have been indebted to a number of individuals and organizations. Mention should first be made of the Nuffield Foundation which generously funded the study, and we are particularly grateful to its Deputy Director, Patricia Thomas, for her assistance and advice throughout the period of the research.

His Honour Judge Byrt, QC, who was the President of Social Security Appeal Tribunals at the time of our study, offered us every encouragement as we set about our enquiry, and his seven Regional Chairmen, who were freely consulted on many occasions, similarly did much to ease the difficulties that confronted us in our visits to tribunals in their areas.

Officials within the Department of Social Security and Department of Employment provided us with much valuable advice about how we might go about the study, and many officers agreed to be interviewed by us or in other ways to participate in our enquiry. As we report in this book, these officers are as a rule obliged to work under intense pressure, and their readiness to spare time for us was always much appreciated. Tribunal chairmen, members, presenting officers, and appellants also found time to talk to us, despite the inconvenience that our interviews often created for them. We are indebted to all these individuals, and we must concede that, whatever might be the limitations of the study, these cannot fairly be blamed on the people from whom we sought assistance.

Our colleague, Professor John Miller, and Mr John Mesher of Sheffield University, very kindly undertook to read the original manuscript in its entirety, and their many insightful comments, observations, and criticisms have done much to improve the quality of the text. We would also like to thank Richard Hart, Law Editor at Oxford University Press, for his encouragement and support at all stages.

Timothy Boyce, Elizabeth Clark, Kerry Devlin, Polly Durstan, Helen Gillespie, Howard Hymanson, Justin Kopelowitz,

Timothy Moloney, and Wendy Sanders acted as research assistants for various periods, and the conscientious way in which they conducted observations and interviews is gratefully acknowledged.

Mrs Angela Baugh acted as secretary throughout the period of the study, and the cheerfulness with which she bore the many burdens we placed upon her was greatly appreciated.

Finally, we recognize our indebtedness to Kay, Clare, and Rosalind who, with good humour, have tolerated for over three years our obsession with social security adjudication.

We have tried to do justice in this book to the contributions that all these people have made in their differing ways. However, the views we express are ours alone and should not be taken as representing those of the Department of Social Security, the Department of Employment, the Office of the President of Social Security Appeal Tribunals (now the Independent Tribunal Service), or of any other persons to whom we are indebted.

Birmingham JOHN BALDWIN
September 1991 NICK WIKELEY
RICHARD YOUNG

Contents

1

Social Security Policy and Adjudication

T H E importance of social security in Britain can scarcely be over-stated. The budget devoted to it represents the largest single departmental programme, and accounts for nearly one-third of all public expenditure. Over four million households rely on income support and a similar number receive housing benefit. The state retirement pension is paid to approximately ten million people and child benefit is paid to nearly seven million families.[1] Each week the Government spends more than £1 billion on benefits and their administration.[2] Social security, in short, is big business.

Today social security benefits in Britain, as in most other developed countries, fall into two broad categories. The first consists of means-tested benefits designed to relieve poverty, the primary form being income support, a lineal descendant of the old Poor Law. Its previous incarnations were as national assistance (1948–66) and supplementary benefit (1966–88). The second category is comprised of benefits which are designed to meet particular risks or needs irrespective of income levels. This group includes the national insurance benefits, which aim to guarantee a minimum level of income over the life cycle by the collective spreading of risks. This is typified by unemployment benefit, entitlement to which requires a certain level of contributions to have been paid on past earnings.

The central concern of this book is the adjudication of claims for social security benefits. We examine both the initial determination of claims in the offices of the Department of Social Security

---

[1] HM Treasury (1991), p. 14.   [2] Ibid. 1–13. See also Otton (1984).

and the Department of Employment, and the subsequent handling of appeals by social security appeal tribunals. The findings are based on research funded by the Nuffield Foundation, the fieldwork for which was conducted throughout 1989 and in early 1990. Before we discuss the research that we undertook, it is worth placing the research in a wider context.

Although matters of entitlement to benefit are governed by a complex web of legal rules, these adjudication arrangements cannot be regarded as purely legal issues. When staff in local benefit offices claim that they mechanically apply the regulations to the claims before them, or when tribunal members state that their discretion has been eroded, or when claimants complain that their right of appeal is meaningless, each is recognizing, consciously or otherwise, the political constraints within which the social security system operates. Adjudication in the social security field inevitably reflects the concerns of government and policy makers since it is constrained by the legal framework which they establish. As Bradley (1985) has argued, 'the justice that needy claimants now receive can be no more sympathetic than the regulations allow' (p. 439). It would therefore be idle to pretend that one can analyse the workings of the social security adjudication system in an abstract fashion, without having regard to the wider social, economic, and political context within which it operates.

Social security policy

The modern benefit system is still recognizably based on the Beveridge Report of 1942. Beveridge's model for a new system of social security envisaged a central role for universal and comprehensive social insurance, building on the national insurance scheme established by the 1911 Liberal Government. His intention was that the new system of insurance benefits would guarantee a subsistence level of income to cover the major causes of income loss, through unemployment, sickness, and old age, whilst individuals would be encouraged to provide a higher standard of living for their families by voluntary savings. Beveridge hoped that such a scheme would satisfy the needs of most of the population, but accepted that a safety net of residual means-tested assistance would have to be available for those who failed to qualify under the contributory scheme. According to the Beveridge Plan, such a social security system could not be implemented in isolation; the government also had to be committed to introducing family allowances and a national health service, and to maintaining full employment. In this way, Beveridge, like subsequent policy makers, recognized the interrelationship between social security and other areas of government policy.

The subsequent history of the welfare state has demonstrated both the inherent flaws in Beveridge's scheme[3] and the extent to which successive administrations have been either unable or unwilling to fulfil his objectives. The most obvious weakness has been the consistent failure of governments to set the rates of national insurance benefits at levels such that recourse to means-tested assistance would be rendered unnecessary. The effect of this policy has been that increasing numbers of people, in particular those who are unemployed or retired, have been forced to rely upon the safety net of means-tested benefit. This trend became more pronounced in the 1980s, as the Thatcher administrations consistently eroded entitlement to the national insurance benefits, especially unemployment benefit.[4] The upshot has been that the means-tested assistance which Beveridge designed as a benefit of last resort has become transformed into the main source of income maintenance for millions of families. In 1948 about a million people received national assistance, whereas today four times as many receive income support. It is impossible to explain such dramatic changes in the social security landscape without some understanding of the post-war debate on the provision of welfare.[5]

---

[3] The Beveridge Plan assumed, for example, that women would be housewives, with the result that sex discrimination was built into the system. Moreover, its insistence on contributions as the means of entitlement to benefits excluded many people unable to build up a long contributions record, most notably disabled people and recent immigrants. See Wilson (1977) and Atkins and Hoggett (1984) at pp. 162–6.

[4] See Atkinson and Micklewright (1989) and Wikeley (1989).

[5] Underpinning this debate should be the search for an objective assessment of the extent and nature of poverty in contemporary Britain. Successive governments have, however, shown a marked lack of enthusiasm for such an exercise. See Townsend (1979), Mack and Lansley (1985), and Townsend and Gordon (1989).

(i) *Public or private provision?*

The first area of debate has concerned the proper balance to be struck between public and private provision. The emphasis of the Beveridge Plan on collective provision was attacked from the outset by theorists of the neo-liberal right as an unwarranted interference with the naturally efficient workings of the market.[6] The post-war consensus on welfare policy meant, however, that this critique found little political support until the mid-1970s, when the sharp rise in oil prices put Western economies under immense strain. This in turn led to doubts as to whether the developed nations could continue to sustain expenditure on social security on the same scale as before, resulting in a crisis of legitimacy for the welfare state.[7]

The election of Margaret Thatcher's first administration in 1979 is widely regarded as marking a fundamental break with the bipartisan commitment to the Beveridge model of the welfare state.[8] The Conservatives promised to 'roll back the frontiers of the state' and to restrain public expenditure. Yet social security spending rose throughout Mrs Thatcher's first term of office, principally because of the effects of a rigid monetarist policy on unemployment. Since then expenditure on benefits has continued to increase, and, in an attempt to control the rate of such increases in spending, the Government has concentrated on restructuring the welfare state. The ideology which was marshalled to justify this cost-cutting exercise was that fundamental changes were needed to rid people of the 'benefit culture' and to promote personal responsibility. This ideology found its fullest expression in the 'Fowler review' of the mid-1980s.[9] This resulted in a whittling away of the State Earnings-Related Pensions Scheme (SERPS), and a major campaign was launched (with the incentive of rebates from the national insurance fund) to encourage individuals to purchase their own private pensions.[10] Other changes were more immediate. One striking example was the abolition

[6]   See, for example, Hayek (1944).
[7]   See Mishra (1984) and Ringen (1987), ch. 3. The literature is reviewed by Moran (1988).
[8]   See further Silburn (1991).
[9]   See the Green Paper (DHSS, 1985*a*) and the White Paper (DHSS, 1985*b*).
[10]   Some £1,806 million of expenditure from the national insurance fund was met from general taxation, equivalent to about 1.5p on the basic rate of tax. House of Commons Committee of Public Accounts (1991), para. 33.

of single payments from the supplementary benefits scheme (which had provided one-off lump sum grants for special needs) and their replacement with repayable loans from the cash-limited social fund.[11] As a result, many claimants had to budget for major items out of their basic weekly benefit, or go without. In practice many have been driven to seek help from charities or less reputable sources, including illegal money-lenders.[12]

Whilst the attack on SERPS and the introduction of the social fund are indicative of a direct abdication of state responsibility, the Government has also divested itself of the administrative responsibility for the provision of social security in various ways. The most important example was the introduction of the housing benefits scheme in 1983, when liability for meeting most of the housing costs of supplementary benefit claimants was transferred to local authorities, resulting in widespread administrative chaos. The Government has similarly shifted on to employers the onus of administering short-term benefits for sickness and maternity. An attempt to do the same for family credit, as proposed in the 1985 Green Paper, failed in the face of an unholy alliance of business interests and the women's lobby. A less obvious manifestation of this zeal for privatizing the administration of social security can be seen in the extensive use of new postal claims forms. The introduction of these lengthy and detailed forms has emphasized that the responsibility for documenting a claim rests not with the Department but with claimants themselves.[13]

(ii) *Universal or selective benefits?*

The second area of debate on welfare provision has focused on the question of how far benefits should be universal rather than selective in nature. Historically the distinction between universal contributory insurance and selective means-tested assistance is said to have 'emerged within the context of the Edwardian obsession with the deserving and undeserving poor'.[14] In 1948 there were only three means-tested benefits:

---

[11] For extended discussion of the social fund arrangements, see Bolderson (1988), Drabble and Lynes (1989), Mullen (1989) and Mesher (1990).

[12] On this, see Howells (1990).

[13] See Walker (1987).

[14] Deacon and Bradshaw (1983) at p. 6.

the non-contributory pension, national assistance, and free school meals. Since then the range of means-tested benefits has been extended, most notably by the introduction of rent and rate rebates, and rent allowances (all now subsumed within housing benefit), and the creation of Family Income Supplement, a benefit for people in low-paid work with family responsibilities (now Family Credit). Whereas Labour governments have reluctantly accepted the increased use of means-testing as an unfortunate compromise dictated by the pressures of economic stringency, selectivity has been welcomed by Conservative governments as a means of preserving work incentives within a distinctly minimalist conception of social welfare.[15] Indeed, using the phraseology of Townsend (1979), the more prominent role of means-testing today marks a shift from minimum rights for the many to conditional welfare for the few.

Selective benefits offer a number of advantages for any government. In particular, the lower take-up rates for such benefits produce savings in public expenditure, and the perpetuation of the ideological distinction between the 'deserving' and 'undeserving' poor creates a political climate in which restrictions on the scope of such assistance can be implemented with minimal opposition. The incremental cuts in housing benefit since its introduction in 1983 are a recent illustration of this phenomenon. As an American sociologist has observed, 'programs targeted on the poor are far more vulnerable to political attack than programs with universal coverage and hence larger and more diverse constituencies'.[16]

The importance of 'targeting' resources effectively (an insidious semantic change from means-testing) to meet the needs of the poorest in society was a recurrent theme of the Fowler review.[17] The principal means to this end was the replacement of supplementary benefit by income support. The extra weekly additions to supplementary benefit, known as additional requirements, for recurring needs such as heating, special diets, and extra baths were abolished. Instead the basic level of income support was supplemented by a range of premiums, for example for families, pensioners, and disabled people. Simultaneously

---

[15] Digby (1989) at p. 69.   [16] Coughlin (1988) at p. 206.
[17] See, for example, DHSS (1985a), vol. 1 at p. 18.

the right to claim a single payment grant was replaced by the possibility of a loan (and sometimes a grant) from the discretionary social fund. The universal and contributory benefits were further marginalized, for, as Lister (1989) observes, the Fowler review explicitly presented means-tested benefits as the 'fulcrum of the system'. Child benefit was frozen, the death grant and the maternity grant were abolished, and the remaining national insurance benefits (especially industrial injuries benefits) were further eroded. The Fowler review thus represented a massive retreat from the ideals of Beveridge.[18]

(iii) *Rules or discretion?*

Once the emphasis has shifted from contributory or universal benefits to means-testing, the question arises as to the proper balance to be struck between regulation and discretion in the administration of benefits. On a preliminary note, it should be recognized that the distinction between 'rules' and 'discretion' is something of a false antithesis.[19] Many social security rules provide ample scope for the exercise of discretion, such as the provision which renders claimants who are dismissed for misconduct, or who leave their jobs without just cause, liable to be barred from unemployment benefit for up to twenty-six weeks.[20] The duration of the disqualification may be any period from one day to the full twenty-six weeks, the only guidance being that the authorities must take into account all the circumstances of the case and exercise their discretion in a judicial and sensible fashion.[21]

Conversely the law may appear to allow considerable scope for discretion in paying benefit when in fact little or none exists. For example, the apparent discretion under the pre-1980 single payments regime to meet 'exceptional needs' was curtailed in practice by a complex body of internal rules devised by the Supplementary Benefits Commission, the quango then responsible

---

[18] For critiques of the Fowler review, see in particular Child Poverty Action Group (1985), Walker (1986), Berthoud (1987), and Dilnot and Webb (1988). One of the first steps taken by the Major administration in 1990 was to unfreeze child benefit.

[19] See generally Davis (1969) and Galligan (1986).

[20] Social Security Act 1975, s. 20(1).

[21] *R(U) 8/74* and *R(U) 4/87*.

for administering benefit. In reality, therefore, rules often make provision for the exercise of discretion, whilst discretion becomes fettered by the development of rules. The important issue is the right balance to be struck between discretion and rules, and this is not something that can be determined in the abstract. As Cranston (1985) observes: 'it cannot be said a priori that rules are better than discretion in social welfare legislation: the crucial issue is to determine for the particular circumstances the right mix of rules and discretion' (p. 185).

Traditionally there has been a clear distinction within the social security system between national insurance benefits and means-tested national assistance. The former were 'earned' by claimants by virtue of their contributions records and were the subject of rights enshrined in primary and secondary legislation. Payment of the latter was dependent upon the discretion of the National Assistance Board. This dichotomy was increasingly questioned by writers on social policy in the 1950s and 1960s. Marshall (1950) developed the idea of a right to welfare as part of a new concept of social citizenship, and Reich (1964) argued that the citizen had a new property right in welfare benefits provided by the state.[22] Inspired by such writers, the emergent poverty lobby attacked the discretionary elements of welfare as a cloak for arbitrary and irrational decision making, which discriminated between the 'deserving' and the 'undeserving' poor. Rule-based entitlement, modelled on the arrangements for national insurance benefits, offered the prospect of clear and legally enforceable rights. Poverty campaigners also hoped that the notion of a right to welfare would avoid the stigma attached to means-tested assistance, and that this in turn would improve the take-up of benefits.

This campaign met with apparent success in eroding the formal distinction between contributory and means-tested benefits. The process started in 1966 when national assistance was replaced by supplementary benefit, entitlement to the basic rate of which was for the first time made a matter of statutory right. Yet this move away from discretion towards rules was only partial, and the basic scale rate of supplementary benefit could be enhanced by additional weekly amounts for extra needs and lump sum

[22] See also Reich (1965) and, for more recent analyses, Sampford and Galligan (1986) and Detmold (1989), ch. 10.

grants for one-off exceptional needs. The award of these amounts was dependent upon the discretion of individual officers, albeit exercised within a complicated code of internal instructions. The discretionary element within supplementary benefit was further reduced when the scheme underwent a major overhaul in 1980, following an internal structural review.[23] Entitlement to the weekly additions to the basic benefit rates and to the lump sum grants now depended upon criteria laid down in regulations rather than in internal codes.

It may be argued that the shift of emphasis in means-tested benefits from discretion to regulation had more to do with administrative convenience and the need to contain costs than with the poverty campaigners' aim of making the system fairer to claimants. Any form of means-testing necessarily involves a labour-intensive process of checking the eligibility of claimants. It is not surprising, therefore, that the drift from universal to means-tested benefits that has occurred has been accompanied by a phasing out of discretion. A regulated system is, at least in principle, simpler to administer than one based on discretion.[24] As far as cost cutting is concerned, the transition to rule-based entitlement provided the potential for tighter controls on supplementary benefit expenditure.[25] At every stage in this transition, a concern to contain costs has been evident. The 1980 changes, for example, were explicitly introduced on a nil-cost basis, which meant that any improvements in benefits had to be met by savings elsewhere in the system. This strategy worked for a year or two, but, as claimants and welfare rights workers became more familiar with the new system, so the numbers of additional requirements and single payments awarded began to rise again. This trend was exacerbated by the steep rise in unemployment in the recession of the early 1980s, and was particularly marked in respect of single payments. The number of

[23] DHSS (1978). For an analysis of the changes, see Beltram (1984).

[24] See, for example, the comments of the then Secretary of State for Social Services when announcing the 1980 overhaul of the system: 'The present discretionary system has become unmanageable. Unmanageable for claimants who do not understand it, unmanageable for the staff at my Department who cannot operate it; and unmanageable for the public who suspect it of abuse. Setting down the Supplementary Benefit scheme in regulations will give a firmer and clearer framework within which the staff can operate.' DHSS Press Release, 27 July 1980.

[25] See Jowell (1975), p. 19, and Mesher (1981).

awards fell from 1.2 million in 1978 to 0.8 million in 1981, but then rose again to almost three million in 1984.[26]

The Fowler review of the mid-1980s can also be seen as an exercise in containing the growth in public expenditure on social security. Thus additional requirements were abolished, and their loss was only partially compensated by the various premiums built into the new system of income support. Simultaneously, single payments, which had already been seriously eroded by a tightening up of the regulations in August 1986, were replaced by the cash-limited social fund. The 1985 White Paper maintained that the regulatory framework had not worked satisfactorily for the provision of help to meet special but intermittent needs: 'Experience has shown that it is often difficult and at times absurd to try to meet special needs—and one-off needs in particular—by matching personal circumstances to a set of legal criteria' (p. 7). The social fund, administered separately from income support, would, it was claimed, enable staff to respond to individual needs as they arose in a flexible manner, so that 'decisions will not be constrained by a very detailed framework of rules and precedents' (p. 37). Despite this rhetoric, the guidance actually issued to social fund officers in the voluminous *Social Fund Manual* could just as easily have been drafted as statutory regulations, and this lends credence to the view that the social fund was introduced primarily as a way of cutting costs rather than of improving the service to the claimant.[27]

There are other reasons for questioning whether the shift away from discretion has led to such an improvement. A perennial problem with a purely rights-based approach is that it depends for its success on the willingness or ability of individuals to assert their rights[28] (and assumes that the rights themselves are worth asserting). The introduction of a legal entitlement to a means-tested benefit, given that certain criteria are satisfied, has not been enough to erase the long history of stigmatization attached to the Poor Law and its successors. Indeed, in many ways a rule-based system may be subject to precisely the same criticisms as one founded on discretion. Goodin (1986) has demonstrated that the problems of arbitrary decisions, uncertainty, insecurity,

---

[26] DHSS (1985*a*), vol. 2 at p. 15.
[27] Drabble and Lynes (1989), p. 304 and Mesher (1990).
[28] See Beltram (1984), pp. 56 and 192.

and intrusiveness into claimants' private lives, all of which are potential features of a system based on discretion, may equally well exist under a regulatory scheme. He notes, for instance, that, 'insofar as the rules that replace discretion attempt to capture the same range of considerations, their operation may (at least from the client's point of view) be as unpredictable as the discretionary caseworker's' (p. 251).

In any case the protection afforded to claimants by a rule-based system can prove largely illusory since, if the Government wishes to restrict eligibility to social security benefits as a means of achieving wider social and economic objectives,[29] it can simply use its parliamentary majority to force through the desired legislative changes. Similarly, where decisions of the tribunals or courts concerned with social security have had the effect of expanding entitlement to benefit, the value of such decisions as precedents has often been nullified almost immediately by the laying of statutory instruments designed to close such unexpected 'loopholes'.[30] The utility of a rights-based system should not, therefore, be overestimated and it would be mistaken to regard welfare rights as ends in themselves.[31]

Finally, it is important that the the shift away from discretion should not be overstated. Even where there appears to be no discretion vested in those responsible for making the decision, questions of judgement are inevitable in the application of rules, as this can never be a mechanical or automatic process. Thus it is a question of judgement to determine whether a claimant has indeed been dismissed for 'misconduct' or has voluntarily left a job without 'just cause'. In exercising this judgement, adjudicators have considerable leeway both in interpreting the evidence and attaching significance to their findings of fact. Where the rules themselves are not settled, or do not obviously cater for the circumstances of a particular case, the adjudicator

[29] These objectives might include, for example, the enhancement of work incentives, the encouragement of 'realism' in wage negotiations, the enforcement of labour discipline or the control of public expenditure.

[30] The record from the issuing of a decision of the Commissioners to the laying of amending regulations is said to stand at just 72 hours: see Smith (1988) at p. 29.

[31] See Prosser (1981) at p. 170, who argues that welfare rights may be used as 'resources' to pressurize government. One illustration of this is the bringing of test cases against the Department of Social Security in order to arouse public awareness of specific problems. See on p. 31 for a good example.

will have greater room for manœuvre in deciding how best to develop the rules in order to determine the appeal.

To summarize, the 1980s witnessed a restructuring of the welfare state away from an ideal of universal benefits based on common citizenship to a residual notion of state welfare, based on means-tested benefits for the marginalized poor. The encouragement of private provision over collective insurance, the emphasis on selective as opposed to universal benefits, and the deployment of a regulatory approach as a means of capping social security spending, are all important features of this process. It should not be forgotten, however, that political pragmatism served to temper the ideological fervour of Thatcherism. On a number of occasions, the Government had to abandon or modify proposals which proved too controversial. We have already mentioned one of the few Government concessions on the Fowler review proposals, namely the withdrawal of the proposal that employers should administer family credit. Whereas this proposal was dropped following well-orchestrated lobbying by pressure groups, other changes have had to be rushed through to assuage more widespread public discontent. For example, the upper limit for capital resources disregarded for the purpose of housing benefit was swiftly raised from £6,000 to £8,000 following Conservative backbenchers' representations about the hardship caused to their pensioner constituents.[32]

Whilst the emphasis on selective benefits serves to marginalize claimants and to make their position the more vulnerable, there are clearly limits beyond which it is politically unacceptable to go, even if these limits shift with time. Much depends upon the character of the claimant population involved. For example, the Government has been far more successful in withdrawing benefit entitlement from under 18-year-olds than it has been in curtailing social security benefits for pensioners. The reappearance of young beggars on the streets of London and other cities in the aftermath of cuts in the benefits available to teenagers

---

[32] The subsequent increase in the limit to £16,000 with the introduction of the ill-fated community charge in England is also of importance. The community charge had been implemented a year earlier in Scotland without such a generous rebate system. The Government quickly caved in to pressure and, to put a stop to the accusations of unfair discrimination, introduced retrospective arrangements north of the border.

has aroused, if somewhat belatedly, public concern at the consequences of this policy.

The pursuit of the Government's social and economic objectives may therefore be constrained by the need to maintain support both within and outside Westminster. The tension between these competing objectives and constraints is manifested in the absence of any coherent approach to the reform of social security. The Social Security Act, like the Finance Act, has become an annual ritual in Parliament, comprising a number of piecemeal measures to achieve limited objectives. The frequent amendments to the statutory instruments governing the detailed benefit rules are likewise characterized both by their narrow objectives and by their obscure drafting. All too often further statutory amendments are necessary as inadequacies and inconsistencies in earlier legislation become evident. The way the benefit system is administered and claims for benefit adjudicated also reflects these tensions. It is to this issue that we now turn.

Social security adjudication

The prime focus of the research reported in this book is the process by which claims for social security benefits are determined. The first part of our investigation involved visits to forty-two of the local offices of the Department of Social Security where most claims for benefit are handled.[33] These offices are divided for operational purposes into two main types of work, covering respectively income support and contributory benefits. Until 1984 the staff deciding claims for contributory benefits were known as 'insurance officers' and were generally regarded as being more independent than their counterparts on the means-tested side, the 'benefit officers'. Today, both are known as adjudication officers. We also visited eleven offices of the Department of Employment where claims for unemployment benefit

---

[33] Some benefits are handled centrally. Child benefit is dealt with in Washington and family credit in Blackpool. Since April 1991 both local and central benefit offices have been run by the Benefits Agency, a freestanding executive body enjoying a degree of autonomy from the policy making branch of the Department. Similarly, the Employment Services Agency is now responsible for administering benefits within the Department of Employment.

are determined.[34] The offices were selected to provide a reasonably representative sample of offices throughout England, Scotland, and Wales, and a total of 158 adjudication officers were interviewed.[35]

Certain issues which arise in connection with claims for benefit are decided not by adjudication officers but by the Secretary of State, or rather by civil servants acting on his behalf. In most cases these civil servants are also adjudication officers.[36] This gives rise to the curious phenomenon of an individual acting in two conceptually distinct capacities. The implications of the legal status of adjudication officers and the way they actually make decisions on claims are explored in Chapter 2.

If a claimant appeals against a decision reached by an adjudication officer, the original determination is always reviewed as a matter of departmental practice by either the original officer or an officer of the same grade. Many appeals are resolved at this stage, with the initial determination being revised in the claimant's favour, and this process of internal review forms the subject of Chapter 3. Assuming that the earlier decision is not revised, the case is listed for a hearing before a social security appeal tribunal. Whilst the tribunals deal with only a tiny proportion of all benefit claims, they constitute none the less one of the most important forms of civil justice in the modern legal system. Apart from the magistrates' court, no other court or tribunal holds as many oral hearings.

The second part of the project involved attending tribunal hearings to observe the proceedings and to interview the participants. Our target was to observe fifty hearings in each of the seven tribunal regions in England, Wales, and Scotland, divided in

[34] The Department of Employment effectively acts as an agent for the Department of Social Security in this regard: see further Wikeley (1986a).

[35] At each Department of Social Security office visited, we interviewed an income support adjudication officer, a contributory benefit adjudication officer, and an income support appeals officer. To take account of the differing size of offices, we interviewed one other income support adjudication officer in the two busiest offices in each of the seven departmental regions. We also visited one office in each of the eleven Department of Employment regions in England, Scotland and Wales and interviewed two unemployment benefit adjudication officers at each location.

[36] See Partington (1991). Most adjudication officers are drawn from the civil service rank of executive officer. They are graded as Local Officer Is, or LOIs, to reflect the greater demands and stresses of the job compared to other types of executive officer work in the civil service.

each region between a large urban tribunal (25 cases), two medium sized tribunals (10 cases each), and one small rural tribunal (5 cases).[37] In the event, because of the vagaries of time-tabling hearings, we observed a total of 337 cases, split fairly evenly between the seven regions. Just over half of these hearings were at the busy urban tribunals, 39 per cent were at medium sized tribunals and about one-tenth were at the smallest centres: a pattern that is broadly reproduced on a national level. Chapter 4 outlines the key features of hearings before these tribunals, and in Chapters 5, 6, and 7, we consider the roles of the chairmen and members, the appellant, and the presenting officer.

The appeals process for deciding social security claims does not end with the hearing before a tribunal. Both the claimant and the adjudication officer have a right of appeal (with leave) to one of the Social Security Commissioners. This right of appeal exists only on points of law, not fact. The Commissioners deal with only about 1,000 appeals and 2,000 applications for leave to appeal a year, but have an important role in developing a body of case law binding on tribunals. There is then a further right of appeal (with leave) from the Commissioner's decision to the Court of Appeal and from there to the House of Lords. In practice very few social security cases enter these higher reaches of the traditional court structure. Indeed, the House of Lords has to date heard only two appeals concerning unemployment benefit in the last eighty years, and the first of these was not until 1983.[38] We did not extend the empirical work to the levels of appeal beyond the tribunal.

There are three principal exceptions to this overview of how claims for benefit are determined. First, there are special arrangements for the determination of the various medical issues which can arise in connection with certain benefits.[39] Secondly, as explained earlier, housing benefit is administered by local authorities rather than directly by the Department of Social Security. Thirdly, applications for payments from the social fund are administered outside the normal system of adjudication officers and

[37] Since our fieldwork was concluded, the number of tribunal regions has been reduced to six with the amalgamation of the two London regions.

[38] *Presho* v. *Insurance Officer* [1984] A.C. 310, H.L.

[39] See Sainsbury (1988), and see now Disability Living Allowance and Disability Working Allowance Act 1991.

tribunals. These matters did not fall within the scope of our research.

(i) *Initial decision making and bureaucratic justice*

There can be no doubting the critical importance of the first stage in the benefit adjudication process. In 1989, for example, on the income support side alone, adjudication officers dealt with over four million claims for benefit and over ten million reviews of benefit following changes in claimants' circumstances. In contrast, about 160,000 appeals are lodged with social security appeal tribunals each year, of which only about half actually proceed to a hearing. Thus in practice less than one per cent of all claims for benefit are challenged on appeal. The fact that so few claims proceed to an appeal makes it imperative that there be adequate internal checks on the quality of first tier decision making, since most claimants will not have their case considered outside the Department. Furthermore, the standards of first-tier adjudication also have implications for the work of the tribunals, for, as Bradley (1985) observes, 'the appeals system would break down unless most decisions were acceptable to the claimants most of the time' (p. 408).[40]

In his analysis highlighting the importance of initial decision making, Mashaw (1983) examined the process of dealing with claims for social security disability benefits in the United States. He developed a threefold taxonomy of possible justice models. The first, which he calls 'bureaucratic rationality', is aimed at implementing governmental objectives, is hierarchical in structure and is legitimized by its claims to accuracy and consistency. The second, 'professional treatment', has client satisfaction as its goal, is interpersonal in form and is predicated upon service to the client. The third, 'moral judgement', is designed to resolve conflicts, is independent in status, and has procedural fairness as its legitimating value. It should be stressed that these three models are ideal types: they are not mutually exclusive although where one model is emphasized, there is less scope for the operation of either of the others. Bureaucratic rationality (which

---

[40] In what sense decisions are regarded as 'acceptable' is another matter. A failure to appeal should certainly not be equated with an acceptance that a decision is correct.

works on the basis of processing information) is the principal model for administrative decision making; professional treatment (which involves the clinical application of knowledge) is more appropriate for decisions involving questions of health care, whilst the paradigm for the moral judgement model is the traditional court of law.

Using Mashaw's typology, the processing of benefit claims by adjudication officers at first instance is clearly an example of the model of bureaucratic rationality. Adjudication officers work within an organization which has its own distinct goals and which stresses the need for cost effectiveness. The Department of Social Security has, for example, placed increasing emphasis in recent years on various performance indicators, such as targets for the clearance of work. Cost effectiveness is a particularly important feature of the model of bureaucratic rationality, as Mashaw explains:

Given the democratically (legislatively) approved task—to pay disability benefits to eligible persons—the administrative goal in the ideal conception of bureaucratic rationality is to develop, at the least possible cost, a system for distinguishing between true and false claims. Adjudicating should be both accurate (the legislatively specified goal) and cost-effective. (p. 25)

The position which social security appeal tribunals seek to occupy is much more analogous to the moral judgment model, in that they stress their independence from the executive (as do the ordinary civil courts) and accord paramount importance to procedural fairness. Although tribunals have themselves become increasingly concerned about their own clearance rates, such matters are none the less regarded as less pressing at the appellate level. The appeals process has different goals, structures and legitimating values from those of initial decision making, and there is evidently scope for tensions to arise between the two levels of adjudication.

These differing perspectives of first- and second-tier decision makers render the extent to which tribunal decisions have an effect on determinations by adjudication officers at least questionable. Indeed, Mashaw's conclusion is that internal quality controls have far greater potential for maintaining and improving upon the quality of adjudication standards than an outside appeals system. So far as the performance of adjudication officers is concerned, internal monitoring is carried out on two main levels: first, by immediate superiors, and, secondly, by the Chief Adjudication Officer's staff. The effectiveness of these forms of quality control is discussed in Chapter 2, while the influence of tribunal decisions on adjudication officers is considered in Chapter 3.

(ii) *Tribunal decision making*

Social security appeal tribunals were created by merging national insurance local tribunals and supplementary benefit appeal tribunals as part of a general overhaul of adjudication arrangements in 1984. Until that date, the existence of separate appellate systems for national insurance and means-tested benefits reflected the same distinction which has traditionally pervaded the Department itself. Just as insurance officers were widely regarded as more independent than benefit officers, so the national insurance tribunals were seen as a superior form of tribunal to their poorer cousins. In the 1970s, a number of empirical studies were heavily critical both of the conduct of the proceedings and the quality of adjudication in supplementary benefit appeal tribunals.[41]

In the face of these criticisms, the Department of Health and Social Security commissioned Professor Kathleen Bell to carry out a major research project into the workings of supplementary benefit appeal tribunals.[42] The Bell report proved to be a landmark in the evolution of social security tribunals, elaborating as it did upon a number of the findings of earlier studies. She observed that supplementary benefit appeal tribunals were often unable to distinguish properly between matters of law and questions of policy and that there were wide variations in the way in which issues of discretion were determined. It was also apparent from Bell's research that the tribunals' capacity for independence was seriously compromised by their close administrative

---

[41] See in particular Herman (1972), Lewis (1973), Lister (1974), Adler and Bradley (1975), Frost and Howard (1977), and Fulbrook (1978).

[42] Bell's full report has never been published. A summary of her findings is contained in Bell (1975), and the cryptic style in which it is written has been a source of frustration to many. See, for instance, Bull (1981).

links with the Department. As part of a strategy for improving
the quality of adjudication in these tribunals, Bell made a series
of recommendations. Her most important recommendations
were for the appointment of more lawyers as chairmen[43] and
the provision of more training and guidance for the lay tribunal
members. Bell was also responsible for bringing about the introduction of a presidential system, which divided the country into
a number of regions, each with a full-time chairman at the head,
together with a national President. The introduction of a right
of appeal from supplementary benefit appeal tribunals was a
first step towards their integration with the national insurance
local tribunal appellate structure, Bell's final important structural
recommendation.

The Department of Health and Social Security phased in these
reforms during the late 1970s and the early 1980s, culminating
in the establishment of social security appeal tribunals in 1984.
These changes were widely welcomed, and appeared to meet
most if not all of the complaints levelled against the old supplementary benefit appeal tribunals. Reservations were expressed
about some of the details,[44] but this did not seriously detract
from the generally favourable reception given to the new
arrangements.

It is important to bear in mind that the first years of the social
security appeal tribunals were a period of great flux. In particular,
as Table 1 shows, there was a marked increase in the number
of single payments appeals heard by tribunals, which more than
doubled in the space of four years.

The immediate cause of the upsurge of single payments
appeals in 1986 was the Government's decision to make savings
in expenditure by restricting the eligibility rules for such grants.
This in turn prompted welfare rights groups to organize campaigns to encourage claimants to apply for single payments
before the rules were narrowed. The outcome was a dramatic
increase in the tribunals' workload within a short space of time.
As staffing levels within the tribunal system were not adjusted

---

[43] Most chairmen of supplementary benefit appeal tribunals were lay people,
whereas their counterparts in national insurance local tribunals were almost
invariably legally qualified.
[44] The abolition of the two panel system of wing members was, for example,
seen as potentially undermining the contribution of trade unionists to tribunals.

TABLE 1: *Workload of social security appeal tribunals 1985–9.*
Appeals (and references) heard and decided according to type of work

	1985	1986	1987	1988	1989
Supplementary benefit					
Single payments	45,684	54,184	96,375	103,383	8,321
Other payments	32,050	34,342	33,758	34,705	10,395
Income support	—	—	—	6,133	27,761
Unemployment benefit	21,058	21,218	20,528	22,402	16,966
All other benefits	15,758	16,094	14,646	17,262	20,080
TOTAL	114,550	125,838	165,307	183,885	83,523

Source: DSS, *Social Security Statistics*

with commensurate speed, the inevitable consequences were long delays before cases could be heard.[45] This was followed by an equally dramatic fall in the volume of appeals after the abolition of single payments in April 1988. By 1989 the new income support scheme was generating less than a quarter of the number of supplementary benefit appeals heard in 1988. It was against this background of a sharp fall off in hearings that our research took place.

The types of case we observed are set out in Table 2. The largest single category consisted of income support appeals, which accounted for two out of every five appeals. Unemployment benefit cases comprised almost one-quarter of the sample. Although our field work did not commence until nine months after the April 1988 changeover, there remained a substantial number of the old supplementary benefit appeals in the system, most of which concerned single payments. The way in which the tribunals dealt with these appeals provided a useful counterpoint to those under income support. It is clear that, whilst the main means-tested benefit continues to provide the bulk of the tribunals' workload, appeals in relation to unemployment benefit and the centrally determined benefits (such as family credit and child benefit) are beginning to form a more important part of the tribunals' work.

[45] These delays only began to be cleared by dint of the efforts by tribunal chairmen, members, and staff.

TABLE 2: *Breakdown of hearings observed by type of benefit*

	Number	Per cent
Supplementary benefit or single payment	45	13.4
Income support	138	40.9
Unemployment benefit	82	24.3
Family credit	22	6.5
Invalidity or sickness benefit	14	4.2
Child benefit	12	3.6
Mobility allowance	6	1.8
Other benefits	18	5.3
TOTAL	337	100.0

(iii) *Social security adjudication and the rule of law*

The implicit assumption underlying the calls for reform of the old supplementary benefit appeal tribunals was that a more court-like process of external review offered greater potential for advancing claimants' rights and might at least make first level decision-making more accountable. A clear parallel can be drawn with the debate in the 1960s and 1970s in which the poverty lobby had pressed for social security to be based more on regulation than on discretion. Cranston (1985) has identified the common thread between these movements:

The replacement of discretion by definite and public rules, and the trans-formation of social welfare tribunals, can be regarded as bringing social welfare administration more into line with conventional formulations of the rule of law. (p. 163)

The problem is that, since the British constitution is unwritten and that, in general, the courts remain wedded to the doctrine of the supremacy of Parliament,[46] the rule of law offers only an uncertain and contingent protection for the substantive and procedural rights of claimants. It cannot prevent the right of appeal to the reformed social security tribunals being withdrawn

[46] The doctrine is undergoing some modification, particularly in the economic sphere, as a result of the United Kingdom's membership of the European Community. See Collins (1990), ch. 1 for a discussion of the position, and *Factortame Ltd and others* v. *Secretary of State for Transport (No. 2)* [1991] 1 All E.R. 70.

in certain areas, or even abolished completely. For example, when housing benefit was introduced in 1983, the right of appeal formerly enjoyed by claimants on matters relating to their housing costs simply disappeared. In its place was established an unsatisfactory process of internal review within the local authority responsible for the initial decision.[47] The abolition of single payments and the exclusion of social fund decisions from the jurisdiction of the social security appeal tribunal provides another notable example. As we have seen, this development resulted in the tribunal's workload being more than halved at a stroke.

The exclusion of any form of independent review from entire categories of administrative decisions suggests that the Government's commitment to improving procedural justice for claimants is less than wholehearted. None the less, the funds expended over the last fifteen years in judicializing the tribunal system makes it unlikely that abolition of all rights of appeal would seriously be countenanced. Prosser (1977) has argued that the existence of an independent right of appeal fulfils an important function in providing legitimacy for the social security system as a whole. It coats the system with a veneer of procedural fairness which may serve to deflect attention from the severe and rigid nature of many of the benefit rules which lie beneath it. Any discontent with the application of those rules can be channelled into the politically innocuous avenue of an appeal. The process of appealing has the effect of individualizing claimants' grievances, and it reduces the likelihood of group action to draw attention to their plight. By the time the appeal is listed for a hearing, the initial sense of grievance of many claimants will have dissipated. Any anger which remains can only be directed at tribunal members who have no power to amend or suspend the application of the rules which form the focus of the complaint. Viewed from this perspective, the tribunals fulfil an ideological and practical role for governments anxious to insulate themselves from criticism.[48]

---

[47] See further Wikeley (1986*b*) and Ch. 8 of this book.

[48] In relation to the introduction of the social fund, Mesher (1990) notes that it was the strong desire of Government to clamp down on demand-led expenditure which made it 'worthwhile to lose the important legitimating effect of the existence of a right of appeal . . .' (p. 55).

It is clear that the new appellate structure can offer no real relief from the increasingly restrictive nature of substantive benefit rights. Its role is delimited by the regulations which must be applied. As Judge John Byrt QC, the first President of the Social Security Appeal Tribunals, himself recognized in 1989:

Social security law is essentially based upon a political statement, and, on the peripheral margin, it encapsulates in unmistakable form the philosophy and economic priorities of the day. . . . When the time is reached for the evaluation of the evidence and the application of the law, there can of course be no place for sympathy and the tribunal must apply its professionalism.[49]

In the light of these considerations, it was decided that a central feature of this research should be to examine the extent to which claimants appreciated the legal constraints under which tribunals worked and how this affected their perceptions of the system's fairness.

Any analysis of how claimants initiate and use the appeals process ought to cover the one recommendation in the Bell report which has never been implemented. She called for the development of broadly based and accessible advisory facilities, including the services of lawyers and an expansion of facilities for representation of claimants before tribunals. These proposals were echoed in subsequent reports by the Royal Commission on Legal Services (1979), the Lord Chancellor's Advisory Committee on Legal Aid, and the Council on Tribunals.[50] Fifteen years later, no such service exists. A hotchpotch of agencies, including Law Centres and Citizens Advice Bureaux, do their best to fill the gap, but the extent to which these agencies offer representation facilities inevitably depends to a large extent on the resources and priorities of each advice centre.[51] In practice only one-quarter of all claimants are represented before social security appeal tribunals.

During his period as President of the Social Security Appeal Tribunals, Judge Byrt sought to compensate for the paucity of representation facilities by developing an imaginative philoso-

---

[49] House of Commons Social Services Committee (1989), pp. 32 and 37.
[50] *33rd Legal Aid Annual Reports* (1982/3), *35th Legal Aid Annual Reports* (1984/5), and Council on Tribunals (1989).
[51] On this, see Baldwin (1989).

phy for tribunals, drawing on the Bell report and other sources.[52]
He believed that tribunals should take an active part in eliciting
the material facts and identifying the relevant law, rather than
relying on the points made by claimants or presenting officers.
This approach obviously contrasts with the adversarial traditions
of the ordinary courts. As Judge Byrt expressed it: 'The underlying principle is that the tribunal should in all things conduct
itself so as to enable the appellant to maximise his performance
and himself to feel that he has done so.'[53]

Given the concurrent shift towards legalism in substantive benefit law and the judicialization of the appeals structure, the idea
that claimants can play a central role in presenting their appeal
may be unrealistic. It is surely more likely that these wider developments will pull more strongly in the other direction, marginalizing claimants who have little understanding of the law and
legal processes.[54] There is already strong evidence from a study
by Genn and Genn (1989) that the inquisitorial role advocated
by Judge Byrt is no substitute for the wider availability of skilled
representation for claimants.[55] None the less, the development
of such a tribunal philosophy is ambitious, and Chapter 4
explores the extent to which social security appeal tribunals are
acting in accordance with it.

Conclusion

The last decade has seen the implementation of a series of
structural measures designed, on one analysis, to strengthen
the independence, professionalism, and quality of decision making of the first two tiers of the adjudication system. Very little
is known about how well the new system of adjudication officers
and tribunals is functioning, and the principal objective of the
research reported in this book has been to analyse how these
changes are working out in practice. In theory these reforms
can only be to the advantage of claimants seeking to establish
their entitlement to benefit. Yet throughout this period the sub-

---

[52] For example, Byrt's own experience in the field of adult education and the
Camden Working Men's College: see Fulbrook (1989).
[53] See further House of Commons Social Services Committee (1989) at p. 37.
[54] See in particular Harris (1983).
[55] For comment on the report by Genn and Genn, see Young (1990).

stantive rules of entitlement to the main social security benefits have been tightened and the right of appeal to an independent tribunal has been eroded.

Although our study is concerned with the system for determining social security claims and appeals, our findings have to be seen within the overall framework of analysis that we have outlined. Throughout this book will be seen examples of conflicting aims, tensions, and inconsistencies which can only be understood by reference to the wider political, economic, and social context. All governments, whatever their political hue, have to make decisions on how to allocate scarce resources. The way in which they allocate those resources is never a neutral activity but a highly politicized one, which can reveal much about policy making and the use of legal and administrative structures by governments.

2

Adjudication in Local Offices

As noted in Chapter 1, the initial decision on most claims for benefit is the responsibility of an adjudication officer, a civil servant employed by the Department of Social Security or the Department of Employment and appointed by the Secretary of State under the Social Security Act 1975. In the Department of Social Security, there are some 15,000 adjudication officers working in the network of 480 local offices, and a further 500 are based in the specialized sector adjudication offices of the Department of Employment. Each year adjudication officers make millions of decisions of crucial importance to claimants, many of whom are surviving on the margins of society. In the vast majority of cases, these determinations are final in the sense that the claimant does not seek to appeal against them. Despite the central importance of the adjudication officer's role, there has been surprisingly little research into this stage of decision making, and most attention has been focused on the appeal tribunals. We examine the reasons for this shortly, but first consider the evolution of the role of the adjudication officer and the legal framework within which they work.

From insurance officer to adjudication officer

The origins of the adjudication officer can be traced back to the creation of insurance officers prior to the First World War. The political nature of the forces which shaped the role of the insurance officer was evident from the outset. Under the National Insurance Act 1911, insurance officers were given the task of determining claims for benefit as part of the new unemployment insurance scheme. A government department, the Board of

Trade, assumed overall responsibility for administering the scheme, but it was not considered desirable that the Board itself should be responsible for particular decisions, not least because of the implications for ministerial accountability. In devising the notion of an insurance officer, the Government was able to avoid responsibility for the determination of individual claims.

This was achieved by making insurance officers independent statutory authorities. It was not a true independence, however, since the insurance officer remained a civil servant and thus took on a complex dual-role. In terms of the administration of claims, insurance officers were responsible to their superiors in the Board of Trade. In terms of the adjudication of claims, the same civil servants were independent decision makers, with the duty of determining claims on the basis of legislation laid down by Parliament.[1]

This position was maintained under the post-war Beveridge reforms, as a result of which there were insurance officers in both the Ministry of Labour (which had assumed control of unemployment insurance) and the new Ministry of National Insurance (for contributory benefits). As part of the revised scheme, a national post of Chief Insurance Officer was established in order to give insurance officers advice and guidance on the exercise of their statutory responsibilities. Although this post was invariably filled by a senior civil servant on secondment, the creation of the office was designed to reinforce the concept of the independence of the insurance officer from line-management control. Despite the real possibility of a conflict of interests, the role of the insurance officer in practice was regarded by most observers as a success. One former Chief National Insurance Commissioner concluded, for example, that they 'render excellent civil service to the cause of justice'.[2]

The quasi-judicial traditions of the insurance officer certainly

---

[1] Beveridge (1930) refers to this as an ingenious side-tracking of responsibility. As he observes: 'The ultimate responsibility for refusing benefit in individual cases—and of explaining in Parliament why it had been refused—was thus removed from the [Minister]' (p. 268). This means of deflecting responsibility is not unique to the social security field and analogies can be drawn with the position of an Inspector of Taxes in the Inland Revenue or an Immigration Officer at the Home Office.

[2] Micklethwait (1976) at p. 67. See also the acknowledgement by Mesher (1983) of their 'long history of independence and objectivity' (p. 135).

compared favourably to those prevalent in means-tested decision making. The main such benefit went through several guises, in the forms of unemployment assistance, national assistance and then supplementary benefit, before being transformed into income support in 1988. These benefits were administered respectively by the Unemployment Assistance Board, the National Assistance Board, and until 1980 the Supplementary Benefits Commission. Until that time, the insurance officer concept was quite alien to the means-tested benefit adjudication process. Claims were dealt with on an administrative basis by civil servants following internal guidelines, giving both the Board (or the Commission) and officials considerable scope for the exercise of discretion.[3]

There was no attempt to portray these staff as acting in any sense independently of the Board or the Commission: their task was to implement official policy in benefit administration. Put crudely, whereas the insurance officer owed his allegiance to the law, these civil servants were little more than agents of government. This sharp dichotomy began to be eroded with the shift in 1980 towards a more regulatory basis for supplementary benefit. The Supplementary Benefits Commission was abolished, and decisions on benefit entitlement were made by supplementary benefit officers in their own right on the basis of the legislation, which also provided a right of appeal to a Commissioner on a point of law. At the same time a Chief Supplementary Benefit Officer was established to provide guidance to these officers in the exercise of their functions. The aim was evidently to introduce into the regime for means-tested benefits the well-established model for national insurance adjudication.

This process was taken a step further by the Health and Social Services and Social Security Adjudication Act 1983, which gave the title of adjudication officer to both insurance officers and supplementary benefit officers. This was essentially a semantic change since the organizational divide between the adjudication of contributory benefits and of means-tested benefits was maintained within the Department of Health and Social Security. However, to emphasize the common nature of the tasks of all adjudication officers, the roles of the Chief Insurance Officer

---

[3] See Hill (1969).

and of the Chief Supplementary Benefit Officer were combined into a new post of Chief Adjudication Officer.[4] It was hoped that this innovation would inculcate in decision makers on the supplementary benefits side of the Department an independent approach, and that some of the insurance officer's traditions would 'rub off' on them.[5]

The status of the adjudication officer: a legal conundrum

The evolution of the first tier in social security decision making highlights the fundamentally ambivalent character of the role of adjudication officers. They are office holders appointed by the Secretary of State to perform statutory functions in deciding claims for benefit, yet they are required to do so independently of that Minister.[6] In accordance with these principles, adjudication officers are conventionally described as the first stage in the hierarchy of independent statutory authorities. Their function is quasi-judicial in that they are required to arrive at a decision on the merits of a claim, applying the statutory provisions as interpreted by the courts and the Commissioners. Once an adjudication officer has determined a claim, that decision cannot be overturned by a superior within the Department. It may only be changed on a review by an adjudication officer (on specified grounds) or on appeal by the claimant to a social security appeal tribunal.

Notwithstanding this apparently quasi-judicial task, adjudication officers remain civil servants and may well have departmental responsibilities, such as supervising or training junior staff, which make pressing demands on their time. The Chief

[4] The Chief Adjudication Officer is a senior civil servant or lawyer seconded from within the Department of Social Security.

[5] See Mesher (1983) who suggested that there was then no real awareness within the Department of the supplementary benefit officer playing an independent role. As he put it: 'it is far from clear that the implications of this status are appreciated down at the initial decision-making level or before tribunals' (p. 135).

[6] The intention that adjudication officers act independently of the Department is reflected in the structure of the Social Security Act 1975. In Part III of the Act, which deals with the determination of claims, there are quite distinct provisions dealing with adjudication by the Secretary of State on the one hand and by adjudication officers, tribunals, and Commissioners on the other.

Adjudication Officer has asserted that 'the adjudication function is quite separate from the receipt and preliminary investigation of claims which is for the Secretary of State'.[7] Whilst this is a correct statement of the legal position, it belies the reality of everyday life in a local office, where the same official may have to switch between the roles of adjudication officer and Secretary of State continually.[8] A more realistic view was taken by Bradley (1976) who described the insurance officer, the adjudication officer's immediate predecessor, as 'an adjudicating animal who is so well camouflaged within his natural habitat that he is easily mistaken for an administrative or executive official' (p. 115).

The courts have never been happy with the idea of civil servants exercising judicial functions, so their approach has been to depict the adjudication officer's job as being essentially administrative in nature. This approach was reaffirmed by the Court of Appeal in *Jones* v. *Department of Employment*.[9] A claimant sued the Department of Employment for the allegedly negligent decision of one of its adjudication officers. Initially the Department's sole defence to the claim was that the adjudication officer was exercising a judicial function, and was therefore immune from legal proceedings by virtue of the Crown Proceedings Act 1947 or at common law. The Court of Appeal, whilst dismissing the appeal on other grounds,[10] indicated its disagreement with this argument, preferring instead the reasoning of Diplock LJ on the position of the insurance officer in *R.* v. *Deputy Industrial Injuries Commissioner ex p. Moore*:

His duties are administrative only; he exercises no quasi-judicial functions, for there is, at this stage, no other person between whose contentions and those of the claimant he can adjudicate.[11]

---

[7] See affidavit evidence of the Chief Adjudication Officer in *R* v. *Secretary of State for Social Services ex p. CPAG* [1989] 1 All E.R. 1047, C.A. at p. 1050.

[8] As was recognized by Lord Justice Woolf in *R* v. *Secretary of State for Social Services ex p. CPAG*, ibid., observing that 'most adjudication officers do not spend all their time on adjudicating functions but are also engaged on other departmental duties including supervising other staff, paying benefits and interviewing and visiting claimants' (p. 1051).

[9] [1988] 2 W.L.R. 493, C.A.

[10] The Court held that the 1975 Social Security Act excludes any right to bring proceedings at common law, given the existence of the statutory appeals mechanism, and that in any event adjudication officers do not owe a common law duty of care to claimants in deciding claims. See further Swadling (1988).

[11] [1965] 1 Q.B. 456 at p. 486.

Whether the role be characterized as judicial or administrative, it may be argued that the chief safeguard of accurate and fair adjudication lies in the independent status of the adjudication officer, and that any compromise to that status will prejudice the standards of justice that claimants receive in the determination of their claims for benefit. Yet as we shall explore in this chapter, the notion that adjudication officers operate independently of departmental constraints and influences is viewed by adjudication officers themselves as decidedly problematic.

The legal regulation of the adjudication officer's work

On the face of it, the legal rules governing the disposal of benefit claims appear to place a heavy burden on both the Department of Social Security as a whole and its officers as individuals. The law requires that a claim for benefit be 'submitted forthwith' to an adjudication officer for determination, who shall then 'take it into consideration and, so far as practicable, dispose of it . . . within 14 days of its submission to him'.[12] In fact the interpretation accorded to these provisions by the Court of Appeal in *R. v. Secretary of State for Social Services ex p. CPAG*,[13] decided in 1988, means that the duty is somewhat less onerous than it might seem.

In that case, the applicants[14] were concerned about the long delays being experienced by many claimants in having their claims decided, especially those for single payments. These delays were caused by a number of factors, not least the shortage and high turnover of staff and the large volume of claims. The applicants' argument was that, properly interpreted, the statute obliged the Department to transmit a claim to an adjudication officer as soon as it had been received, and that the officer then had fourteen days in which to make a decision. This limit could, it was conceded, be exceeded for reasons peculiar to the particular claim, if, say, further enquiries needed to be made of a

---

[12] Social Security Act 1975, ss. 98(1) and 99(1).
[13] [1989] 1 All E.R. 1047, C.A. See Wikeley (1988).
[14] The Child Poverty Action Group, the National Association of Citizens Advice Bureaux, and two inner London boroughs.

claimant's former employer. The Court of Appeal, however, held that the relevant parts of the statute could not be construed in so rigid a fashion. The duty of the Secretary of State to refer a claim forthwith only arose when the claim itself was in a fit state for determination, so a claim lacking some essential information did not require immediate referral. Furthermore, the reasons for exceeding the fourteen-day time limit were not confined to matters relating specifically to the claim. They also included external factors, such as the number of staff available and the overall volume of claims. The Court also ruled that the Secretary of State was not under any open-ended obligation to appoint as many adjudication officers as were necessary to comply with the statutory timetable because the Act made it clear that appointments were subject to the consent of the Treasury.[15]

Decision making by adjudication officers is based entirely on the papers, that is, a person's claim form and any other relevant correspondence and documentary evidence. Claimants are not entitled to an oral hearing in front of the officer, a facility which must be offered by social fund officers if they are minded to turn down an application for assistance. Traditionally, adjudication officers (especially on the contributory benefits side) have avoided any face-to-face contact with individual claimants, although this may sometimes occur, as for example when they double up as section supervisors and see claimants at the public counter in that capacity.

In deciding a claim, adjudication officers have three options. Claims can be allowed, disallowed, or referred to an appeal tribunal for it to decide the case, the last option being rarely used. In the case of claims for unemployment benefit and the other contributory benefits, claimants must be notified of the decision in writing with the reasons for that decision, whereas in income support cases, in the absence of an express request by the claimant, there is no legal requirement to give reasons. This reflects the continuing dichotomy between the two sides of the Department, two differing traditions that continue to have a marked bearing upon the way that claims are determined.

---

[15] Although the application for judicial review was unsuccessful, the applicants none the less gained a considerable amount of publicity to highlight the problem of delays in local offices, and the Court of Appeal was itself at pains to stress the importance of expedition in dealing with benefit claims.

The 'construction' of claims for benefit

Adjudication officers are usually drawn from the executive officer level of the civil service hierarchy, but they rely heavily on more junior staff within the office to produce the materials which form the basis of the claim on which they must adjudicate. This preliminary activity by clerical staff has been the subject of two observational studies which highlight the importance of this stage of the decision making process.

In a detailed examination of a social security office in Northern Ireland, Howe (1985) observed that there was a large gap between departmental policy on administering welfare benefits and local office practice. Guide-lines required officials to provide every claimant with an explanation of entitlements under the social security scheme, to give courteous and prompt attention to all claimants, to ensure that the claimant was asked about any possible needs, and to give proper consideration to exceptional circumstances. The basis of local practice, however, was to place the onus on claimants to ask for an explanation of their entitlements and to draw attention to their needs and circumstances. The preoccupation of staff was to discourage claims, not to facilitate them. Interviews were accordingly perfunctory and concerned with recording the information presented by claimants. Little information or explanation was offered on what other benefits or allowances might be available. To put it bluntly, if claimants didn't ask for a benefit, they didn't get it.

Howe identified two main factors which explained this phenomenon. First, the time available to officers to conduct interviews with claimants was grossly inadequate because there were simply too many cases for them to handle satisfactorily. Consequently staff had to keep interviews as short and as uncomplicated as possible, aware that, if they imparted more information to claimants, it might trigger further queries or claims, thereby prolonging the interview and adding to the already massive workload within the office. Secondly, and providing a justification for the practice of discouraging claims, there was a set of beliefs and attitudes held by officers about claimants. Primary amongst these was the view that fraud and abuse were rife and that to provide more information about benefits was to invite an avalanche of unmeritorious claims. Officers saw abuse in very wide terms, encompassing those who claimed their entitlements to the full range of benefits in a persistent or assertive manner. Claimants who were passive and did not seek to claim all their legal entitlements were seen as 'deserving'. But most were classed as 'undeserving' since, as Howe puts it, 'the average claimant is not perceived as a pawn manipulated by an oppressive and complex system but as someone who actively and cunningly exploits it' (p. 64). Howe's analysis of the consequences of the practice fuelled by this belief was that:

> many claimants get less than they should under the law, whilst only some receive their full legal entitlement ... local practice effectively penalizes most claimants, either by creating circumstances in which it is unlikely that needs will be exposed or, if they are expressed, by not examining them in sufficient detail. (pp. 67–8)

A similar conclusion was drawn by Cooper (1985) in the only other study in the literature involving observation of local office procedures. As in Howe's study, Cooper focused on the administration of the supplementary benefit scheme, and noted that 'most of the time, the emphasis was on getting the work done at all, rather than doing it well' (p. 8). He detected practices which closely resembled those that Howe described. For example, visiting officers, making calls to homes to assess claims for single payments, faced the possibility that a more lengthy and general reassessment of the claimant's position might be necessary should the claimant, during the course of the visit, draw attention to changed circumstances or further needs. But, as Cooper observed:

> In practice, the rapidity of interviews, a reluctance to make general welfare enquiries and the adoption of a minimalist approach appeared to discourage requests that added to the workload and may, subconsciously, have been intended to do so. (p. 25)

The distinction between 'genuinely needy claimants' on the one hand and 'unscrupulous exploiters of the system' on the other was again noted by Cooper. He argued that 'the treatment of claimants could vary according to a judgement made about them by officers, on the basis of very little information and a brief acquaintance' (p. 51). Sympathetic treatment would be given to needy claimants making single payment claims whilst those regarded as unscrupulous would, with varying degrees of subtlety, be discouraged from pursuing their claims. Thus, it was apparent that moral evaluations of claimants could be just as important as fine legal distinctions or technical regulations in making decisons. Cooper concluded that the 1980 reform of supplementary benefit, which began the process of replacing a discretionary scheme with a regulated one, had not removed the possibility of personal judgement playing a major part in welfare administration.

These findings demonstrate the importance of studying the administration of welfare claims in terms of the interrelationships between the various stages. Adjudication officers can only make decisions on the claims which are put before them, yet many claims are strangled at birth by lower level staff. Such staff lack the training and experience of adjudication officers and any notion of their playing an independent or impartial role is alien to them. This means in practice that an inestimable number of claimants fail to get the money to which they are legally entitled. An assessment needs to be made as to how far the beliefs and personal judgements held by those within social security offices affect the process of adjudication itself. It should be noted that the single payment visiting officers whom Cooper observed were all adjudication officers and they often determined claims with reference to moral evaluations. Since Cooper completed his study, however, single payments have been abolished, the amount of visiting undertaken by adjudication officers has been curtailed and the new income support system is more tightly regulated than the supplementary benefit scheme it replaced. The scope for personal judgement in adjudication, although it has by no means been eliminated, appears to have been much reduced.

The relative paucity of literature on first-tier adjudication is due in part to the Department having been in the past protective to the point of secrecy about the work of its officers. It also stems from the fact that until recently researchers concentrated their attention on the more visible processes of adjudication before the appeal tribunals. Far fewer problems of access arose, and there was more of a tradition of researching the behaviour of courts and tribunals to draw upon.[16] Mashaw's influential book, *Bureaucratic Justice*, published in 1983, represents a landmark in reorientating interest towards administrative decision making.[17] The idea that criteria based on the concept of 'administrative justice' can be developed and used to evaluate the performance of bureaucracies is novel and has enormous potential, and the present study has been much influenced by this new direction in research.[18]

Not much, then, is known about the work that adjudication officers do, despite the fact that their decisions profoundly affect the quality of life of many thousands of families every day. Yet the little material that is available suggests that their performance leaves much to be desired. Although Cooper's (1985) study was not of adjudication *per se*, it provided many useful insights into first-tier decision making procedures. In particular he drew attention to the infrequency with which adjudication officers consulted the legal regulations upon which their decisions were supposedly grounded. As he put it:

getting the job done, with people waiting in the queue, or a pile of cases to be dealt with today, did not seem to include checking carefully on the regulations applying to each decision. Officers gave a clear impression of knowing, and consciously applying, the main clauses of the most frequently used regulations; but equally, their knowledge of the finer points of detail appeared very hazy. (p. 17)

The most important source of information about how adjudication officers perform is found in the Annual Reports of the Chief Adjudication Officer.[19] Adjudication officers have been criticized year after year by the Chief Adjudication Officer whose reports, based as they are on independent monitoring of samples of decisions, serve to indicate the shoddy standards of adjudi-

[16] It was not until the 1960s, with the development of a separate discipline of socio-legal studies, that the work of courts and tribunals attracted the critical attention of large numbers of legal and sociological researchers in this country.

[17] See Ch. 1 for discussion of Mashaw's ideas. In 1986 the Economic and Social Research Council launched a major review in this area: see further the valuable review of socio-legal research on administrative justice conducted by Rawlings (1986).

[18] For a rigorous and illuminating application of Mashaw's thesis in a British welfare context, see Sainsbury (1988).

[19] A useful analysis of these reports, together with a review of the first four years of the Office of the Chief Adjudication Officer, is contained in Sainsbury (1989).

cation that appear to obtain in most local offices. This unsatisfactory standard has improved little since the first Annual Report was published in 1985. In his report for 1989/1990, for instance, the Chief Adjudication Officer concluded that 'adjudication standards remain low on many benefits' (para. 1. 14) and 'appeals work in DSS local offices mostly deteriorated further this year, with many deficiencies in submissions to appeal tribunals' (para. 1. 13). The catalogue of failings identified in this report parallels those noted in earlier years: officers basing decisions on insufficient evidence, making wrong findings of fact, applying the law incorrectly or applying the incorrect law, and a general lack of knowledge of changing legal provisions.

The Chief Adjudication Officer has identified in successive Annual Reports those factors which he believes have the greatest bearing on improving these poor standards: simpler rules, less frequent change in regulations, better guidance, greater specialization, and better supervision. In the 1988/9 report, he included another factor—the creation of 'a climate in which good adjudication practices are actively pursued, measured and recognized by management at all levels' (para. 1. 14). He added that 'too often management regards adjudication as subsidiary to, or even standing in the way of, the main job of seeing that claimants get their benefit' (para. 1. 15). The following year he felt compelled to note that 'the Departments' progress on this has not been lit with great enthusiasm' (para. 1. 14).

So much for the views from above, what do adjudication officers themselves say about their situation? How do the officially prescribed concepts upon which the principles of adjudication are based get translated into the daily decision making of adjudication officers? Do they translate at all? It was with these questions in mind that we set out to talk to adjudication officers across the country.[20]

The research findings

We were largely given a free hand in interviewing adjudication officers. The interview schedule that was devised ranged widely

---

[20] An outline of the research sample is given in Ch. 1.

over many aspects of the work that adjudication officers do, including the main problems they experienced, the way they coped with the pressure of work, the level of supervision they received, the adequacy of their training, the practical meaning of independence, and the sources of guidance available to them.[21] Given the confidentiality surrounding particular claims, we were not able to ask about individual cases, although during the course of the interview, respondents frequently illustrated their answers with reference to specific cases with which they had dealt. Almost all of the respondents agreed to be tape recorded, so that a complete record of each interview was available. In our discussion we shall draw freely on the qualitative materials that were collected.[22]

It will come as no surprise to those with any familiarity with the vast socio-legal literature of recent years to learn that we found a marked discrepancy between the formal legal position of adjudication officers and the way that they said they carry out their work. This body of literature shows clearly how the behaviour of officials such as police officers, lawyers, court officers, and tribunal personnel very commonly deviates from the formal rules.[23] The same was true of the adjudication officers to whom we spoke in the course of this study.

Before we describe our findings in detail, a word should be said about our selection of material from the vast amount that we collected. There is no doubt that some adjudication officers, usually those working with fewest distractions in the smaller offices, find the task of adjudication easy and uncomplicated. They said to us that they could cope with their work with ease, found the guides, manuals, and regulations simple to operate, received good and sufficient training, and had adequate guidance and support within the office. For a majority, however, things are very different and most adjudication officers reported a lengthy catalogue of problems. It is known that standards of adjudication are generally poor, and we noted earlier how the

---

[21] The interviews also dealt with review and appeals work: see Ch. 3.

[22] Since we were able to tape record most of the interviews we conducted, the extracts from interviews that we reproduce in this and subsequent chapters are cited *verbatim*, modified slightly only where we seek to preserve the anonymity of individuals or cases.

[23] See the provocative discussion of this tradition in McBarnet (1978).

Chief Adjudication Officer has been outspoken in his criticisms of these standards in recent years. We shall therefore concentrate in this chapter on why this is so and what kind of difficulties adjudication officers face in their work. The material that we quote from interviews is intended to give a good idea of how the average adjudication officer goes about the business of adjudication.

Bureaucratic rationality or conveyor belt justice?

In the previous chapter, we discussed the competing models developed by Mashaw (1983) to provide a framework within which to analyse administrative systems. Mashaw contends that in particular contexts one of these models will tend to dominate. His study of the disability programme in the United States suggested that 'bureaucratic rationality' was the dominant model—that is, that accuracy and fairness were achieved through the application of detailed rules and guidelines combined with internal systems of management and control to achieve consistency. Mashaw himself argued that this model provides a better guarantee of justice for claimants than the 'moral judgement' model which emphasizes the value of external systems of review and appeal such as courts and tribunals provide. Ogus (1987), while welcoming the development of these ideas, has cautioned against naïvety in their application by pointing to the practical difficulties which impede the achievement of bureaucratic rationality by officials operating welfare systems. He writes:

With the current high levels of unemployment and public spending cuts, the DHSS staff have been stretched mercilessly in processing social security claims. To envisage greater information flows and 'cultural engineering' in such circumstances may not be realistic. (p. 315)

The difficulties of achieving accuracy when under pressure to process claims quickly was perhaps the strongest point to emerge from our own survey of adjudication officers. In the interviews, we pressed them about how they tried to balance speed and accuracy. How did they maintain reasonable standards of accuracy whilst processing claims with expedition? Only about a half replied that they gave priority to accuracy and more than a quarter immediately conceded that their priority was speed.

The interesting point here was that there were very marked variations between the different types of adjudication officer. While
less than 10 per cent of contributory benefit and unemployment
benefit officers indicated that speed was their priority, fully a
half of income support officers admitted that accuracy took
second place to speed. Table 3 shows these remarkable differences between types of adjudication officers.

TABLE 3: *Striking a balance between speed and accuracy according to type of work*

| | Department of Social Security | | | | Department of Employment | | | |
| | CB AOs | | IS AOs | | UB AOs | | Total | |
	No.	%	No.	%	No.	%	No.	%
Accuracy given priority	33	80.4	13	24.1	14	66.7	60	51.7
Accuracy and speed given equal priority	4	9.8	14	25.9	6	28.6	24	20.7
Speed given priority	4	9.8	27	50.0	1	4.7	32	27.6
	41	100.0	54	100.0	21	100.0	116	100.0

Note: Column headings refer to types of adjudication officer.
(CB = Contributory Benefit, IS = Income Support, UB = Unemployment Benefit)

We also asked adjudication officers how difficult it was for
them to balance these two main objectives. It was again significant that, whereas 39 per cent of contributory benefit officers
said they encountered no difficulty at all in balancing speed and
accuracy, only about 15 per cent of both unemployment benefit
and income support adjudication officers claimed the same thing.
Another notable difference was that, while a half of income support and unemployment benefit adjudication officers said they
had constant problems in striking the right balance, only a
quarter of contributory benefit adjudication officers said they
experienced such difficulties. It is not, in our view, that contributory benefit adjudication officers find it easier to strike the right
balance: rather it is that they have a different attitude to their
work. While they tend single-mindedly to plod through their
work and not to worry overmuch about striking a balance with

speed, income support and unemployment benefit adjudication
officers are more concerned with getting work done quickly but
are perturbed about sacrificing accuracy to achieve this. They
see their work as piling up on a relentless conveyor belt of cases.
The main difference between the two latter groups is that income
support officers are, it seems, far readier to make such sacrifices
to keep the conveyor belt moving than are unemployment benefit
officers.

We carried out various analyses to see whether these differences in approach could be explained by other factors, such as
the officers' length of service or the region in which the office
was located. None of the factors, however, produced any statistical differences, and we were forced to conclude that the key
variable in explaining these differences in attitude was simply
the type of work adjudication officers carried out. It will be
important, therefore, in the ensuing discussion to focus on the
context in which each category of adjudication officer works.
Consideration will be given first to adjudication officers working
in the Department of Social Security, and we shall pay particular
attention to income support officers, since they formed the
largest group of respondents and appeared to experience the
greatest problems in carrying out their work. We shall then examine the differing experience of contributory benefit adjudication
officers, before analysing the extent to which both these types
of adjudication officer adhere to the notion that they are
'independent' adjudicating authorities. Finally, the distinctive
arrangements for adjudication in the Department of Employment
will be discussed.

(i) *Income support adjudication officers: running to stand still*

Within the Department of Social Security, adjudication officers
are divided into two main groups—those who adjudicate on contributory benefits and those whose staple work is income support. In addition to acting as adjudication officers, where they
are applying the law, they take various decisions relating to
claims for benefit on behalf of the Secretary of State, where they
must follow departmental guidance. Adjudication officers are
integrated into the local social security office so that their independent status is not at all obvious to an observer. Contributory

benefit adjudication officers have traditionally had a private room away from the distractions of the open-plan office and have been able to concentrate on adjudication work. On the income support side, on the other hand, an adjudication officer (an LOI in departmental parlance) supervises a team of clerical officers (LOIIs), all grouped around adjoining desks. In practice, income support adjudication officers must field a constant stream of enquiries (and complaints) from claimants and staff alike throughout the day. This inevitably means that their ability to give considered attention to adjudication is seriously impeded.

It quickly became apparent as we interviewed staff that many income support adjudication officers regarded the process of adjudication as no more than checking or authorizing the work of the clerical staff working under them. This practice is encouraged by the existence of departmental targets requiring adjudication officers to carry out checks on the provisional assessments made by their clerical team. All new claims are meant to be checked, but officers are only required to check 10 per cent of those cases where the assessment is being reviewed for some reason, such as a change in the claimant's circumstances. Thus, the emphasis in an income support adjudication officer's job is on checking, not adjudication, and respondents tended to see accuracy in these terms. This means that accuracy is not an issue in 90 per cent of review cases, as is illustrated by the following quotes drawn from our interviews with officers working on income support:

All you're supposed to do is check all the brand new cases and 10 per cent of the others that involve changes. But of course I find that I can't cast more than a cursory eye over what is there. I suppose you can do a passable job, what's expected of you, but you can't do as good a job as you'd want. You can't give the quality in the time that you've got. Sometimes, you just sort of close your eyes and sign it, and that's all. (Interview 43, North East)

You can't aim for accuracy because you are only checking one in ten of the review cases. You really can't guarantee accuracy. The bottom line for us is that we have to pay benefit and occasionally you have to let accuracy slip to get the benefit paid. (Interview 60, North London)

All I do on claims is authorize them. I have clerical staff who look at the forms, check that they've been completed fully and do the assessment. As far as accuracy is concerned, I'm only required to do a 10 per cent check on existing cases. So there you are. (Interview 67, South London)

We have to do a 10 per cent check on all change of circumstance type things and a 100 per cent check on all new claims. The rest of the time, if you want to, you can just sign the stuff without really looking at it. A lot of the time you are just signing things and you don't even have time to check the mathematics. You are just a rubber stamp. That isn't the way it's supposed to be. It's not the way you are taught to do it at adjudication courses. But you just don't have any choice. You have to remember that this is not a busy office. The situation will be ten times worse in a busy inner city office. Some offices are literally months behind and the truth of it is that they are forced to chuck checking out of the window. You can't even do the 100 per cent check on new claims. You just have to sign the stuff and even then that's not enough. If we can't do it, what chance do they stand? (Interview 78, South West)

The truth of the matter is that most income support adjudication officers do very little adjudication: they simply authorize with their signature the decisions taken *de facto* by junior staff. The responsibility for taking decisions is in practice delegated to a level lower than is officially intended. The likelihood that mistakes will be made is great, especially since these low level clerical staff receive no special training in adjudication, in how to use the Adjudication Officers' Guide, or in how to interpret the complex regulations to be applied. It is not a case of adjudication officers seeking to shirk their responsibilities: they simply do not have the time to carry out more than a superficial check, and then it involves only a minority of all the claims passing through their sections. In this situation, to expect an adjudication officer to consider the claimant as a 'whole person'[24] and investigate all possible needs, circumstances and entitlements is quite unrealistic. Officers do not even have time properly to investigate and consider those specific claims that are put before them. As one respondent conceded:

Speed unfortunately comes first, the accuracy tends to come later. Sometimes you know that a mistake is going to happen and that you've got to try and pick it up at a later date because you just don't have

[24] The term derives from one of the objectives set out in the Department of Health and Social Security's operational strategy published in 1982 (DHSS, 1982). The idea is that claimants should not be treated in a compartmentalized manner but as people who could be helped in a range of ways through the social security scheme.

time to go thoroughly into the case. Most adjudication matters need a lot more evidence than we've got time to find out about with the pressure of the work here. But if we are going to meet our targets, and if people are actually going to get their money, then we've got to adjudicate wrongly on the basis of incomplete information. It's normally because people don't fill the forms in correctly. If we spot something, then perhaps we can clear it up. But you get so many boxes unticked, and we are supposed to clear claims within five working days. (Interview 73, South London)

Adjudication officers often raised in interview this question of targets set by superiors, by office managers, and by regional or head office. But revealingly none made reference to the statutory requirement of dealing with a claim within fourteen days 'so far as practicable', nor did they show any awareness of the stipulation that claims, once received by the local office, should be submitted to them 'forthwith' for determination. This demonstrates that the statutory yardsticks have minimal impact on the behaviour of adjudication officers when compared to the practical importance of departmental goals. The increasing importance attached to 'performance indicators' serves only to heighten pressure upon staff and to make the tension that exists between speed and accuracy the more acute. As one officer observed:

In these days, where there is a tremendous amount of pressure and work, certainly there is very much of an impetus on to achieve productivity to reach performance indicators and it's got to be to the detriment of decision making. With the pressures and importance of performance indicators now, where it's related to office performance and even linked, or will be in the long term, to merit pay, it's obviously not in the interests of quality decision making. (Interview 77, South West)

In his 1988/9 report, the Chief Adjudication Officer recommended the institution of a new performance indicator to measure the achievement of accuracy. The introduction of yet another target to be met by hard-pressed adjudication officers seems as likely to promote nervous breakdowns as accuracy in local offices. The stress of working in social security offices under such pressure should not be underestimated. The responsibility of interpreting legal regulations weighed heavily on many of the adjudication officers to whom we spoke, and they frequently pointed out that they held no legal qualification to do such work. One income support adjudication officer, when asked what qualities were needed for the job, replied:

A lot more than I've got! I think we need some basic legal training. I don't really think that people like me, educated up to O level standard, are really capable of interpreting the law because of the way it's written. When I first joined the Department, I didn't expect a clerical officer with seven O levels to be required to perform this kind of work. To be quite honest about it, I often have sleepless nights because of the responsibility. It can spoil your whole weekend if a difficult case drops on your desk on a Friday afternoon. It's too great a responsibility for someone like me. (Interview 57, Midlands)

It will only be by slowing down, taking more care, and investigating claims more thoroughly that decisions taken by adjudication officers involved in income support will become more accurate. If other factors remain constant, accuracy will inevitably continue to take second place to speed, and new performance indicators will not change that situation.

The need for speed is deeply entrenched within local office culture, however, and in an important sense it is right and proper that it should be so. Speed is vital to claimants and this is recognized by adjudication officers. As one officer from Wales remarked, 'With income support we are the last straw, the last place people can go. The necessity for speed is always there, so we accept it as second nature without saying that something is urgent. Everything is urgent.' People who are obliged to claim income support are in dire financial straits, frequently lacking the means even to buy food or keep a roof over their heads. A ponderous system providing 100 per cent accuracy has little merit in such circumstances. Naturally, claimants also want to receive their full entitlement so have an interest in accuracy too. Given the fact that the resources available to the system are limited, some compromise between speed and accuracy has to be struck, and a central question confronting policy makers, managers, and adjudication officers themselves is how a satisfactory compromise can best be achieved. What level of inaccuracy in decisions should be tolerated in order to maintain acceptable expedition?[25] With current levels of staffing on income support, the balance in our view is too heavily tilted in favour of haste. 'We still pay lip service to adjudication,' commented one exper-

---

[25] As Sainsbury (1989) notes, the Chief Adjudication Officer has shied away from specifying what he would consider to be an acceptable standard for adjudication, preferring to talk in rather vague descriptive terms such as 'unsatisfactory' or 'disappointing'.

ienced officer acidly, 'we are here basically to pay people benefit: if we are lucky we can get the assessment right at the same time.'

Two further factors exacerbate the problems that income support officers face in coping with their workloads: the demands of acting as supervisors and the limited supervision that they themselves receive from superiors. Adjudication officers dealing with income support were often scathing about having to combine the roles of adjudication officer and supervisor. They told us that in practice the duties of acting on behalf of the Secretary of State generally took precedence over the requirements of careful adjudication. The following quotes give a flavour of the stressful environment in which these officers work.

The problem with an adjudication officer on IS is that the majority of your time is spent purely as a checking officer and organising the staff that you've got. You need to take up work and ensure that it's done quickly and got out. You've got the responsibilities of supervisor and everything that entails for the five staff you've got: influx of work, checking on boxes, doing reports, and all the major and minor crises that come up as when somebody goes off sick or whatever. So I find that there's very little time to adjudicate properly. You hope that you are adjudicating correctly but, because of the time constraints on you, you are in some cases just sitting there, crossing your fingers and signing, and hoping it's right. We should have adjudication and supervision totally separate. They don't marry at all. (Interview 48, North East)

It is extremely difficult. You find that there are constant interruptions all day and you don't have the time to study the really difficult case, plus you lack somewhere quiet to study a case since we don't have an office of our own. Your staff have to ask you things because they have people in the reception area who want an immediate decision about whether they can get payment or not. In those circumstances you are almost obliged to make an instant decision, especially if it is late in the afternoon. The same applies to telephone calls. If people think they are entitled to money and they haven't got any, they are obviously in a desperate situation so you are almost forced again to give a hasty decision. (Interview 57, Midlands)

In making decisions, income support adjudication officers received little support from their superiors and considerably less than officers adjudicating on other benefits. While a quarter of contributory benefit and unemployment benefit adjudication officers said that their superiors had little or no involvement in their work, twice as many of officers working on income support made this claim. As a further illustration of their differing experiences, nearly four times as many contributory benefit officers as income support officers indicated that their superior was someone to whom they could turn on a day-to-day basis for advice and guidance. Income support officers much more often saw themselves as forced to be self-reliant.

Many of the superior officers (who hold the rank of higher executive officer, commonly referred to as an HEO) in income support have little or no experience of assessing claims under the new system, and they are in any event preoccupied with managerial responsibilities. In consequence, adjudication officers tend simply to call across the desk to a colleague for advice. To seek advice from an HEO, let alone from adjudication specialists based externally in the Regional Offices and within the Office of the Chief Adjudication Officer (OCAO), is too time consuming and the rewards are rarely seen as being worth the effort. No more than 7 per cent of respondents working on income support (compared to 14 per cent of unemployment benefit officers and 39 per cent of contributory benefit officers) had sought specialist advice or guidance from either the Regional Office or OCAO on more than a handful of occasions in the previous twelve months, and nearly 20 per cent had never approached these sources. Working under intense pressure, income support officers want speedy and definite answers to their queries, and they tend to be put off from seeking specialist assistance either because they have to submit their request in writing or through a superior or else because the advice they receive is often equivocal, no doubt out of respect for the independent status of adjudication officers. These points were commented on in forthright terms by the income support officers we interviewed, as can be seen from the following quotes:

It's become more difficult to go to the OCAO for further guidance. Before, if you wanted to do that, you sounded out your HEO first, and if they couldn't throw any light on it, it was a question of picking up the phone and asking for the appropriate person. Now we have to go through line management, and we have to do a submission on why we want the information, and they're not as accessible as they once were. I think that's a shame because it is a complicated subject and you can never know it all and time is a great factor. People want their money and they need it now. So to make things more difficult to get is not a good thing. You need the expert advice to be as accessible as possible. It's quite rare that I go to the Regional Office or OCAO nowadays because it's become such a rigmarole. (Interview 62, North London)

I don't think we always get the full support [from HEOs] that I would like, mainly because they are harassed and they find it time consuming. And often it comes back, 'Well, what do you think? You are the adjudication officer. Get on with it.' Beyond that, I've contacted Region more often than OCAO but often you don't get the degree of co-operation you would like there either. They don't come back to you quickly enough; they don't seem to realize the urgency of our job. I don't know whether they have experience of working in a local office, I think it would help if they did. Their general attitude is that we should know and why are we bothering them? (Interview 70, South London)

As you are probably aware, the higher up you get, the less familiar you become; you lose touch with adjudication. So they [HEOs] would probably admit that they're not as good at it as we are. They do a monthly check on a selection of cases, but there's not an awful lot of involvement really. (Interview 82, North West)

We have all these sources of advice or guidance but, I have to be perfectly honest, as LOIs we don't use these things all that often. Unless you have a really complicated case, the LOIs will just discuss things amongst themselves. (Interview 94, Scotland)

So it is rare for decisions to involve sources outside the immediate section of the office in which the adjudication officer works. Officers try to get by on their own or else enlist the assistance of those working alongside them. It seems that the pressure of work is such, at least for officers working on income support, that they do not even have time (or indeed, the inclination) to consult the law, and only exceptionally turn to their guide to this law—the Adjudication Officers' Guide (AOG). This guide, produced by OCAO, was often referred to as 'the Bible' during our visits to local offices, yet just 20 per cent of officers working on income support were unreservedly positive about the guide. The same proportion regarded the guide as of only very limited value.[26] In practice, a high premium is placed on experience, the instant help available from colleagues, and on getting the work done.

There are serious dangers in this situation. Relying on each

[26] This compares with around 45 per cent of contributory benefit and unemployment benefit adjudication officers who expressed great satisfaction with the Adjudication Officers' Guide, and 5 per cent of these two groups who saw the guide as of little or no value to them.

other's experience may simply perpetuate or exacerbate bad pat-
terns of decision making and cause erroneous interpretations
of the law to spread through the office. In addition, the failure
to refer to the standard reference works or manuals containing
law and guidance in relatively straightforward cases means that
adjudication officers remain unfamiliar with these sources and
are incapable of making effective use of them when they
encounter more complex matters.[27] Those officers who make
frequent use of the Adjudication Officers' Guide tend not to
read the law and guidance in tandem but rather to treat the
guidance as the final word on the subject. These points are
vividly illustrated by the following passages drawn from our
interview material:

We have the Blue Book which contains the law relating to IS but you
will find that the IS AO on a section very rarely has regard to that.
We mainly have regard to our AOG and our IS manuals which are
our lifeline in the running of our IS sections. (Interview 46, North East)

Basically you rely a lot on experience. You're only going to refer to
Codes and legislation if you come across an area you're unsure of,
or if there are facts about a particular case that you can't deal with
straight off. Although you are an adjudication officer when you authorize a claim, you're really dealing with it in terms of the Secretary of
State in the sense that it's all straightforward and done automatically,
more or less, unless there is something you need to check up on. (Interview 51, Midlands)

Because you don't do adjudication very often, it's difficult. I suppose
we are adjudicating all the time in theory, but we don't think of it
in those terms, we just sign and authorize the claims. Although that
strictly speaking involves a number of decisions, you do it automatically.
It's when you get a difficult case that you have to go to the books
and start looking things up, and because you don't do that very often,
you tend not to be very good at it. We don't look things up very often
because we don't have the time. (Interview 59, North London)

The evidence we collected indicates that, while the quality of
guidance provided by the Office of the Chief Adjudication Officer

---

[27] The Guide was also seen as too cumbersome to use on a routine basis.
It comes in several volumes, and officers commonly complained that it was
difficult to find the information that they required and that the index was poor
with subjects listed under obscure or confusing headings.

is not a major factor affecting the standards of accuracy achieved by adjudication officers, the lack of time to make effective use of that guidance is. Nor did it seem to us that a lack of good training in adjudication techniques lay behind the infrequency with which the law and the attendant guides were consulted. Rather, methods taught in training could not realistically be followed given the limited time that was available to officers to deal with each claim. One respondent summarized the dilemma well:

I'll try and look at the mechanics of everything, but, if you are too busy, you just can't do it. The actual adjudication work has to be done mainly out of your head and the only time you end up going to the law or the AOG is if you get something you don't know the answer to. When we go on our adjudication courses, we are told that with any decision we should start with the law, to go through all the Acts, which you just can't do in practice. The course itself is very good. But when you actually get back to the office, in practice you can't do what they are telling you to do which is to sit down and dissect every single aspect of the case and make a separate adjudication decision on each applicable amount or on each fact. (Interview 78, South West)

Income support adjudication officers develop ways of coping with their situation as best they can, and one of these mechanisms deserves mention—the belief that the vast majority of claims are straightforward and can be dealt with on the basis of experience alone. That this belief is mistaken was explicitly recognized by one respondent from the north-east who told us that in training 'away from the office, you could see that it's a very complicated subject, which tends not to come across in the office.' Or, as an officer based in north London put it, 'training opened your eyes to how much you don't know rather than how much you do: you realize that you're just scratching the surface, and you find that it's actually complicated and so involved'. However, the pressures within the system are so great that, if adjudication officers were to treat every claim put before them as a complex matter requiring careful attention, the system of adjudication would soon break down under the weight of all the accumulated cases on the sections. Adjudication officers are well aware of this, as was made clear in an internal review of appeals handling in the Department of Social Security: 'A widespread view pervading [local offices] was that it would be neither possible, nor cost effective, for AOs to treat every case at the first tier adjudication level as if it was a potential appeal' (DHSS, 1987, para. 3. 3).

It might be thought that the position of the income support officer has become much easier since the system of income support was introduced in 1988. This was intended to be simpler to understand and to operate than the supplementary benefit regime that it replaced. Two qualifications, however, need to be made about this. First, the removal of a broad band of discretion in decision making has meant that decisions will now tend to be unequivocally wrong or right. Whereas under supplementary benefit, a rough and ready view of a case could be taken by an adjudication officer with little risk that the decision might be impugned as clearly wrong, this is no longer the case. Once the facts have been established, the rules either require payment of benefit or forbid payment of benefit, with no margin for superficial consideration of claims to be disguised as a legitimate exercise of discretion. In this sense, income support poses more, not less, of a problem for adjudication officers. Secondly, the new system may have been designed to be straightforward, but the execution and development of that blueprint have undermined much of the intended simplicity.

As discussed in Chapter 1, welfare policy making is a highly political activity, and is subject to a number of conflicting pressures. The frequent and often rushed amendments to the income support regulations are testimony to this and to the difficulties that are faced by those responsible for designing a scheme which will not provoke a political outcry. There is inevitably an acute tension between having a system which is easy to operate and one that is fair in the sense of taking full account of a claimant's circumstances. Any simple scheme will be rough and ready, and a just scheme will require an elaborate and complex body of regulations to operate. Governments striving to strike an acceptable political balance face a difficult task. The implementation of a relatively straightforward system like income support is bound frequently to throw up gross and manifest injustices, and particularly so when the rates of benefit are less than generous. Adjudication officers find themselves at the sharp end and must daily bear the brunt of these underlying political tensions. They are the ones who are expected to cope with the tangle of new regulations, and, as the following quotes show, it is not easy for them:

One of the things which is difficult for AOs on the ground is the wealth of information which you have to absorb, and the amount of changes that occur. It's often very difficult to keep pace with it because you can have various circulars advising you of changes, and just trying to keep tabs on them all is extremely difficult. There's the Blue Volumes, there's the AOG, there's IS circulars, you get internal circulars and various other things. You tend to find that you see a case and you think, 'Oh, I know something about that somehow. Now where the hell did I see that?' (Interview 51, Midlands)

The Government tends to spring changes on us without much warning, for good political reasons in their eyes. Like the pensioners' enhanced premiums coming in at the end of October. Many pensioners were worse off when income support came in so the Government has bowed to political pressure and is paying extra premiums for those over seventy five from October. That creates a lot of extra work for us, and we haven't got any extra staff to do it. This Department knows it's a political football and we are prey to such decisions. (Interview 67, South London)

I sometimes feel that the AOG (especially the most recent one) hasn't been written as well as the previous guides. The English is so poor in the Guide, it has double meanings and you can interpret it in different ways. With the income support legislation being rushed through, the Guide was written as fast as they could, and I don't think the drafting is as good as it should be. (Interview 86, North West)

The number of changes we get is one of the major problems. The staff are just used to working one way and then we get something else coming through. That doesn't help. With income support, we were told that there were going to be less sort of changes now and that doesn't seem to be the case. (Interview 95, Scotland)

To summarize, income support adjudication officers tend not to regard adjudication as playing more than a minor or even a marginal part in their daily work. They conceive of themselves as performing largely administrative tasks, chiefly organizing, checking, and authorizing the work of their sections. They view the processing of most claims for benefit as 'straightforward', 'automatic', and 'routine'. Their priority is to 'get people paid', 'shift the work', 'meet targets'. Accuracy 'comes later' or is achieved 'through luck' or 'by chance'. They work largely 'out of their heads' with scant reference to the official channels and sources of advice and guidance, let alone the law which they are obliged to apply. These factors, in our view, go a long way to explaining the official figures on the poor standards that pertain in income support adjudication.

(ii) *Contributory benefit adjudication officers*

Officers adjudicating on contributory benefits are fully integrated into local Department of Social Security offices but their outlook is the product of a very different tradition from that which underpins the work of their colleagues working on income support. As we have noted, they say that their first priority is accuracy and that they are much less concerned with striking a balance with speed than their counterparts working on income support or unemployment benefit. Similarly they consider themselves to be better supported by their superiors within the office, and are certainly more prepared to seek guidance from the Regional Office and the Office of the Chief Adjudication Officer. The preoccupation with achieving accuracy can in part be attributed to the more highly developed legalistic tradition of these officers. Furthermore, the frenetic atmosphere which pervades income support work is largely absent here, because people claiming contributory benefits tend not to be in such dire financial straits as those seeking income support.

One might expect, then, to find that standards of accuracy in the adjudication of contributory benefits would be considerably higher than those achieved in income support. Yet this does not seem to be the case. The Chief Adjudication Officer concluded in his 1989/90 report that the 'overall standard of [contributory benefits] adjudication was variable, with an improvement in disablement benefit offset by a continuing unsatisfactory standard on short-term benefits' (para. 1. 9). Moreover, the statistics in that report indicate that there is no real difference between the two types of adjudication officer working in the Department of Social Security in this respect.[28] This suggests that those features which income support and contributory

[28] OCAO 'raises an adjudication comment sheet' if the process of adjudication on a decision is deemed to have been deficient in some way. The ratio of comment sheets to decisions provides a guide to adjudication standards in each area of work, albeit a rough and ready one: see Sainsbury (1989). The comment ratio for income support and contributory benefit work currently stand at 37 and 39 per cent respectively: Chief Adjudication Officer (1991), App. 1 and 6.

benefit adjudication officers have in common may be more significant than those which distinguish them.

Chief amongst these common characteristics seemed to be the difficulties of combining adjudication with supervisory duties, described as a major problem by over half the officers working on contributory benefits to whom we spoke. In addition, like their income support colleagues, they are constantly struggling to keep up with the frequent changes to the regulations they must apply. Contributory benefit officers evidently have an even more complex job than their counterparts in income support inasmuch as they must master and apply the law relating to a whole range of benefits.[29]

In some offices, we found that contributory benefit adjudication officers had been released from supervisory duties, and this seemed to have made the task of adjudication much simpler and relieved the pressure so as to make the attainment of accuracy more likely. Yet in other offices the trend was towards making adjudication officers responsible for supervising a contributory benefit section. The latter policy jeopardizes good adjudication practices, not least because of the threat that such integration presents to the independence of adjudication officers.

(iii) *The 'independence' of adjudication officers*

Both types of adjudication officer within the Department of Social Security regarded the notion of their independence as extremely problematic. Independence in this context involves the weighing-up of evidence and the application of the law in an objective and impartial manner. It means also that adjudication officers should resist the temptation to make moral judgements and should ignore any prejudicial comments that are made about particular claimants within the office. Finally, it means that officers should resist any departmental policies or pressures which conflict with their duty to apply the law as fairly and as accurately as possible.

When we asked staff to explain what independence meant to them in practice, we found a wide spectrum of views among

---

[29] These include disablement, invalidity, maternity, and sickness benefits as well as retirement and widows' pensions.

adjudication officers, varying from those who appeared to have a good understanding (even if tempered with some scepticism) to others to whom the idea seemed entirely foreign. In the light of what has already been said about differences between adjudication officers dealing with the different types of benefit, it is not perhaps surprising that the highest levels of confusion and misinterpretation were found among officers working on income support. An appreciation of the idea of independence and its importance in decision making seems to be most highly developed amongst those working in Department of Employment offices, as Table 4 shows.

TABLE 4: *Understanding of the meaning of 'independence' among adjudication officers in different departments*

	Department of Social Security				Department of Employment			
	CB AOs		IS AOs		UB AOs		Total	
	No.	%	No.	%	No.	%	No.	%
Full understanding of meaning of independence	14	34.1	10	18.5	17	81.0	41	35.3
Full understanding but sees it as compromised	11	26.9	9	16.7	0	0.0	20	17.2
Misinterpretation of meaning of independence	14	34.1	25	46.3	4	19.0	43	37.1
No idea that independence plays a part in the job	2	4.9	10	18.5	0	0.0	12	10.4
	41	100.0	54	100.0	21	100.0	116	100.0

Note: Column headings refer to types of adjudication officer.
(CB = Contributory Benefit, IS = Income Support, UB = Unemployment Benefit)

It is worth exploring the main sources of confusion and misinterpretation, and this discussion will focus on adjudication officers working within the Department of Social Security, as their experience of the problems of acting independently is quite distinct from those of unemployment benefit adjudication officers working for the Department of Employment.

The most common way that officers misinterpret the notion of independence is to assume that it just means that no one within the Department can change any of their decisions, though the precise nature of this confusion varies a great deal from officer to officer. The concept of independence at best rests uneasily in the minds of adjudication officers as they are engaged in their daily office routine. Officers inevitably find it difficult to preserve a lofty detachment from the rest of decision making in a local social security office, not least because they are physically part of that office and are very commonly working immediately alongside those from whom they are expected to be detached. Indeed, the very people from whom adjudication officers should be independent are those most ready and accessible when it comes to seeking advice or help with particular decisions. In most cases adjudication is just one part of the job, and is not seen as needing in any way to be differentiated from other duties or to be removed from the general hurly-burly of office life. This was particularly true of those income support adjudication officers who, working on sections, had especially onerous supervisory duties to perform. As Table 4 shows, about one in five of these officers had no idea what independence meant in relation to their job. Only just over one-third had a proper understanding of the concept. Some officers, indeed, appeared dumbfounded that we should be asking them questions about it at all.

As with similar organizations,[30] an office culture develops, and it seems to us quite unrealistic and artificial to expect adjudication officers to remain aloof from it. Yet the opinions, beliefs, and prejudices that are traded throughout the office contaminate the process of adjudication. 'You're indoctrinated in the Department's way of thinking' is how one officer in Scotland expressed it to us, and another in the Midlands described himself as 'part

[30] There has been a long tradition in sociological research which has examined the complex interrelationships between formal and informal structures in influencing the behaviour of individuals and groups. This work covers a variety of different groups from police officers to factory workers. See, for example, Skolnick (1966), Cole (1979), and McConville and Baldwin (1981).

and parcel of the group'. A third officer expressed her reservations more graphically:

I think it's possible to be independent to a degree, but basically I think it's a bit of a joke and I'm not surprised that claimants don't accept it. I am paid by the Department, work for the Department, my supervisor works for the Department. I am, to all intents and purposes, a DSS employee. (Interview 12, Contributory Benefit Adjudication Officer, Midlands)

Other officers, particularly those working on income support, conflated the concept of independence with that of discretion. This group argued that decision making is nowadays so hidebound by the legislation that any scope for independent decision making is in effect stifled. These officers understood independence to mean that they had the freedom to take whatever decision they thought proper, and that, if they so wished, their personal assessment of the claimant and the claim might be a legitimate consideration.

It must be said that adjudication officers rarely express the view that they are under pressure to toe a particular Departmental line in decision making:[31] rather it is that officers, insofar as they consider the question at all, think that the potential for independent decision making is heavily circumscribed by a combination of factors, prominent amongst which are constraints imposed by ever-tightening legal regulations, daily contacts with junior staff with whom they share an office, and by the insidious pressure of simply being an employee of the Department (feeling the Department, as one adjudication officer put it, 'sort of sitting on your shoulder'). Some impression of the reservations that adjudication officers themselves held is given by the following quotes from their interviews:

It's difficult to be independent because you are in the local office and people come to us and say they have got a case involving someone who causes a lot of trouble by always ringing up and complaining. I used to work out there anyway so a lot of the names I know. You'd have to ask claimants about how independent we can really be. Really you haven't got very much leeway in what you do. The law is laid down and you've got to apply it. There's not much discretion to be exercised. I'd be rather sceptical myself about all the talk about 'indepen-

[31] Only three of the adjudication officers to whom we spoke said that they felt they were put under overt pressure to act in particular ways.

dence', to be honest. When a claimant rings up and is told an adjudication officer is someone who works in the office but is independent, it must be very hard to believe. (Interview 17, Contributory Benefits Adjudication Officer, North London)

Independence often doesn't mean that much, though I do try not to be influenced by other people on the section. I just make sure that I only consider the evidence and apply the law. If you don't do it like that, you're not worth having there. But sometimes I feel that I am out of step. I get criticized a lot in the office for decisions I make. There's no way that sitting behind a desk here I am independent of other staff in the office. I come into contact with them every day of the week yet, supposedly to preserve my independence, I'm cut off from the claimants. That must in a lot of cases make it impossible for an AO to be unbiased. I was on the dole myself for nine months so I know what it's like not to get your giro or to have got troubles with the Department. You can do without someone who's supposedly independent being biased against you. (Interview 31, Contributory Benefits Adjudication Officer, North West)

I don't think independence means a great deal really. Obviously we've got the freedom to make decisions, but on the other hand we're bound by the regulations. So really we have no discretion. At one time there was a much greater amount of discretion. We weren't bound to the same extent by the rules and regulations that we are now. (Interview 47, Income Support Adjudication Officer, North East)

I don't see how you could be independent. There's the law, that's the law and you just apply it. There's no question of saying that you'll change the law on a particular day. The law is there and you apply it as it's written down. That's especially true nowadays where the law is very much black and white. There used to be more leeway for personal interpretation prior to income support. Nowadays in 99 per cent of cases, the law is cut and dried. People either qualify or they don't qualify, regardless of how I might feel about it. (Interview 86, Income Support Adjudication Officer, North West)

We have noted that adjudication officers are not under much pressure from senior levels in the Department to make decisions in a particular way. Indeed, one might wonder whether it might not be desirable for there to be greater involvement of more senior staff in routine decision making. It is much more common for there to be no real involvement of superiors in officers' decision making (reported by 37 per cent of those we interviewed) or else for there only to be involvement when an adjudication officer takes the initiative. Consultation with either the Regional Office or the Office of the Chief Adjudication Officer is likewise a very infrequent occurrence for most adjudication officers, with 79 per cent saying that these sources of guidance were rarely, if ever, used in their experience. Routine monitoring of a proportion of adjudication officers' decisions is, it is true, carried out by the local office. But again, if the perceptions of the adjudication officers themselves are to be believed, this rarely has any bearing on the way they approach their task. No more than 14 per cent told us that such monitoring was an important influence upon their decisions, whereas two-thirds said that it had no effect whatever.

In this sense, the independence of adjudication officers might be more appropriately viewed as an isolation from superiors. The natural consequence is that, in the average busy office, it is junior colleagues who fill the vacuum. One of the most revealing points to emerge from the interviews we conducted concerned the procedures that adjudication officers follow when they get stuck on cases. Most officers indicated that they would first of all consult others working in the same room. This seemed an almost universal response, almost too obvious to be worth discussing. Yet adjudication officers are not for the most part highly trained individuals.[32] The essence of the job for the majority is to pick it up as they go along, sitting with a more experienced colleague to learn the ropes, and then struggling on their own as best they can with the numerous guides, volumes of legislation and Commissioners' decisions. Being 'thrown in at the deep end' is how adjudication officers commonly characterized this process. In these circumstances, it is not surprising to find that two-thirds of the sample saw the experience they acquired working on the job as more important than the training they received. It is no surprise either to find that, in what is for many a disagreeable and stressful position, adjudication officers are thrown upon each other or upon the junior staff for

---

[32] It is apparent that the training that adjudication officers receive varies enormously from office to office and that the amount of training they are given depends upon a number of factors, such as the staffing levels in a particular office, pressure of work at a given time and the length of time officers have spent in the job. A third of respondents viewed the training they had received as inadequate, and it was disturbing to find that five officers claimed to have received no training whatsoever and that a further 25 (16 per cent) said they had only received tuition within their own office, perhaps supplemented by a self-instruction package.

mutual support and assistance rather than upon their superiors. It is in this way that a potent office culture develops, and the notion of 'independent decision making' comes to look decidedly precarious and unrealistic. For most, indeed, independence is a luxury that they cannot seriously entertain.

(iv) *Department of Employment adjudication officers*

The situation is very different amongst adjudication officers working in the Department of Employment. These officers had a much more highly developed sense of what independence means, and not one of them viewed the concept as compromised by influences within the Department.[33] Official recognition of the independent status of adjudication officers is also much more marked in the Department of Employment. Since 1987 adjudication has been carried out in sector adjudication offices, physically and organizationally separate from the unemployment benefit offices at which claimants are interviewed, lodge their claims for unemployment benefit, and sign on each fortnight. Unemployment benefit office staff are responsible for the initial collection of information on a claim and for transmitting it to the sector office for an adjudication officer to consider. Adjudication officers may then make further enquiries in writing or ask the local benefit office staff to interview the claimant in question to elicit more details before taking a decision.

Adjudication officers in the Department of Employment specialize in adjudication: they do not have any supervisory or other Secretary of State functions to perform. This means that they are not subject to the kinds of conflicting interests and pressures experienced by their counterparts in the Department of Social Security. It is true that many adjudication officers began their careers in local unemployment benefit offices, but they seem swiftly to adopt the different perspective needed for adjudication on leaving those offices, as the following quotes well illustrate:

You obviously need to be fair because, initially, all the AOs come from the UB office. When you work there, even if you are not actually

[33] Adjudication officers in the Department of Employment appeared to have received better training than their counterparts in the Department of Social Security and to be considerably more positive about the content of the training programme.

anti-claimant, there is a feeling, when you send a case to adjudication, that you want to see the claimant disallowed or disqualified. When you come on to adjudication, you have to separate that away totally and you've got to give a decision based solely on the evidence before you. If that means allowing someone who, from the tone of their replies, you don't particularly like, you've got to put that aside and simply apply the law. To my mind it's imperative that adjudication officers be independent. Although we are not truly independent in the sense that we are still employed by the Department and housed in offices of the Department of Employment, and we're all people who worked in UB offices, I think it's as much as anything something that you've got to set in your own mind. If you believe in your own mind that you are independent, then you give your decisions according to the Acts and regulations, based only on the facts that are before you. (Interview 109, Wales)

In practice our independence means that we've got to be objective in looking at what's presented to us. And we've got to remember as well that, although we're employed by the Department, we don't take the Department's side in giving decisions. We have learnt to view evidence provided by the local Unemployment Benefit Office quite critically really. All of us here have worked in UBOs and we know the sort of things that go on there, and we know the sorts of misleading information which is put out by them to claimants. We're not on the side of the UBO, but we should be fair to the claimants who claim benefit. (Interview 114, North West)

The physical separation of adjudication officers from local office administrative staff clearly encourages officers to think and act independently. Furthermore, unlike their counterparts in the Department of Social Security, adjudication officers working on unemployment benefit commonly perceive themselves as having to judge which of two opposing stories, the employer's or the employee's, should be believed. In determining entitlement to unemployment benefit, it is often crucial to decide whether the claimant left a previous job voluntarily. In doing so, the claimant's evidence must be weighed against any provided by the former employer. As one adjudication officer put it, 'you have to gain all the available information from both sides, claimants and employers, and make a fair decision on the information in front of you'. The distinctive nature of unemployment benefit adjudication appears, then, to reinforce a sense of playing an independent quasi-judicial role.

We have already noted that adjudication officers working in the Department of Employment attach great importance to accurate decison making. The great majority told us that accuracy must take precedence over speed. It is arguable, however, that this emphasis on accuracy serves merely to disguise the reality of everyday decision making by hard-pressed adjudication officers. Departmental targets concerning the amount of work that each officer is meant to clear each day are at odds with the expectation that a high standard of accuracy be achieved. One adjudication officer described these conflicting pressures:[34]

On the regional staffing scheme, which determines our staff complement, we are allowed sixteen minutes per case, which isn't realistic at all ... Sometimes it can take sixteen minutes to read through it, just to devise your first batch of questions. We are also charged with gathering all the evidence we possibly can, not to leave out any evidence that is necessary. That goes against speed as well. ... So yes, we do need more time. I don't like to give duff decisions. But it's a difficult balance and you have to trade off accuracy against speed all the time. (Interview 104, South London)

In addition to the sheer pressure of work, other factors militate against accurate decision making. Much of what has already been said about Department of Social Security adjudication officers applies with equal force to those working on unemployment benefit: they must cope with frequent changes to the relevant legislation; they receive little support from superiors; they rarely seek specialist guidance from Regional Office or the Office of the Chief Adjudication Officer, and they tend to rely heavily on their own or their colleagues' experience. We have already argued that this situation is not conducive to good adjudication. Indeed, despite the greater recognition of the independent role played by adjudication officers and their emphasis on accuracy, standards of adjudication within the Department of Employment are currently lower than those achieved by adjudication officers working in the Department of Social Security.[35]

---

[34] The 16 minute time allowance referred to by this officer has now been abandoned for one which varies according to the type of question involved.

[35] The latest figures available show that adjudication decisions on unemployment benefit attract a comment ratio of 53 per cent (see n. 28 above). It is worth noting that the central offices of the Department of Social Security, set up to specialize in particular benefits, generally achieve much higher standards of adjudication than the local offices (with the exception of family credit): see Chief Adjudication Officer (1991), para. 1. 11 and statistical tables set out in the appendices.

Conclusion

The adjudication of claims for benefit is not easy work, and it is unrealistic to expect that adjudication officers, who are after all relatively low grade civil servants, will be able readily to master the art. It is, in essence, a quasi-judicial function, which at the very least involves having a good understanding of how to weigh evidence, how to remain impartial in determining the merits of a claim, and how to apply the appropriate standard of proof. These are difficult concepts and to assume that relatively junior officials will be able to apply them is in our view quite fanciful. As we went around the country, visiting a range of different types of office and talking to adjudication officers of all levels of experience, it became evident to us that such a judicial approach was signally lacking. Many adjudication officers, it is true, are able to recite the standard textbook prescriptions taught to them on a course. But in many cases this reflects only a superficial understanding and is very different from a proper absorption of all that is meant by playing a judicial role.

While it may be unrealistic to expect adjudication officers to fulfil the lofty expectations set for them, it is surely not unreasonable to expect higher standards than those that seem presently to apply. Adjudication officers make decisions which have a great impact on the livelihood of millions of individuals who find themselves in serious financial difficulty. For them, decision making is not routine or administrative. But while it seems that for most adjudication officers good training programmes and reliable sources of advice and guidance are available, what is lacking is the time to make effective use of them. This, together with the complexity of the system they have to operate and the frequent legal changes that have to be mastered, make it difficult for staff to reach a competent standard of adjudication, particularly when they are having to combine this work with supervisory duties. All in all, it is a sorry picture. And it emerges not just from our own observations and impressions: it is also well supported by the detailed monitoring conducted by the Office of the Chief Adjudication Officer to which we have referred in this chapter.

Our findings suggest that an awareness of the need to think independently and a concern with accuracy are necessary but not sufficient pre-conditions of good adjudication. In practice the efforts of adjudication officers to adhere to the independent role that they are meant to play are systematically undermined by a variety of factors, not least of which is the failure of successive governments to fund the number of officers needed to adjudicate fairly and accurately on much obscurely drafted legislation rushed through Parliament at frequent intervals. Poor decision making is not the fault of the individuals concerned, most of whom doubtless strive to do their work competently. It is rather a natural consequence of a system which is under-resourced and in which hurried decisions are not merely tolerated but expected. High quality decision making will remain an elusive goal as long as the political will is lacking to make the system work properly. Yet those groups in society affected by this system tend to be those whose voices, if they are raised at all, can most easily be ignored.

3

Internal Reviews and Appeals Work in Local Offices

THE previous chapter has highlighted the central importance of initial decision making in the social security system. We turn now to consider the way in which appeals against those initial decisions are handled within the local offices of the Department of Social Security and Department of Employment. Less than one per cent of the decisions taken by adjudication officers each year are challenged through the appeals system. None the less, this percentage represents the considerable figure of some 160,000 appeals, and the system for processing appeals within local social security offices is worthy of study in its own right. Moreover, one of our basic working assumptions is that the different levels of the social security adjudication hierarchy should not be viewed in isolation but rather seen as intermeshing parts of a process. It is our contention that the system for handling appeals has a wider significance in that it affects the approach adopted by adjudication officers when making initial decisions.

In this chapter, we examine the procedures that are brought into play when a claimant challenges a decision to refuse benefit. So far as the legal position is concerned, there are two courses of action open. In the first place, the aggrieved claimant may ask the adjudication officer to reconsider the decision by way of a review.[1] Alternatively, or following an unsuccessful request for a review, the claimant may lodge an appeal against that decision. In principle, these are two very different processes. A review is carried out within the local office and usually by

[1] All developed social security schemes have such a review procedure, in which the relevant agency will reconsider the initial decision at the claimant's request. See Skoler and Zeitzer (1982).

the same adjudication officer who took the original decision, whereas an appeal is heard by a social security appeal tribunal. Moreover, a decision may only be reviewed if certain statutory conditions are satisfied. No such limitations apply to decisions which are appealed and these are considered entirely fresh by a tribunal. In practice, however, the lodging of an appeal may trigger a successful review. On the receipt of an appeal it is standard practice in both the Department of Social Security and the Department of Employment for an informal review to be carried out in order to establish whether the initial decision can still stand. This reconsideration may establish that there are grounds for a formal review of the determination. It is with reviews triggered by an appeal that this chapter is primarily concerned.

The rules governing formal reviews reflect the legal principle that adjudication officers are the first tier in the hierarchy of independent statutory authorities for social security decision making. In law, once an adjudication officer has reached a decision, it can only be altered either on a review or on an appeal. It cannot simply be reversed by senior management within the Department, and may only be changed by an adjudication officer if it was based on a mistake or ignorance as to some question of fact or of law, or if there has been a subsequent change in circumstances.[2]

A review offers three main advantages over an appeal proper. In the first place, reviews represent a simpler, speedier, and less formal means of reversing a decision. This is particularly valuable if the adjudication officer's original decision had clearly been based on some misunderstanding as to the facts or law at issue. Secondly, reviews can be sought at any time, even years after the event, whereas appeals generally have to be made within three months of the decision in question.[3] Thirdly, a review effectively offers the claimant two bites of the cherry. Even if the adjudication officer declines to revise the initial

---

[2] Social Security Act, 1975, s. 104. This provision also enables the adjudication officer to initiate a review regardless of whether there has been any request from the claimant.

[3] Social Security (Adjudication) Regulations 1986 (S.I. 1986, No. 2218), reg. 3 and Sched. 2.

decision, the claimant can still appeal to a tribunal against that refusal.[4]

It is worth emphasizing that, if a decision is only partially revised in the claimant's favour, the appeal must still go before a tribunal. The appeal only lapses if the revised decision is the same as if every ground of appeal had succeeded.[5] This is indicative of the lack of room for compromise within the system of social security adjudication. Either the appellant gets everything that is sought or the tribunal must hear the case. There is precious little scope for an adjudication officer to settle a case by agreeing with the claimant to 'split the difference' as often happens in the criminal process (as where, for example, the accused agrees to plead guilty to a lesser charge) and in other civil jurisdictions where, say, compensation is in issue (as happens in industrial tribunals).[6]

If the original decision is not fully revised in the claimant's favour, then an appeals submission is written for the use of the social security appeal tribunal.[7] This is sent to the tribunal and the claimant prior to the day of hearing. The submission is meant to summarize the facts of the case, to cover the grounds of appeal and to cite the relevant statutory provisions, Commissioners' decisions and any other applicable case law. It should also explain how the decision in issue was reached and draw attention to any new evidence or authority that has come to light in the meantime which may place a different complexion on the case.

We noted in Chapter 2 that little has been written about initial decision making on social security claims. Even less material is available on the reviews process. The only independent study carried out in this country was undertaken in 1971 by Coleman, who monitored the handling of appeals in local offices over a

---

[4] There may none the less be compelling reasons to seek leave to appeal out of time rather than ask for a review: see Rowland (1991) at pp. 185–6.

[5] Social Security Act 1975, s. 104(3B).

[6] See the discussion on this point by Mashaw (1983) at p. 94.

[7] The submission is sent with its supporting documents to the Office of the President of the Social Security Appeal Tribunals (OPSSAT) where the case is listed for hearing. Copies of the submission and documents are prepared at the appropriate OPSSAT Regional Office and distributed to the claimant, the tribunal members and the presenting officer from the Department. The notification of the hearing and the appropriate documents must be sent to all parties at least ten days before the scheduled hearing date: Social Security (Adjudication) Regulations 1986, reg. 4(2).

twelve-month period. He found that about one-third of all appeals lodged were resolved, not by a quasi-judicial hearing before an appeal tribunal, but by the administrative pre-hearing process. He also discovered that almost twice as many of the revised decisions were altered administratively as were overturned by a tribunal. In other words, twice as many claimants won their cases at the internal review stage as succeeded at a formal appeal hearing. Coleman concluded that:

From the point of view of the citizen who is aggrieved by a decision of a public authority, the administrative processing of his complaint may be as important as any actual hearing before a quasi-judicial body . . . the administrative process itself, and its problems, both require and are worthy of greater attention than they traditionally receive. (pp. 13–14)

This viewpoint has gained some recognition over the twenty years since the publication of Coleman's findings. Today the Chief Adjudication Officer monitors appeals processing on a routine basis and the Department itself publishes statistics on the matter. Departmental figures for 1989 show that 140,865 appeals were disposed of in that year, of which 25 per cent were superseded due to an adjudication officer revising the original decision. A further 14 per cent were withdrawn by appellants whilst 19 per cent were decided in favour of the appellant by the social security appeal tribunal, and 40 per cent were dismissed at the tribunal hearing.[8]

Thus more than one-third of all appeals lodged with the tribunal never reach the hearing stage, and more appellants win their appeals at the administrative stage than do so at a tribunal hearing. The combination of a significant rate of decisions being superseded and a low overall rate of appeals reinforces the point that it is imperative that adjudication within local offices be effectively scrutinized. One income support appeals officer put the point forcefully in interview:

If you look at the figures and find that 20 per cent of cases are superseded, in my opinion that shows that those decisions were mostly wrong, and it makes you wonder how many people who don't appeal have been the victims of incorrect decisions. There are many times the

---

[8] DSS (1991), Table H6. 01. The remaining 2 per cent of appeals were either not admitted or struck out by the tribunal because, for example, they fell outside its jurisdiction.

number of people who appeal who just accept the decision that they are given. I think this particularly applies on overpayments. I've checked the overpayments decisions that came my way, and I found that 50 per cent of them were wrong. This means that 50 per cent are probably paying back money that they shouldn't be asked to pay back. It makes you cringe! (Interview 145, Wales and South Western)

We discussed in the previous chapter the reorientation of academic interest away from appellate structures towards initial decision making. The above analysis suggests that, even at the appellate stage of the social security system, the bureaucratic processing of appeals by the Department is of greater importance to claimants than the judicial stage represented by the tribunal. Most meritorious appeals are filtered out by an adjudication officer accepting that every ground of the appeal should succeed, and reviewing the decision accordingly. In some cases, this is because fresh evidence is produced by the appellant; in others, the review process itself reveals an error in the initial decision.

The Department's processing of appeals is far from flawless, however, as is indicated by the critical comment it has attracted from the Chief Adjudication Officer. In his 1989/90 report he reported that 'the overall standard of appeals work is poor' (para. 5. 16), while in relation to appeals submissions prepared by the Department of Employment he noted that 'there was no sign of improvement in standards' (para. 1. 13). Persistent weaknesses identified in appeals submissions include the failure to cite relevant statutory provisions and case law, the provision of an incomplete or inaccurate summary of facts and a lack of or deficiency in argument. The Chief Adjudication Officer has also expressed concern at continuing delays in the preparation of appeals submissions for use by social security appeal tribunals. In the following pages we explore these problems in detail, describe how appeals are processed by local offices, and consider the influence the tribunal exerts on the carrying out of reviews.

There is an important difference in the arrangements for processing appeals in the areas of work covered by this study. Broadly speaking, contributory benefits and unemployment benefit adjudication officers review their own decisions, write the appeals submissions, and appear before the tribunal to present the case. In income support cases, however, a specialist adjudication officer, known as an appeals officer, carries out these functions rather than the first-line adjudication officer. The high number of appeals which supplementary benefit historically generated allowed for such specialism, and the larger local offices often had a team of three or even four appeals officers. Although the number of appeals has fallen since the inception of income support, local offices have nevertheless maintained the practice of using specialist appeals officers. This policy has lately come under threat as lower staffing complements have forced local office managers to combine appeals work with other duties. On the non-means-tested benefits, by contrast, the number of appeals received each week in offices has always been low, and there has never been any scope for engaging officers full time on appeals duties.[9]

It is not just the methods used for processing reviews that differ according to the type of benefit, but also the results produced by the review procedures. In 1989, for example, 31 per cent of all income support appeals which were cleared were disposed of by an adjudication officer revising the original decision. The relevant supersession rates for unemployment benefit and contributory benefit appeals were 24 per cent and 14 per cent respectively.[10] These considerable disparities cannot be explained in terms of differential error rates in initial decision making, since the Chief Adjudication Officer has found that the error rate for income support (37 per cent) is lower than that pertaining in either contributory benefit (39 per cent) or unemployment benefit work (53 per cent).[11] More importantly, the differential error rate argument fails to take into account the number of appeals upheld at tribunals considered as a percentage of all appeals lodged. The figures for 1989 by type of benefit are: income support—12 per cent, unemployment benefit—27 per cent, and contributory benefit—31 per cent.[12] If one adopts

---

[9] See further DHSS (1987) at paras. 3. 17–3. 18.

[10] DSS (1991), Table H6. 01; see also Tables A2. 41 and C1. 10. The contributory benefit percentage is based on the figures for those non-means-tested benefits which are administered in local as opposed to central offices. These figures are slightly distorted by the inclusion in the calculations of referrals, which amounted to 2 per cent of all cases registered at the social security appeal tribunals in 1989. Due to the way in which the statistical data are published it is impossible to separate out the referrals from the appeals.

[11] Chief Adjudication Officer (1991), Appendices 1, 6, and 15.

[12] DSS (1991), Table H6. 01.

as a working hypothesis that, broadly speaking, the number of appeals superseded on review added to the number of appeals upheld following a hearing represents the total number of appeals possessing legal merit, then a more subtle explanation of the supersession rates emerges. This is that the review process on income support is simply more effective at weeding out meritorious appeals than that employed for unemployment benefit and contributory benefit appeals. In other words, a larger proportion of appeals is upheld at an earlier stage of the adjudication process for income support cases than for other types of benefit, with consequent savings of time, money, and inconvenience for all concerned.

What is it about the income support review process which makes review by an appeals officer more effective than self-review by a contributory benefits or unemployment benefit adjudication officer? To explore this matter in more depth it is helpful to consider the two main types of review procedure—review by an appeals officer and self-review.

Income support appeals officers and internal reviews of decisions

As explained above, reviews of income support decisions are carried out by specialist appeals officers. When a letter of appeal is received in a local office, it is directed to the income support appeals officer rather than to the adjudication officer on the section responsible for making the original decision. The appeals officer may seek further evidence and will consider carefully how the relevant law applies to the facts as established. If the appeals officer concludes that the determination ought to be revised, then the formal decision to do so should be taken by the original adjudication officer. Typically, the appeals officer speaks to the adjudication officer concerned to point out any new evidence that has emerged and to draw attention to the applicable legislation and any relevant Commissioners' decisions. On this basis the adjudication officer determines whether the original decision can still be sustained. Apart from this involvement, an income suppport adjudication officer need play no part in the review or appeals process. It is the appeals officer who prepares the appeals submission if it is decided that the case should proceed to a tribunal for a hearing.

Appeals officers enjoy a favoured position in decision making, for not only do they come fresh to the case, but they usually have their own room in which to work, away from the distractions of the rest of the office, or at least a desk in a quieter part of the office. Whilst they may have other duties to perform, such as training or computer liaison, they do not have the day-to-day administrative responsibility of running an income support section. They are thus better placed to undertake a more detached consideration of a claim for benefit than the original adjudication officer. They also tend to be more experienced, most (if not all) having previously worked as adjudication officers for some years. Furthermore, unlike adjudication officers working on income support, they are exposed directly to the scrutiny of the social security appeal tribunals. It was an important objective of our study to discover whether these differences were reflected in the way in which adjudication and appeals work on income support was done. To this end, we carried out interviews with forty-two appeals officers (one from each of the local offices visited).

We found from these interviews that appeals officers had markedly different views from income support adjudication officers on a wide range of topics, and it was clear that they approached their work in a quite distinct fashion. For example, 83 per cent of appeals officers said that they gave priority to accuracy over speed, compared with only 24 per cent of income support adjudication officers. Appeals officers also told us that they found little difficulty in balancing the conflicting requirements of speed and accuracy in their work. Over half stated that this was not a problem at all since they had ample time to prepare appeals, and only 7 per cent considered that achieving such a balance presented them with a major problem. This perception was in stark contrast to that held by income support adjudication officers who considered themselves to be under such intense pressure to do work quickly that they were prepared to sacrifice accuracy to do so.

Given their background within the Department, it is not surprising that appeals officers were acutely conscious of their distinctive approach to their work and of the problems faced by adjudication officers. Appeals officers made these points to us repeatedly when we asked them about such matters as the qualities needed for appeals work, how they balanced the conflicting requirements of speed and accuracy, and how they carried out reviews. The following quotations from interviews illustrate how appeals officers recognize their advantageous position as far as decision making is concerned:

I think the pressure on adjudication officers by line management to clear claims and clear cases leads them to cut corners when they're investigating and obtaining evidence. They don't obtain the evidence they should obtain. Corners are cut all the time. I know only a certain percentage appeal but, as they reach me on appeal, one very often finds evidence of corner cutting and the correct evidence has not been obtained. If I can be perfectly honest, the general standard of adjudication that reaches an appeals officer is not always of the highest and does need a lot of correction. It isn't a question of receiving a letter of appeal, picking up a pen, and writing a submission. There's often a great deal of work to be done. You need to find out things, to check the decision to see whether it's right, and if it isn't, to have it put right. (Interview 121, North East)

AOs reach a decision sort of automatically sometimes and you may have to sort out what the decision was, what the basis for the decision was, where the documents are, and that can take a while. You've got the assessment of the case to work on, but that's it really. It's a mathematical calculation, and from that you've got to work out how the AO reached the decision to award a premium or housing costs or whatever. For speed AOs don't always log every decision they reach or set out their reasons. An AO perhaps does it automatically, or rather the admin. officer does the assessment, and the AO is just saying automatically, 'Well, yes, that seems right', whereas an appeals officer has to justify it by using the regulations. It's very much a detective job, appeals. (Interview 123, Midlands)

I don't suffer from the same pressure that other people in the office have. It's very easy for me to sit here in my nice quiet room and make a few phone calls and write a few letters, but the adjudication officers have very little time to collect a lot of facts on some cases. I gather the facts for them and send it back to ask them to consider the new facts. I'm not on the public counter having people swearing at me. I have the time to consult Commissioners' decisions and I'm in a very, very favoured position from that point of view, as far as appeals are concerned. If necessary, I can take all afternoon on just one case. (Interview 128, Midlands)

The difference between an adjudication officer and an appeals officer is that the appeals officer has more time. In practice the adjudication officer in this Department isn't the wonderful figure that you imagine, that comes across from the literature. Most of the time he's supervising staff. So really an appeals officer needs the qualities which an adjudication officer would ideally have, not different ones particularly. An appeals officer needs the same attention to regulations that an adjudication officer should have. AOs are not really sitting down and thinking about it and looking at this decision and that decision. Because they are necessarily only doing one in ten checks, they are just signing nine out of ten of them so it's not really adjudication. The appeals work is when the adjudication really seems to come in. (Interview 135, London North)

As can be seen from the above quotes, by interviewing appeals officers we gained an insight not just into the way in which they carried out internal reviews but also into initial decision making by income support adjudication officers. Indeed, the comments of appeals officers taken as a whole represented a harsh indictment of the standards of first level decision making. Clearly the much greater time available to appeals officers allows them to investigate each claim and appeal much more thoroughly than adjudication officers are able to do. Such investigation is essential because of the superficial approach which adjudication officers frequently are forced to adopt in considering claims. Appeals officers are sometimes at a loss to know what decision has been made and why. In practice most find it essential to work through the entire adjudicatory process afresh.

But why are appeals officers allocated so much more time within the local office? This is not to be explained by reference to the fact that there are far fewer appeals than claims, since the crucial factor in working out staffing complements is the amount of time allowed per case. It is obvious that adjudication officers are expected to clear a much greater number of cases per hour than are appeals officers. The most likely explanation for this differential treatment is that, at the stage of an appeal, the Department must justify its handling of a case before an external body, namely a social security appeal tribunal. It is this external accountability which ensures that appeals officers are given the time to do their work properly.

This accountability shapes the way that appeals officers approach their work, particularly in their use of the law governing entitlement to benefit. As we saw in Chapter 2, adjudication officers only exceptionally consult works of reference in deciding claims. When they do want to look something up, they are far more likely to turn to the Adjudication Officers' Guide than to the law itself. The reverse is true of appeals officers. They frequently check the legal basis for decisions and turn directly to the regulations and Commissioners' decisions. Their approach is moulded by an awareness that the Adjudication Officers' Guide cannot be cited before the tribunal. It makes sense, therefore, to work exclusively with the law (or 'the Blue Books' in local office parlance). Unlike adjudication officers, they have the time to get to grips with the relevant case law, Acts of Parliament and delegated legislation. Far from finding this a disagreeable chore, appeals officers appeared to prefer the style and language used in regulations to that employed in the Adjudication Officers' Guide. The following quotes from our interviews with appeals officers are instructive on the use in local offices of the law and the official guidance to that law:

When I was a group supervisor, I just used to use the AOG and I thought it was OK, although in some areas it wasn't very specific. I've always been wary of using the actual Act. But now I'm working on appeals where I have to use the Acts, I find them a lot easier to interpret than the AOG. The fear of using the Act is unfounded because I think the AOG contains a lot of misleading information. The law hits the nail on the head. (Interview 125, Midlands)

A major problem is not that decisions are made that are wrong in law, but that people make decisions without referring to the law and without quoting the law. They quote the AOG rather than the regulations. So I have a problem of getting people actually to refer to the law. Adjudication officers are taught in training to start with the Act and regulations and then to go to the guidance but, to be honest, it always starts the other way around. That's understandable because who wants to get bogged down in the technicalities of the law if you think you can go to something that's written clearly. But it's really a back to front way of looking at things. It is a problem to break down people's resistance to using the law despite the fact that it's just as simple to look things up in the law as it is in the AOG. (Interview 128, Midlands)

Because we are tending to work to the law for the majority of the time, we get used to using the legislation and, when you are used to the language, in many ways it's clearer and more to the point than the AOG is. In fact, in many places the AOG is a straight reproduction of what the legislation says anyway. But it is simplified in places to an extent which is not accurate enough for what we have to do. (Interview 132, London North)

The fact that decisions will have to be explained before an independent tribunal also has a marked bearing on the amount and quality of the monitoring undertaken by line management of an appeals officer's work. It is standard practice for all appeals submissions to be checked by a higher executive officer before they are forwarded to the tribunal.[13] While this level of monitoring is generally perceived as being helpful by appeals officers, they do not commonly regard their approach to their work as affected by it.[14] Much more important is the salutary effect produced by the knowledge that they will have to appear in front of a tribunal consisting of a legally qualified chairman and two lay members.[15] For some appeals officers, exposure to tribunals had led to a reorientation of their attitude to adjudication. It was not simply that they took much greater care in the making of decisions but that they had adopted an entirely different philosophy in their work. The tribunal looms large in the thinking of appeals officers, as is well illustrated by the following quotes:

I don't think monitoring affects my work on appeals because I find that appeals is a very high profile aspect of our work anyway. And I think the fact that your submission goes to an independent body, and that the claimant, the claimant's adviser, the chairman, they all see your submission and your decisions, I think that in itself makes you want to get it right. You don't feel any additional pressure with someone from Regional Office or whatever coming to have a look at it. (Interview 120, North East)

It seems that there's almost a natural view that, when you start sitting in this seat, you start seeing things differently from an adjudication officer. I think that adjudication officers tend to think that, so far as claimants are concerned, they've got their hands on the purse strings and they are perhaps not as objective as they should be in interpreting their instructions and regulations. From this seat, you know full well that you've got to put a case in front of a tribunal and, although it's not your decision, the tribunal does view it as your decision. (Interview 133, London North)

[13] Although, as the Chief Adjudication Officer has observed, 'as almost a quarter of income support submissions were deficient in some respect, this check was not as effective as it should have been': Chief Adjudication Officer (1990) at para. 5. 8.

[14] Over three-quarters of appeals officers said that internal monitoring by a higher executive officer or by Regional Office had no effect on their work.

[15] Two-thirds of appeals officers said that their approach to a review was influenced by the attitude they thought a social security appeal tribunal might take.

What really made me diligent of course was getting it in the neck from the tribunals. The chickens really come home to roost then. I found that embarrassing. It's not really internal monitoring that makes you careful so much as tribunals. If the chairman says, 'You don't seem to know the law here', it only needs to happen once. (Interview 135, London North)

Appeals officers are not meant to change decisions themselves no matter how strongly they may feel that a decision ought to be superseded at the review stage. It is for the officer who made the original decision to determine whether it should be changed or not. The interview material suggests, however, that appeals officers develop subtle techniques of persuasion in their dealings with adjudication officers in order to bring about the desired result. They enjoy three main advantages which tend to give them the upper hand: a better technical grasp of social security law; more time to unearth further evidence and facts relating to the decision; and more experience of appearing before tribunals, enabling them to make plausible predictions about how a tribunal is likely to approach a particular case.

The negotiating power of the appeals officer appears to have been considerably enhanced since the replacement of supplementary benefit by income support. In 1988, 22 per cent of supplementary benefit appeals were disposed of by way of an internal review and a further 20 per cent were upheld by the tribunal following a hearing. The respective figures for income support in the following year were 31 per cent (revised on review) and 12 per cent (overturned following a hearing). The effective source of decision making in income support cases has thus shifted significantly from the tribunal towards the appeals officer.[16]

Why should this be so? The distinctive feature about the

---

[16] DSS (1991), Table H6. 01. The overall figures quoted for supplementary benefit appeals in 1988 disguise a significant difference between appeals relating to single payments and those concerning other matters. Only 17 per cent of single payment appeals were superseded by administrative action, whereas 22 per cent were allowed by tribunals. For other supplementary benefit appeals, 32 per cent were revised internally whilst only 15 per cent were changed by tribunals. These figures support the argument that a lack of discretion within the new income support system, effected primarily by the abolition of single payments, has shifted the effective source of decision making in appeals.

replacement of supplementary benefit by income support was the marked reduction in discretion it entailed for decision makers. Under the old system, adjudication officers were able to resist the exhortations of appeals officers to revise decisions by saying it was all 'a matter of opinion'. Appeals officers had no answer to this other than to warn adjudication officers that the tribunal would be likely to exercise its discretion more generously. The introduction of income support left adjudication officers more exposed by depriving them of the opportunity to dress up rushed decisions as legitimate exercises of discretion. Appeals officers are more frequently able nowadays to establish objectively that a decision is wrong and to persuade adjudication officers to toe the line.

With the marked differences in approach and attitudes between adjudication officers and appeals officers, there is scope for disagreement between them on the correct course of action to be taken on a review. We were interested to find out about such disagreements and, in particular, which party had the final say on superseding a decision. On most occasions it was clear that adjudication officers were happy to be guided by the appeals officers. One-third said they had never disagreed with an appeals officer's view of a case, and less than 5 per cent claimed to have had frequent disagreements. The same was broadly true of appeals officers: 74 per cent said that only rarely was there any conflict between them and adjudication officers, although 17 per cent said disagreements occurred quite often.

Where there was an unresolved disagreement on a decision, around one-third of both appeals officers and adjudication officers thought that the latter should not have the final say on the matter. In such circumstances, they thought that the appeals officer should have it (a view held by one-fifth of adjudication officers) or else that the issue should be settled by involving line management. This represents a departure from the formal position that the decision is the adjudication officer's prerogative. The attitude of those appeals officers who demand the final say is understandable since it is they who will have to appear before the tribunal to explain the decision. Some appeals officers were more circumspect. They were prepared to present appeals even though they disagreed with the adjudication officer's decision, but they made little attempt to hide their disagreement before the tribunal. This seemed to guarantee a result favourable to the claimant.[17]

The dynamics of the review process and the importance of the appeals officer's advice are illustrated by the following series of quotes drawn from interviews with adjudication officers and appeals officers:

Normally the appeals officer will give you the tribunal angle when they bring the case back down again. They will say, 'Although I can see your point, I think if it went to the tribunal they are going to say this, and could you bear this in mind.' They never say that you ought to change your decision, but just that you ought to bear it in mind. They ask you to look at it and give it back to them. Obviously what they've said can influence you. (Interview 55, Income support adjudication officer, Midlands)

It can happen that we are at loggerheads on a particular decision and I have, once or twice, dug my heels in. I think I am influenced by the personalities of different appeals officers. If there is a personality clash, an adjudication officer might tend to dig their heels in more, simply because they don't like the appeals officer. The previous appeals officer in this office didn't call us in to discuss a particular case; he would just write abrupt notes pointing out the relevant part of the Act, and the tone of his notes made me feel that I really didn't want to change any decisions. That can be an important factor. (Interview 65, Income support adjudication officer, London North)

I can't force them to change their decision. I've always been told that it's not ethical, although to my mind it's crazy. Some appeals officers do change AOs' decisions, some don't. I have done that on occasion. I don't like justifying a decision which I think is grotty. There are not many but they do creep in now and again. I feel I won't justify something that I don't personally agree with. In that sort of case I just say what the facts are, and if the tribunal says, 'Well, what about this though?', I say that that's my opinion too. (Interview 131, Income support appeals officer, London North)

I use the tribunal as a sort of threat to adjudication officers in order to try and put some leverage on them in order to supersede decisions. In areas like delayed claims, where the tribunal has got some discretion (and that's about one of the only areas where they still have any discretion), the tribunal will usually swing in the claimant's favour if there is any area of doubt. So I do point that out to adjudication officers in the hope that they will revise the decision and save it going to appeal. If they won't revise it, then sometimes you can go along to your HEO and say that you've spoken to the adjudication officer and you think that this is a very poor case. Then it's obviously up to the HEO to

[17] This is discussed in Chapter 7.

discuss it with the person concerned because, at the end of the day, it's the adjudication officer who wants to stick with that decision and so be it. (Interview 133, Income support appeals officer, London North)

They tend to agree with me. I usually find something to back it up first and so, if they don't agree, I say, 'Well, take a look at this.' And if they still don't agree, 'Have a look at this too.' We used to have disagreements on overpayments about the balance of probabilities and that was a process of attrition. You show them the textbooks, you show them the AOG, perhaps a Commissioner's decision or two, and then people tend to cave in after that. So ultimately, one or other of us will concede the point. (Interview 135, Income support appeals officer, London North)

The income support review process works relatively effectively from the standpoint of identifying valid appeals at the administrative stage, and by and large it ensures that those decisions which are overturned within the local office on the advice of an appeals officer would also have been overturned by a tribunal. A cynic might suggest that appeals officers have an in-built bias towards supersession since by doing so they reduce their own workloads.[18] For a number of reasons, we doubt that this is a significant problem. First, appeals officers are monitored by their superior officers, and, as one adjudication officer explained to us, 'As well as what the appeal tribunal might do or say about a decision, we have to think about what our management will say or do.' Secondly, appeals officers consider they have ample time to carry out their duties and do not feel under pressure to reduce their workloads. Thirdly, and perhaps most significantly, most appeals officers seem to enjoy presenting cases at tribunals, and indeed regard presenting appeals as their main function rather than a distraction from other duties. In our judgement, the concern of most appeals officers is to secure the legally correct outcome to the case.[19]

The relationship between the appeals officer and the adjudication officer has therefore a decisive bearing on the outcome of the reviews process. In the vast majority of cases, the adjudi-

[18] See further Mashaw (1983) at p. 74.
[19] A word of caution must be added, however, since some appeals officers appear to be unduly swayed by their prediction of how a tribunal would treat an appeal. On occasion, they told us, this had resulted in a decision thought to be correct being revised within the local office to save the time and expense of an appeal. Pragmatism of this kind may be understandable, but it may well on occasion militate against accuracy.

cation officer follows the advice of the appeals officer. From the point of view of promoting accuracy, this is to be welcomed since appeals officers tend to be more experienced, to be more objective in their approach, to provide fresh insight on the case, to rely on the law rather than guidance, and to give priority to accuracy over speed. It is instructive to compare these benefits with the system of self-review as carried out by contributory benefit and unemployment benefit adjudication officers.

Self-review by unemployment benefit and contributory benefit adjudication officers

The review process for unemployment benefit and contributory benefit decisions provides an important contrast with the income support arrangements. The normal procedure is for the adjudication officer who made the original decision to handle any request for a review or appeal. No use is made of specialist appeals officers. As we saw in Chapter 2, contributory benefit and unemployment benefit adjudication officers claim to set high store by accuracy. Not surprisingly then, on the receipt of an appeal, they see little need to go through the entire adjudicatory process again in the way that an income support appeals officer usually does. Adjudication officers engaged in these areas of work rarely supersede their decisions on receipt of a letter of appeal unless it contains some new evidence. If it does not, then they may themselves conduct a further fact-finding exercise. In the absence of fresh evidence, it is unlikely that the decision will be superseded.

The Department's own regional monitoring teams have reported that contributory benefit adjudicators 'show a reluctance to revise decisions, even where the decision is based on incorrect or incomplete evidence.'[20] This is because most of these officers are confident that their original decision was correct and based on sufficient evidence. This is exemplified in the following quotes:

You'd look at it again, just to check you'd done it right, but hopefully, no, you wouldn't review it, because you'd be convinced you'd done

[20] DHSS (1987), para. 3. 21.

it right in the first place. (Interview 1, Contributory benefit adjudication officer, North East)

I'll look at the decision again but there is little likelihood that it will make any difference, because I try to make sure that all the facts are before me when I give my decision. (Interview 9, Contributory benefit adjudication officer, Midlands)

You get quite a lot of appeals where the claimant has never replied to any enquiry. A lot of them you can review after asking a lot of questions. Very rarely have I thought that I could review straight away on receipt of an appeal. You shouldn't find that, because you should have made the right decision. (Interview 116, Unemployment benefit adjudication officer, Scotland)

Yet the self-belief typified by the above quotes is problematic. The Chief Adjudication Officer's criticisms of adjudicatory standards in respect of both unemployment benefit and contributory benefits indicate that the confidence of adjudication officers in their own abilities is often misplaced. One consequence of allowing adjudication officers to review, in effect, their own performance is that the original decision making process is not subject to any critical scrutiny within the Department. Furthermore, it seems self-evident that the likelihood of the same mistake being repeated is higher under a system of self-review than where someone else reconsiders the decision.[21]

On the other hand, one might argue that any reluctance to countenance a review is to some extent counterbalanced by the fact that adjudication officers can save themselves a lot of work if they supersede a decision on receiving an appeal. As with income support appeals officers, one has to consider the possibility that personal goals might conflict with organizational goals. One adjudication officer told us that 'it's a jolly relief to be able to review', while another observed that 'some people rub their hands with glee if they see further evidence come in because it allows them to revise the decision and get rid of the appeal'. The time taken to write appeal submissions was seen as a major problem by nearly all the contributory benefit and unemploy-

---

[21] An acceptance of the drawbacks of self-review seems implicit in the Government's proposals for the disability living allowance. See DSS (1990) at para. 2. 22 where it is stated baldly, 'We think it is important that any review should be conducted by a different AO.' This proposal was implemented by the Social Security Act 1975 s. 100A(10), inserted by Disability Living Allowance and Disability Working Allowance Act 1991, Sched. 1, para. 5.

ment benefit adjudication officers to whom we talked. Unlike income support appeals officers, they have to combine the writing of submissions with the taking of initial decisions, and, in the case of many contributory benefit officers, with supervisory duties as well. Even in ideal conditions, where uninterrupted attention could be devoted to the task, the writing of a single submission can take a day or more. Such ideal conditions are rarely experienced in practice.

On balance, however, the interview material suggests that the desire to arrive at accurate decisions and their confidence in the correctness of their own decisions are the strongest influences on contributory benefit and unemployment benefit adjudication officers. As was noted earlier, a far smaller proportion of these decisions are superseded internally than is the case with income support decisions. Any suggestion that this is because income support decisions are more often incorrect is belied by the critical comments of the Chief Adjudication Officer about decision making across all three types of work, and by the tribunals overturning of considerably more unemployment benefit and contributory benefit decisions than income support determinations. A more convincing explanation is that the use of a specialist appeals officer on income support has considerable advantages over the system of self-review adopted for the other two types of benefit. These advantages largely flow from the appeals officer's greater experience of appearing before the social security appeal tribunal. This raises again the question of the impact that the tribunal system has on the behaviour of the adjudication officers within the Department of Employment and Department of Social Security.

The influence of the tribunal on decision making

We have argued that initial decision making in local offices is of greater importance to claimants than the handling of appeals by social security appeal tribunals. One could take this argument further by contending that tribunals have only a minimal effect on decision making in local offices for two reasons. First, only denials of benefit are ever appealed, so much of the local office's caseload is not subject to the possibility of appellate scrutiny.

Secondly, appeals are heard *de novo* and where an appellant attends a hearing, further evidence is likely to be forthcoming. This means that the case is, in effect, different from that which was before the adjudication officer. Consequently, appellate hearings provide no clear yardstick by which to assess the quality of the initial adjudication, and they offer no useful feedback when the adjudication officer in the case implements the tribunal's written decision.[22]

Yet in shifting the focus of attention away from judicial to administrative structures, we should not lose sight of the considerable indirect influence that tribunals may exert. It may be that the way in which tribunals decide specific cases influences decision makers in their general approach to their work. Moreover, the mere existence of an independent appellate forum may have a bearing on local office practices and behaviour. In exploring these possibilities, we asked adjudication officers whether, when making an initial decision, they were influenced by the prospect that their decisions could be appealed to a tribunal. Affirmative responses were categorized according to whether the respondent contended simply that this prospect would ensure that the adjudication process would be carried out thoroughly and documented fully—a procedural effect, or whether the broader contention was expressed that the decision itself might be swayed by this prospect—a substantive effect. The results are set out in Table 5. It must be borne in mind in the following discussion that a procedural effect may itself make some substantive difference to a decision. The process of justifying a decision (which may, for example, involve carefully checking the law, seeking out more facts, tapping official sources of guidance, etc.) may lead ultimately to a different decision being taken.

Half the adjudication officers (in all three of the areas of work covered by our study) claimed not to be influenced at all by a tribunal's likely response to an appeal. There were, however, important differences amongst those who said that their approach was affected. For example, nearly half of the unemployment benefit adjudication officers said that the prospect of

---

[22] A further reason for this view would be that tribunal decisions have no precedent value; it is only Commissioners' decisions and those of the higher courts that adjudication officers must follow.

an appeal being made led to their taking extra care in reaching a decision. Yet these officers were virtually as one in denying that the outcome of a case could be swayed by any anticipation of a tribunal's likely decision. This reflects the jealously guarded sense of independence shared by these officers.

TABLE 5: *Effect of tribunal on initial decision making according to type of work*

	Department of Social Security				Department of Employment			
	CB AOs		IS AOs		UB AOs		Total	
	No.	%	No.	%	No.	%	No.	%
No effect	24	58.5	27	50.0	10	47.6	61	52.6
Procedural effect	7	17.1	12	22.2	10	47.6	29	25.0
Substantive effect	5	12.2	14	25.9	1	4.8	20	17.2
Other responses	5	12.2	1	1.9	0	0.0	6	5.2
	41	100.0	54	100.0	21	100.0	116	100.0

Note; Column headings refer to types of adjudication officer.
(CB = Contributory Benefit, IS = Income Support, UB = Unemployment Benefit)

By contrast, about one in eight contributory benefit adjudication officers conceded that their own determination could be affected by the tribunal's likely decision. This minority saw their approach as one of realism in the face of what they regarded as the tribunal's willingness to be influenced by sympathy for the claimant.[23] In interpreting the figures in Table 5, it is necessary to bear in mind that nearly a quarter of the contributory benefits adjudication officers interviewed had never presented a case before a social security appeal tribunal.[24] These adjudication officers therefore have no real contact with the appeal

---

[23] Respondents gave the example of 'fit within limits' cases in invalidity benefit appeals, where the tribunal was said invariably to prefer the claimant's evidence, that he or she was not fit to work, to the DSS doctors' view.

[24] A practice has developed in many areas of using a specialist contributory benefits presenting officer who may present all the appeals originating from one office, or, more usually, from a number of offices. This officer does not fulfil the same role as the income support appeals officer since the relevant adjudication officers still review their own cases and write appeals submissions.

tribunal. This is important because of our general hypothesis that the more often an officer presents cases at the tribunal, the more likely it is that there will be an effect on decision making.

Out of the three types of adjudication officer covered by this study, one might therefore have expected that it would have been those working on income support who would have been the least influenced by the prospect that their decision could be appealed to a tribunal since none of them appears before the tribunal to explain their decisions. Our findings do not bear out this hypothesis, however: one-quarter of income support adjudication officers said that the initial decision itself could be affected by the prospect of an appeal being made. The answer to this paradox lies in the mediating role played by the income support appeals officer between the tribunal and the adjudication officer, and it is worth considering this role in some detail.

Appeals officers enjoy a relatively close relationship with the tribunal. Excluding those respondents who did not present cases at appeal hearings, we found that income support appeals officers appeared before tribunals twice as frequently as did contributory benefit and unemployment benefit adjudication officers. Appeals officers had appeared before a tribunal on an average of thirty-two times over the previous twelve months. They also seemed to be the most strongly influenced by the tribunal in their approach to their work. This emerged when we asked adjudication officers and appeals officers whether, at the stage of an internal review of a decision that had been appealed, they considered a tribunal's likely approach to the appeal. The results, categorized in the same way as in the previous table, are set out in Table 6.

By comparing the figures presented in Tables 5 and 6, it emerges that income support adjudication officers, despite the fact that they do not attend tribunal hearings, were more strongly influenced by the tribunal's approach at the review stage than they were when taking the initial decision. The explanation for this lies in the fact that they usually take the advice of appeals officers at the review stage and, as Table 6 demonstrates, appeals officers pay close attention to how a tribunal will approach a case. We have already explored how income support adjudication officers are made aware by appeals officers of how the tribunal is likely to react to a decision, and this awareness seems

TABLE 6: *Effect of tribunal on internal reviews of decisions according to type of work*

	Department of Social Security						Department of Employment			
	CB AOs		IS AOs		IS Appeals		UB AOs		Total	
	No.	%	No.	%	No.	%	No.	%	No.	%
No effect	29	76.3	29	54.7	14	34.1	10	47.6	82	53.6
Procedural effect	4	10.5	5	9.4	12	29.3	10	47.6	31	20.3
Substantive effect	3	7.9	19	35.9	15	36.6	1	4.8	38	24.8
Other responses	2	5.3	0	0.0	0	0.0	0	0.0	2	1.3
	38	100.0	53	100.0	41	100.0	21	100.0	153	100.0

Note: Column headings refer to types of adjudication officer.
(CB = Contributory Benefit, IS = Income Support, UB = Unemployment Benefit, IS Appeals = Income Support Appeals Officer)

to have a bearing on the way in which adjudication officers take decisions, as well as on their attitude towards reviews.[25]

It might have been expected that the tribunal's approach to a case would have a stronger influence on adjudication officers once a decision had been appealed, since at the review stage it is likely that the case will be heard by the appeal tribunal unless the initial decision is superseded. Yet from the figures presented in Tables 5 and 6, it can be seen that this is only true of income support adjudication officers. Unemployment benefit adjudication officers appear to be no more influenced by the tribunal at the review stage than they are when making initial decisions, while contributory benefit adjudication officers are less

[25] Indeed, the influence of the tribunal on the processing of income support claims and reviews would have been even more evident were it not for the fact that eleven out of the forty-two appeals officers we interviewed did no presenting before tribunals because of a departmental practice in some areas of using a specialist presenting officer. Appeals from several neighbouring offices were prepared locally by appeals officers but presented by one specialist officer. Non-attendance at the tribunal was correlated with claiming not to be influenced by the tribunal, meaning that these appeals officers were less likely to advise adjudication officers to fall in line with the tribunal's approach to decision making.

likely to take into account the tribunal's approach at the review stage. We suggest that this attitude, particularly on the contributory benefits side, is consistent with the unwillingness of these officers to countenance the possibility that they took a wrong decision in the first place (or even to concede that some other decision was possible). Their reluctance to supersede their own decisions is reflected in their indifference to how a tribunal might deal with appeals against those decisions.

To summarize, we found that the existence of the appeal tribunal and its distinctive approach to adjudication had a considerable bearing on initial decision making and the review process within local offices. The strength of this 'tribunal effect' cannot be precisely measured and appears to differ according to the type of benefit involved and the particular administrative structures in place within the Departments for making decisions and processing appeals. Yet about a half of all adjudication officers claimed not to be influenced by the tribunal at all. We have our doubts about such claims and suspect that the tribunal exerts a generalized influence on most, if not all, adjudication officers, even if it is not always acknowledged as such. It is a plausible hypothesis that any adjudication officer who appears before a tribunal to present cases will substantiate decisions more carefully—an effect we have called procedural. Moreover, the local office culture we identified in Chapter 2, nurtured by frequent consultations amongst frontline adjudication officers, will help spread working practices and attitudes which are informed by an awareness of the way the tribunal approaches cases.

Whether such a tribunal effect is a positive feature of the system of social security adjudication is, however, more debatable. The complexity of the problem was evident to us in our discussions with local office staff. The interviews with income support adjudication officers, in particular, suggested that the prospect of an appeal was sometimes a negative influence on decision making. Some of those who said that they took into account the prospect of an appeal intimated that this was more likely to lead them to give an inaccurate decision rather than an accurate one, or to lean towards disallowing. For them the tribunal provided a safety net which relieved them of the obligation to be meticulous in reaching a decision. The attitude seemed to be that, if the decision was wrong, the claimant could always appeal. Other officers allowed their approach to be affected rather grudgingly, accepting that they may as well apply the same tests as to the sufficiency of evidence in a case as would the tribunal, notwithstanding that this ran contrary to their 'gut feeling' about a claim. Three quotes drawn from interviews with income support adjudication officers highlight these points:

You get this attitude a lot with appeals officers that, if you go to a tribunal with the case as it stands, then the tribunal are going to decide in favour of the claimant. That can persuade you to think why create a load of hassle, why not just decide in the claimant's favour because, if they go to a tribunal, they will win it in any case. If it's one where you think that the tribunal could go one way or the other, then you tend to think that they will decide it in the claimant's favour. Or you think that you'll only have the appeals officer come down and ask me to change it, so it's less hassle to do it the way you're going to be asked to do it at a later date. (Interview 55, Midlands)

Sometimes, if I'm not sure of something, I'll authorize it hoping it will go to appeal. Well, not hoping it will go to appeal, but saying to myself that I haven't got time to sort this one out, or I give up with this one, and I'll authorize it, and say no, and then hope it will go to appeal and the appeals officer will then do it. (Interview 59, London North)

It does colour your judgement because you know that, if you haven't got enough evidence in that the appeals tribunal would say you didn't have sufficient evidence on which to base your decision, then you would have to give the claimant the benefit of the doubt. You shouldn't do, you should make your decision on the facts. But you know from experience that you wouldn't have a leg to stand on at a tribunal and sometimes, against your better judgement, you give a decision in their favour. (Interview 71, London South)

The fact that a claimant has a right of appeal provides some comfort to hard-pressed income support adjudication officers who may have a nagging feeling that wrong decisions are being made. It can relieve them of the responsibility to investigate claims more thoroughly. It might well be that adjudication officers would be far less prone to this tendency if they had to appear in front of a tribunal to explain how they reached a decision. Instead, on income support at any rate, it is the appeals officer who is left to carry the can. Not surprisingly, the latter generally do their utmost to ensure that suspect decisions are weeded out at the review stage.

The writing of the submission

The final internal stage in the review process is the writing of the submission for the tribunal in those cases which have not been fully revised in the appellant's favour. The study of supplementary benefit appeal tribunals by Bell (1975) concluded that this document:

is rather intimidating and its layout not easy for ordinary people to cope with . . . it often lacks a full and straightforward explanation of the crucial points of the submission in language readily understandable by people unfamiliar with official forms. (p. 12)

Little seems to have improved in the seventeen years since Bell produced her report. The Chief Adjudication Officer's stern criticisms of the quality of submissions have already been mentioned above, and it is clear from our interviews that many adjudication officers and appeals officers found this the most difficult part of their work. Two-thirds of all those officers whom we interviewed said that they experienced problems in writing a submission to the tribunal which would be understandable to the appellant, and most described the task as very difficult or impossible. A further 10 per cent did not even try to make submissions understandable to appellants. In their view, the submission was geared for the tribunal's use and there was no point pretending that an appellant could possibly understand such a technical legalistic document. The following quotes illustrate the problems experienced in writing a submission:

I find it hard because, after you've worked in the Department for a long time, you get to know what things mean and you find that you can read a submission and think, 'Yes, that's fine, I understand that', but then, on reflection, you realize that it won't mean all that much to someone off the street. Commissioners' decisions, legislation, 'I submit that', and all that sort of thing. So you just have to try and bear that in mind and write it so that it doesn't go over the claimant's head. (Interview 39, Contributory benefit adjudication officer, Scotland)

I've yet to hear an appellant at a tribunal say, 'I don't understand this', so I assume they do understand it. However, reading it myself, and trying to put myself in their position, I haven't a bloody clue how they understand it. We are told to lay it out in a certain way, and it's just complicated. I know you've got to have the law down, and explain it to the tribunal, but the language just seems so archaic that we use. (Interview 103, Unemployment benefit adjudication officer, South East)

You have to get very technical at times. I think even the tribunals some-times find them a bit difficult to understand! They've got to be geared to the tribunal rather than the appellant because it's the tribunal that's going to make the decision. In most cases, I don't suppose the claimant stands much chance of understanding them. Once you start quoting the regulations and sub-paragraphs, I'm sure they get lost. Anyone would. It's experts writing to other experts really. (Interview 145, Income support appeals officer, Wales and South West)

In recognition of these problems, the Office of the Chief Adjudication Officer has issued model submissions to adjudication officers to assist them in their work. These set out standard paragraphs which can be used for particular types of appeal. The danger here is that the model will be followed slavishly, in the same way that the Adjudication Officers' Guide is treated as the final word on the question of how to determine a claim, rather than as mere guidance. As one adjudication officer reveal-ingly put it, 'the vast majority of paragraphs in a submission are really just standard paragraphs, and there are really only two or three where you have to put some thought into them'. Another argued that model submissions increased the difficulty inherent in the task of trying to make comprehensible the appli-cation of a complex body of law to particular facts. As she put it:

It's quite difficult really because we are given these guidelines to use. I can't say these guidelines are all that brilliant. If you're not careful, there are great chunks of it that are not all that relevant and there is a temptation to copy it all out without thinking all that carefully about what you are saying. When you actually see a submission typed up, it can go on and on and on and, when you read it through, you think it's a bit of a mouthful. What it must mean to someone else, I don't know. (Contributory benefit adjudication officer, Interview 17, London North)

The Chief Adjudication Officer has himself noted in his report for 1989/90 'a tendency to make the appeal fit the specimen rather than adapt the specimen to suit the appeal' (para. 5. 6), and he adds that 'as in previous years AOs continued to rely too heavily on my specimen submissions' (para. 5. 28).

There can be little doubt but that the movement away from discretion towards entitlement on the basis of legal rights has made the task of writing appeal submissions even more formi-dable. The vital question—the extent to which appellants themselves are able to follow these documents—is a matter to which we shall return in Chapter 6.

Delays in processing appeals in local offices

The maxim that justice delayed is justice denied applies just as much to tribunals as to the courts. Indeed, in some respects it applies with even greater force, since delays in the hearing of appeals may have grim consequences for social security claimants struggling in the meantime to make ends meet. When the Presidential system was established for social security appeal tribunals, Ministers set a requirement that appeals be heard within four to six weeks of their being lodged at local offices. Since appellants must be given ten days' notice of any tribunal hearing, departmental officials agreed to the President's proposal that appeals submissions should be sent to the tribunal clerk within fifteen working days.

This target has, however, proved to be beyond the capabilities of local office staff.[26] The 1989/90 report of the Chief Adjudication Officer showed that the average time taken to prepare both income support and contributory benefits submissions and send them to the tribunal was twenty three days. The fifteen-day target was met in only 60 per cent of income support appeals and just under a half of those relating to contributory benefits. Less detailed information is available for the Department of Employment although the Chief Adjudication Officer notes that most unemployment benefit decisions were not cleared within the target of fifteen working days.[27]

In many cases delay occurs because an adjudication officer or an appeals officer needs further information before the submission can be prepared. This is particularly true of income support where, as we have seen, the appeals officer is often faced with undertaking the entire adjudicatory process afresh. Income support adjudication officers are simply too short of time to worry overmuch about collecting sufficient information on which to

[26] See DHSS (1987) para. 5. 5.

[27] See Appendices 17 and 19, and paras. 5. 9, 5. 14, and 5. 31 of the Chief Adjudication Officer's report. See also Chapter 6 of this book for an analysis of the delays in writing submissions relating to the sample of appeal hearings observed in this study.

base a decision. If the claimant fails to tick a box on a claim form, or omits to give all the details requested, very often the adjudication officer will make do with what is there. The appeals officer is left to pick up the pieces on those cases that are appealed and it is not surprising that this often takes a good deal of time.

Even so, unemployment benefit and contributory benefits adjudication officers have their own problems. As noted earlier, they have to combine the lengthy business of researching and writing an appeal with what is seen as the more pressing need to take initial decisions. In many instances contributory benefits adjudication officers have to combine adjudication with supervisory duties. The temptation to put the difficult task of writing appeals to the bottom of the in-tray can be very great. Even the most diligent adjudication officer will encounter difficulties in finding an uninterrupted period of time in which to give measured consideration to constructing the submission.

In this situation it is obviously important that hierarchical control be exercised through monitoring the progress of appeals work. This is meant to be achieved in local offices through the keeping of an appeals register which shows when an appeal is lodged, when the submission is sent to the regional tribunal office and when the appeal hearing is held. It also records the date of any supersession of a decision or withdrawal of an appeal and the outcome of the appeal hearing. To obtain some idea of how effective this control is, we were supplied with copies of appeals registers for fifty of the offices we visited as part of this study, for the months of May, June, and July 1989.[28] They make for bewildering reading. The lines of a register are filled in by hand by each adjudication officer, so that each page contains a confusing range of handwriting styles and inks. Some information appears to be missing and much else is virtually indecipherable. The Department of Employment does not even have a standard form for use as the register. Instead such a motley collection of handwritten forms is used that offices differ markedly in the type of information they record.

[28] We are indebted to Ian Thomson at the Department of Employment and Roger Jennings at the Department of Social Security for co-ordinating the collection of this material. We received this information from all eleven DE offices and thirty-nine out of the forty-two DSS offices we visited in our study, making fifty in total.

The most striking point about the registers is that they do not lend themselves to easy analysis. Their main purpose is to allow higher executive officers to identify delays in handling appeals. Yet the registers do not contain meaningful measures of delay: the monitoring officer is merely presented with a string of dates representing the numerous steps that are taken in processing an appeal. Distinguishing the cases where unacceptable delays are building up from those that have just been received or those that are being handled efficiently must be a tedious and unrewarding business. We are not surprised, therefore, to find the Chief Adjudication Officer reporting that the higher executive officer's 'mandatory check of the appeals register is still not particularly effective in ensuring that appeals are dealt with timeously and that, where there are reasons for delay, they are properly recorded'.[29]

The monitoring of appeals seems to be a strong candidate for computerization. With the relevant dates keyed into a computer, it would be a straightforward matter to obtain reports which would quantify precisely the delay in days relating to each stage in processing the appeal. It would also be just as easy to highlight those cases in which exceptional delays were being encountered. The Department has already decided to introduce computerized systems into the whole of the social security network and no doubt is mindful of the problems we have outlined here. These problems are indicative of a massively complex administrative process based on a case-recording system said to date back to 1948.[30] Without modern technology, local office staff will continue to struggle to manage their workloads. Priorities will continue to be dictated more by day-to-day exigencies than by a rational system based on informed monitoring and management. Taking longer to reach decisions does not necessarily make for more accurate adjudication: on the contrary, delays and inaccuracy often walk hand in hand within local offices. An adjudicatory system that can achieve neither speed nor accuracy, let alone a reasonable balance between the two, has little to recommend it.

---

[29] Chief Adjudication Officer (1990) at para. 5. 12. The 1989/90 Annual Report also notes that it is often difficult to ascertain the reasons for delays from the records: Chief Adjudication Officer (1991) at para. 5. 9.

[30] See the discussion by Cooper (1985) at p. 18 on this point.

Conclusion

We have argued that an examination of the way decisions are taken in local offices is of fundamental importance. Such decisions are less 'visible' than those reached in the public arena of the tribunal hearing and they affect a very much greater number of claimants. Yet decision making in local offices is very often a hit-and-miss affair, and, even at the review stage (when it might be supposed that greater care would be exercised), the procedures are seriously flawed. This applies particularly to reviews in contributory benefits and unemployment benefit cases, where the official making the original decision is also responsible for carrying out the review.

Whilst the prospect of an appeal to a tribunal undoubtedly concentrates minds in local offices, this influence is diminished where the adjudication officer making the decision on a claim or review is not the person who will eventually appear before the tribunal. Yet it is important to distinguish what we have termed the 'procedural' and 'substantive' effects when determining whether this influence is to be welcomed. Where the effect is procedural, it can only be beneficial since it means that adjudication officers take more trouble to justify and document their decisions. Where the effect is substantive, however, different considerations apply. There is a tendency amongst some adjudication officers to regard the safety net of the tribunal system as meaning that no harm is done to claimants by cutting corners in decision making since matters can always be put right on appeal. This indicates that the different stages of the adjudication process are not exclusive or watertight compartments: rather the tribunals cast a long shadow over the work done in local offices.

4

Appeals before Social Security Appeal Tribunals

IN the previous two chapters, we have considered initial decision making and the carrying out of reviews within the Department of Social Security and the Department of Employment. In this chapter we consider the third distinctive stage in the process of adjudicating on welfare benefits, the appeal to an independent tribunal. We have already seen how the work of the tribunal can have an important effect on the way in which social security claims and appeals are processed within the Department. Conversely the Department influences the course of appeal hearings before tribunals, not least through having a presenting officer, who is an employee of the Department, present in virtually every case to answer questions about the facts and applicable regulations.[1] Here we focus on the functions performed by the tribunals and the distinctive philosophy which was developed to guide their handling of appeals.

The approach of the tribunals to the cases coming before them has also been moulded by broader trends in the evolution of tribunals generally. In its report published over thirty years ago, the Franks Committee identified a number of characteristics of tribunals which gave them advantages over court procedures.[2] These characteristics were, according to the Committee, 'cheapness, accessibility, freedom from technicality, expedition and expert knowledge of their particular subject' (para. 38). The model tribunal was seen as being one in which the citizen was able to present a case adequately without legal or other specialist

---

[1] The role of the presenting officer forms the subject of Ch. 7.
[2] See Franks (1957*a*).

representation. It has in practice proved difficult for tribunals to live up to these standards, and, since the tendency has been for tribunal procedures to become increasingly 'judicialized', so the differences between tribunals and courts have diminished.[3]

The goal of enabling ordinary people to put their cases to a tribunal has historically proved elusive in the welfare benefits field, and nowhere more so than in relation to supplementary benefits appeal tribunals. A series of extremely critical research studies was published in the 1970s demonstrating how unsuccessful they were in this regard.[4] Claimants, it was said, were made to feel that they themselves were on trial rather than the decisions of the Department, and were expected to adopt humiliating public postures if they were to be viewed with favour by the tribunals.[5]

The Bell report (1975), which proved to be especially influential, referred to the 'enabling' role that chairmen and members ought to be playing in drawing out information from unrepresented appellants. Bell argued that:

there is considerable onus on the tribunal (chairman and members) not only to give [appellants] full opportunity to speak but to ensure that they are asked those questions which help them to bring out their case and are afforded help in concentrating on the significant issues. (p. 17)

Seizing this point some years later, His Honour Judge Byrt, the then President of OPSSAT, stipulated that it was the responsibility of chairmen to enter the arena of dispute. It makes, he said, 'a mockery of the tribunal system to leave [the claimant] totally to his own devices to argue his appeal as best he may'.[6] Chairmen, then, are not just encouraged to assist unrepresented claimants; they are expected to do so. Moreover, tribunals were exhorted in all cases to adopt an inquisitorial approach, and so

---

[3] See, for instance, Dickens *et al*. (1985) and Leslie (1985).
[4] In particular, see Herman (1972); Burkeman (1975); Rose (1975); Lister (1975); Milton (1975); Bell (1975); Frost and Howard (1977) and Fulbrook (1978).
[5] Rose (1975) at p. 152.
[6] See House of Commons Social Services Committee (1989) at p. 36. A very similar approach has been advocated by the Civil Justice Review (1988) in relation to small claims courts (p. 100).

to take the initiative in questioning both parties in an attempt to ascertain all the facts.

These are seductive arguments, and it is difficult even for lawyers reared and trained in the adversarial tradition not to find them persuasive. It seems almost self-evident that a tribunal that strives to be informal in its approach should lend a helping hand to an appellant who is floundering. Yet there are a number of features of hearings at social security appeal tribunals which affect the scope for such an inquisitorial and enabling approach. First, because of the removal of discretion from large areas of that part of the social security system which comes within the tribunal's jurisdiction, the tribunal often appears to have little or no room for manœuvre in reviewing an adjudication officer's decision. Secondly, in about half of the cases coming before the tribunal, there is no appellant present to whom questions can be put and assistance offered. Thirdly, even where the appellant attends, it is rare for there to be a representative to assist in the presentation of the case. Each of these matters will be discussed in turn.

(i) *The erosion of discretion*

There is no doubt that the erosion of discretion within the social security system over the last ten to fifteen years has greatly reduced the tribunal's role in many cases. One consequence is that some chairmen and members evidently see little point in enquiring into the facts of cases which they regard as doomed from the outset because of the rigid nature of the law to be applied. Indeed, in some cases we observed, the tribunal acted as little more than a rubber stamp for the decisions of adjudication officers. The chairman and members appeared resigned to the view that, unless the adjudication officer could be found to have applied the law incorrectly, there was virtually nothing they could do to affect the amount of benefit received by a claimant. There was often an air of frustration about the proceedings, and in many cases the claimant was left with the impression that the tribunal itself did not care much for the rules it was obliged to apply.

Yet in behaving in this manner tribunals often over-react to the undoubted loss of discretion in social security adjudication.

As was argued in Chapter 1, a considerable degree of freedom remains to adjudicators in weighing evidence and determining the facts. As Mesher (1990) has noted, the most significant form of discretion in a bureaucratic system may be in the finding of facts. It follows, he argues, that 'Particularly from the point of view of claimants, the extent of the difference between the pre- and post-1980 systems is often greatly exaggerated' (p. 39).

Based on our observations of tribunal hearings, we attempted to determine the frequency with which tribunals considered themselves to be hamstrung by the rules. In as many as 143 out of the 337 cases we observed (42 per cent), the tribunal appeared to take the view that there was nothing whatever it could do to affect the outcome of the appeal, inasmuch as the evidence before it did not amount to an arguable case. In other words, the rules were regarded as having predetermined that the appellant would lose. In some of these cases, this conclusion was reached only after careful questioning of the presenting officer and, if present, the appellant. But in others it would be fair to describe the tribunal as having jumped to this conclusion. In a further 21 per cent of the hearings, the appellants lost despite having some sort of arguable case in the tribunal's eyes. Details of the outcome of the cases we observed are presented in Table 7. The figures are broken down by whether the case was dealt with by the tribunal on the basis that it involved scope for discretion and judgement to play a significant part or was rather an open and shut matter where the tribunal had little choice but to dismiss the appeal.[7]

We saw in Chapter 3 how the review stage of the appeals process, operated within local departmental offices, is fairly effective in weeding out strong appeals, particularly in income support cases. In consequence, the tribunal generally has to deal with two types of case: those which on paper appear to be weak or hopeless but which the appellant has not withdrawn, and those where the evidence on each side is so evenly balanced

---

[7] It should be stressed that our sample of 337 cases excludes all hearings where the tribunal immediately adjourned the case to give the appellant another chance to attend. These were excluded because we wished to concentrate on the dynamics of an appeal hearing where an attempt was being made to dispose of the case.

TABLE 7: *Results of appeal heard by social security appeal tribunal by whether tribunal treated case as one in which it had discretion*

Result	No. discretion		Some discretion		Total	
	No.	%	No.	%	No.	%
Appellant loses	139	97.2	70	36.1	209	62.0
Appellant wins in part	0	0.0	14	7.2	14	4.2
Appellant wins	0	0.0	90	46.4	90	26.7
Adjourned part-heard	4	2.8	20	10.3	24	7.1
	143	100.0	194	100.0	337	100.0

that the reviewing officer did not feel able to supersede the original decision and give the claimant all that was sought.[8] Some appellants are able to present new information at their appeal hearings and thereby transform what was previously regarded by the Department as a hopeless case into an arguable or even an irresistible one. But this is not always so, and, as roughly half of all appellants fail to attend their hearings, it can hardly be regarded as a frequent occurrence.

To summarize, while the tribunal treats many cases as hopeless because they are hopeless,[9] it is likely that it also treats many other cases as weak in which it could have exercised somewhat greater judgment. Part of the problem seems to be that chairmen and especially members focus on the discretionary powers tribu-

---

[8] This is not to deny that some cases before the tribunal should never have reached that stage. The Chief Adjudication Officer (1991) has commented on the standard of contributory benefits appeals work, for example, as follows: 'AOs continued to support the decision appealed against, although it was often incorrect, and their argument in submissions was frequently absent or deficient' (para. 5. 11).

[9] For example, one elderly and confused claimant with £17,000 in savings appealed against a disallowance of income support. (The capital allowance for income support is £8,000 at the time of writing: Income Support (General) Regulations 1987, S.I. No. 1967, reg. 45.) There were also five unsuccessful appeals against refusals of mobility allowance by pensioners who, having claimed after the age of 65, were bound to fail by virtue of s. 37A(5) of the Social Security Act 1975.

nals have lost in recent years, and underestimate the scope for discretion that remains. We were told by many chairmen and members that they greatly regretted the erosion of their discretion so that they could not do justice as they saw fit. No fewer than 44 per cent of the chairmen to whom we spoke and 68 per cent of the members said that tribunal decision making is now too constrained by legal regulation. Many others took the view that this was a matter for Parliament, not for them, to determine, but only a minority of chairmen (30 per cent) and members (16 per cent) said that they did not think their discretion was now too tightly constrained. We saw how, on occasion, chairmen and their members were prepared to wrack their brains to seek ways of circumventing what they viewed as a particularly disagreeable provision. But, as far as we could see, hardly any were prepared to ignore the law or regulations in order to pursue some broader notion of justice of their own. The following comments on this important subject are typical of the range of views expressed to us:

There are many cases where you would like to do something and you can't. Your hands are tied absolutely. But that, I think, you've got to lay at the doors of Parliament. I think it's a shame that we've moved much more to rigidity than before. There isn't enough discretion, which is sad. (Chairman, North East, Interview 2)

I see certain disadvantages with having a lot of discretion. There is a danger with these tribunals that you get people playing God, feeling it is great to dole out money, playing the role of Lady Bountiful. There has to be some central regulation. But I do sometimes think that the regulations should be more generous. That's really the key problem. I certainly favour a tight regulatory system but I think we need better regulations. There are a lot of people nowadays, especially old people, who are in really dire straits, yet there is no way of giving them any more money. (Chairman, Midlands, Interview 10)

I think we are too constrained. The tribunal now only gets the chance to amend an adjudication officer's decision where the adjudication officer has made a slip (which isn't very often) or where there is new evidence. I would like more room for manœuvre at the tribunal. But administratively the absence of discretion makes it much easier to calculate the social security budget. (Chairman, Midlands, Interview 15)

We sit here sometimes and go home and sit in a darkened room afterwards because we haven't been able to help a single soul. (Chairman, London North, Interview 16)

It is frightening the number of occasions one comes out at the end of an afternoon thinking that one has upheld appeals which were in some sort of ethical sense unmeritorious and turned down ones where people really needed the money. That worries me a good deal. (Member, North East, Interview 61)

You've got to make a decision within the law. That is a very considerable restraint. All the tribunal can achieve is a discussion about the way the law's been applied. We all come up against situations where you've got terrific sympathy but at the same time you cannot uphold the appeal because of the legal constraints. (Member, London South, Interview 104)

The legal regulations tie you hand and foot. You are more or less handcuffed to a decision. You could possibly find a very deserving case sitting in front of you, and yet nothing can be done because of the regulations. No discretion whatsoever! (Member, Scotland, Interview 137)

These comments serve to illustrate the widespread distaste that chairmen and members feel about the rigidity with which they are obliged to apply much social security legislation. In the interviews we conducted, there was a frequent harking back to what were viewed as halcyon days when discretion was the order of the day. Now that the pendulum has swung abruptly in the opposite direction, chairmen (and, even more so, members) lament their impotence to assist the needy.

It is arguable, however, that the lack of discretion in many cases before the tribunal is not objectionable in itself. As one of the chairmen quoted above points out, if the regulations made relatively generous provision for people in financial difficulties, then the treatment of those that fell just outside the scope of the rules would not seem so unjust. It is the perceived harshness of the current social security system, combined with a lack of discretion to alleviate the worst effects of the regulations, that leads tribunal members to question the justice of welfare provision. Yet our findings strongly suggest that tribunals chaired by lawyers can be entrusted with discretion without necessarily operating it automatically in favour of claimants. It is noteworthy that in just over one-third of those cases regarded by the tribunal as allowing some latitude, the decision went against the appellant. Despite the fact that tribunals nowadays have less opportunity to overturn an adjudication officer's decision, it seemed to us that chairmen and members generally thought long and hard before taking that step.

(ii) *Non-attended cases*

Another important source of frustration for chairmen and members is the proportion of cases that they hear in the absence of the appellant. In our sample of cases, appellants were present in 54 per cent of the hearings, compared to the national average of 47 per cent. The failure of appellants to attend is evidently a matter of great concern to those who sit on tribunals, as they explained to us in interview. The most common view expressed was that the tribunal was then restricted to making its decision on the papers prepared by the Department, including a copy of the appellant's letter of appeal and the written appeals submission. There is no legal requirement on adjudication officers to provide tribunals with submissions. The Department's solicitors have argued that the practice of providing submissions has served all parties well, reflecting 'the fact that the character of social security appeals is inquisitorial rather than adversarial'.[10] This characterization of the appeals process is questionable, however, and the influence of the submission on the tribunal should not be underestimated. In practice it defines the issues and sets the tribunal's agenda through the papers being sent to appellants, chairmen and members well in advance of the hearing. It represents a highly organized response by the Department to an appeal and, in its selection and treatment of facts and law, may be constructed in such a way that no other reasonable decision than the one taken by the adjudication officer seems possible.[11]

Our interviews with adjudication officers, appeals officers, chairmen, and members, coupled with our own observations of hearings, all point to the same conclusion: submissions are written to explain and justify decisions rather than to assist the tribunal's inquiry into the possibility of arriving at a different decision. In his report for 1989/90, the Chief Adjudication Officer (1991) observed in relation to the declining standard of income

[10] Prestataire (1978).
[11] On the complexity of constructing cases, see the analysis by Sanders (1987), building on earlier work by Nelken (1983).

support submissions that, 'The most common failing was absent or deficient argument: matters raised by the appellant were often ignored' (para. 5. 4).[12] Where, then, appellants do not attend their hearings to put their side of the story (and since most letters challenging decisions provide only cryptic clues as to the appellant's grounds of appeal), the tribunal may be left with little apparent alternative but to follow the submission and dismiss the appeal. This was seen as highly unsatisfactory by many chairmen and members but only a few of them emphasized the need in non-attended cases for the tribunal to be especially vigilant in its scrutiny of the Department's case. Even this small minority conceded that the absence of the appellant made it unlikely that an appeal would be upheld.[13] Yet the heavy reliance by the tribunals upon submissions is worrying given the comments of the Chief Adjudication Officer regarding the 'many deficiencies' these written documents contain.[14]

The frustration experienced by tribunal panels when appellants fail to attend their hearings highlights one crucial fact: social security appeal tribunals may adopt an inquisitorial approach in the conduct of hearings, but they are emphatically not inquisitorial bodies in the full sense of that term.[15] They have no powers to compel witnesses, appellants, or presenting officers to attend, to require the production of evidence, or to investigate the truth of the matter for themselves away from the tribunal room. While they may assist the appellants to develop their cases at the hearing, they play no part in collecting and preparing evidence prior to this stage. The onus is on appellants to make out their claims, and, if they fail to attend the tribunal hearing, this is usually

[12] The Chief Adjudication Officer (1991) made similar comments regarding contributory benefits submissions (at para. 5. 11). Further evidence of this tendency is provided by the views of the current President of the social security appeal tribunals, as reported by the Chief Adjudication Officer: 'There are still . . . too many instances where the submission fails to deal with all the points raised in the claimant's letter of appeal and does not mention relevant case law especially if favourable to the claimant' (ibid., at para. 5. 33).

[13] It should be noted that it may be tactically advantageous for the appellant not to attend the appeal hearing where the onus lies on the adjudication officer to prove a case.

[14] Chief Adjudication Officer (1991) at para. 1. 13.

[15] For a variety of accounts of the differences between inquisitorial and adversarial systems see Zander (1988) at pp. 291–325. See Logie and Watchman (1989) for a discussion of these differences in the social security context.

not discharged.[16] Ganz (1974) has observed that, 'tribunals though they step into the arena much more than ordinary courts are still very much influenced by the adversary model of procedure' (p. 35). This remains true of social security appeal tribunals today. The dilemma that chairmen face in carrying out their duty to inquire into the case while lacking the means effectively to achieve this is reflected in the following quotes from chairmen and members on the issue of the absent appellant:

I must admit I'm very disappointed with the number of appellants who actually turn up. Far too many don't. There are plenty of people who simply don't want to bother. I always think it's a shame because you're not hearing one side. Part of the job involves evaluating the evidence and that involves evaluating the person who's giving that evidence. Do you believe them or don't you? I don't think you can do that unless you actually hear them. (Interview 2, Chairman, North East)

It's very difficult when the claimant doesn't turn up. You can only look through the papers then and see if there's a flaw. You have to be extra careful in these cases because so often when they do attend, something emerges which wasn't obvious from the papers. So when they are not present, you have to be careful that there isn't something questionable in the papers. But it's pretty difficult to find anything like that, depending on the nature of the case. (Interview 10, Chairman, Midlands)

It makes me quite angry sometimes when they don't come. They lodge an appeal, make the system work in such a way that their case comes before a tribunal, and then they don't even bother to appear. I think they do themselves a disservice. I would like to see some kind of solution to the question, where some pressure could be put on claimants to appear, whether it be by saying to them, 'If you want to appeal, there will be a deposit of £10 which you will get back', or whether you say, 'If you don't go to the appeal hearing and there is no good reason for your absence, you will pay all the costs.' Also, I wish the tribunal could compel witnesses and evidence as it would make things much easier for us to reach a decision. (Interview 49, Chairman, Scotland)

One of the traps for the unwary is that the appeal papers that are sent out prior to a hearing say that the appellant does not need to be present. I think that is bad advice because, on occasion after occasion, the tribunal would have been willing to sustain the appeal if certain points could

---

[16] For a valuable analysis of the burden of proof in this field, see Mesher (1987). In certain cases the burden of proof lies on the adjudication officer rather than the claimant, as where grounds need to be established to disqualify a claimant from unemployment benefit. Yet even here the submission and the oral presentation by the presenting officer may effectively shift the onus on to the appellant.

have been clarified. It should never be suggested that a case can be heard in an appellant's absence. I think it's fundamentally unsound. It's unfair to the appellant, and it doesn't seem to me to take account of the realities of a tribunal hearing. (Interview 50, Chairman, Scotland)

We've studied the papers before the day of hearing and we've made up our own minds. We've just had such a case today. I said to myself, 'If the presenting officer hasn't got anything further to say, then this is what I think.' And if the appellant isn't there, you've no reason to change your mind. (Interview 71, Member, Midlands)

If the appellant isn't there, one can't be as effective as one might otherwise be. All appellants ought to make an effort to attend because if they don't it seems almost like an admission on their part that they think they've lost. It's striking that with appellants who do come, the night before you might have been reading the case and thinking that they haven't got a chance, that it's a waste of time. But within ten minutes of the hearing starting, you begin to realize that there are things that he is saying that the presenting and adjudication officers knew nothing about. (Interview 100, Member, London South)

The success rates for appellants at the tribunal are shown in Table 8 broken down by whether or not they attended. The figures confirm the correlation between presence at an appeal hearing and a successful outcome.[17] None the less, half of the appellants who attended their hearings lost their appeals. While it is undeniable that attendance will improve the chances of success for an appellant with an arguable case, the fact remains that many appeals are so weak that attendance at the appeal hearing will make little or no difference to the outcome. In 64 per cent of the appeals treated by the tribunal as hopeless, the appellants failed to attend their hearings. Could these cases have been transformed into strong cases through attendance? Or had appellants made a realistic assessment of their chances on receiving the Department's written appeals submission after lodging their appeal? This submission represents the first full explanation claimants receive as to why the adjudication officer took the decision in question. The importance of the submission as a trigger for the withdrawal of appeals and as a factor in dissuading appellants from attending their appeals is examined further in

[17] This issue has been analysed in detail in the study undertaken by Genn and Genn (1989).

Chapter 6. Here it is sufficient to emphasize that attendance at a hearing by no means guarantees that a case will be strengthened. Nearly one in three of those appellants who attended hearings presented weak or hopeless cases and had their appeals dismissed accordingly.

TABLE 8: *Results of hearing by whether appellant or representative was present*

	Appellant or rep. present		No appellant or rep. present		Totals	
	No.	%	No.	%	No.	%
Appellant loses	91	49.7	118	76.6	209	62.0
Appellant wins in part	7	3.8	7	4.6	14	4.2
Appellant wins	72	39.4	18	11.7	90	26.7
Adjourned part-heard	13	7.1	11	7.1	24	7.1
	183	100.0	154	100.0	337	100.0

While it seems likely that many claimants correctly concluded that they stood little chance of winning their appeal, regardless of whether they attended their hearing, there was another substantial group of appellants, comprising 40 per cent of those who failed to turn up to their hearings, who appeared on paper to have arguable cases. Of the 63 appellants in this group, 27 lost their appeals, 18 won, 7 won in part and in 11 the tribunal adjourned the case part-heard to give the appellant another chance to attend. These figures suggest that the tribunal's inquisitorial approach often serves such appellants well, since of those appellants in this category, almost as many succeeded with their appeals as lost.

Not all the tribunals we observed gave much attention to non-attended cases, however. Forty per cent of the non-attended cases were heard in under five minutes, compared with 2 per cent of the attended cases. And only 36 per cent of the cases where the appellant was absent took more than ten minutes compared with 89 per cent of cases where the appellant was present.[18] The view was frequently expressed by chairmen and members that cases in which appellants failed to attend would tend to receive a more cursory examination than those in which the appellant appeared in person.[19] This tendency was acknowledged in the passages we quote here, illustrating the negative view that some chairmen and members take of absent appellants:

I always make a point of seeing what, if any, reason they've given us for not coming on the form. If someone says they are too ill to come, then I will perhaps give them a bit more of my time and attention than someone who has failed to respond at all. (Interview 15, Chairman, Midlands)

There is a tendency there, particularly with wing members, to say, 'If they are not coming, that's their own fault, so I don't see why we should find in favour of them.' (Interview 43, Chairman, North West)

There is a difference when they don't come. Some of these chairmen say, 'Well, no reply . . .' I've had many a row with chairmen in that situation and I try to put my foot down. One chairman said, 'He can't even be bothered to turn up—he'll get nothing.' I said, 'Hang on a minute, Mr Chairman, we've not even gone over the papers yet.' (Interview 68, Member, Midlands)

If they just don't attend and don't reply to any of the papers sent by the Department, then to me they're just not interested. So why should we bother? I personally feel that they're not worth bothering with. (Interview 83, Member, London North)

I always wonder, when they don't turn up, why they haven't turned up, and I tend to take the view that, if they can't be bothered, then neither can I. It's a matter of courteousness. There's been a lot of money spent preparing this appeal for hearing, and, if somebody doesn't turn up, then it's all just wasted. (Interview 88, Member, London North)

Absolutely there's a difference when they don't come inasmuch as they have asked for the appeal, we have attended and they haven't bothered. So I don't think we would lean over backwards to help them. (Interview 126, Member, North West)

Such attitudes as these help to explain why most non-attended

[18] The brevity of hearings in non-attended cases would not matter if the tribunal panel discussed the issues raised by the appeal before or after the hearing. Pre-hearing discussions did not appear to be common, however, and the brevity of post-hearing deliberations (which took five minutes or less in two-thirds of non-attended cases) suggests that these cases were dealt with somewhat peremptorily.

[19] This point was also made in the earlier literature. See, for example, Frost and Howard (1977) at pp. 53 and 59, Flockhart (1975) at p. 106, and Rose (1975) at p. 147.

cases were dealt with so swiftly by tribunals. As half of all appellants fail to attend their hearings, this finding is a cause for concern.

(iii) *Low rates of expert representation*

Another salient feature of tribunal adjudication is the high proportion of appellants without expert representation. Only 17 per cent of all appellants (whether they attended or not) were represented by agencies such as advice centres or Citizens Advice Bureaux. Whereas the erosion of discretion and the low rate of attendance at hearings were viewed by chairmen and members as greatly reducing the scope for an inquisitorial approach to hearings, the lack of expert representation was seen by them as making their active intervention to assist the appellant essential.

A number of problems, however, arose in connection with representation. First and foremost was that some respondents told us that they would not be inclined to intervene if a representative proved to be incompetent. This seems an adversarial stance, or at least reflects a certain awkwardness as to the proper function of the tribunal in this situation. Secondly, we noticed that, where there was a representative at a hearing, the atmosphere was more formal and businesslike, and this may not always have been in the appellant's best interests. In such cases the tribunal focused narrowly on the legal issues, paying little attention to possible extra-legal solutions to the appellant's plight. Thirdly, most respondents recognized that the absence of a representative meant that proceedings became more drawn out, and that the inquisitorial approach could not compensate for the lack of preparation of an appellant's case which a good representative would have undertaken prior to the day of hearing. Fourthly, the fear was expressed by a few chairmen and members that, by becoming too involved in assisting the unrepresented appellant, they would lose their objectivity and become biased in the appellant's favour. The following comments illustrate the range of views expressed to us on the issue of representation and the inquisitorial approach:

It's much more difficult when they're not represented. You've got to in those circumstances do all you can to help the appellant present his or her case while at the same time maintaining an unprejudiced attitude. It's a difficult trap because, by assisting, you become biased towards his or her case. That's a danger you've got to be concerned about. (Interview 2, Chairman, North East)

I see a difference between the CAB and a lawyer. I wouldn't particularly interfere with what a lawyer would put forward. If he wants to put forward the case and he makes a mess of it, so be it, that's his fault. (Interview 4, Chairman, North East)

If the appellant attends without a representative, I would take more of a leading role in extracting information than if he was represented, where I would feel sometimes that I was treading on the toes of the representative. Certainly we go to pains to make sure that a claimant who is not represented is not under any disabilty as a result of it. (Interview 13, Chairman, Midlands)

If the appellant's represented, you can take a number of short cuts and concentrate on the issues much more quickly. You can say to the person that's representing, 'It seems to me that the nub of this case is such and such. Should we be addressing ourselves to just this or is there anything else?' Also you can clear out of the way certain preliminary issues where the facts or the interpretation are agreed between the presenting officer and the representative. So it's obviously very much easier for a chairman if the claimant is represented. (Interview 28, Chairman, London South)

I feel particularly for unrepresented elderly people who don't really understand the thing at all. One's got to bend over backwards to try and extract the case they're trying to make, and put it back to them in question form—either to make sure one's colleagues have picked it up or to be sure in one's own mind. It does put an extra strain on the tribunal. But every chairman I've sat with has always bent over backwards to bring the appellant's case forward. (Interview 116, Member, Wales and South West)

The overall message which came out of our interviews with chairmen and members is that the inquisitorial approach is seen as being most relevant in cases when an appellant attends a hearing, but has no representative. In cases where a representative is present, or an appellant is absent, the inquisitorial approach is much less in evidence. Indeed, in some instances, it is abandoned altogether.

How far inquisitorially minded chairmen can compensate for a lack of expert representation is an interesting question. Genn and Genn (1989) have argued that such compensation as can be offered is inadequate, but the Lord Chancellor's Department has shown little enthusiasm for their proposal that a publicly funded representation service be set up. Instead, it seems, the preference is for chairmen to be encouraged to enter into the arena of the dispute still further in order to assist the appellant.[20] Even if one leaves aside the objection that the appellant needs help to prepare a case before the hearing, it must be recognized that the inquisitorial approach does not necessarily work to the unrepresented appellant's advantage. At the heart of such an approach is a search for the truth, and it may not always be in the interests of the appellant for the truth to come out. It must be remembered that the tribunal's primary task is to establish the appellant's correct entitlement according to the law. As one experienced chairman put it when asked if there was any difference in his role when the appellant had no representative:

Oh yes, very much so, it's much harder work then. I do very much think that it's the duty of the tribunal to in a sense act for the claimant, but with one reservation. That is that of course an advocate would leave well alone the answers that were going to be detrimental to him. But because it's an inquisitorial role, you've got to get answers to those questions which may be against him as well as those which are going to help him. (Interview 31, Chairman, Wales and South West)

The point might be made that the interests of justice demand that the truth should be discovered through such an inquisition, but this merely begs the larger question of whether a more inquisitorial or adversarial system of trial produces the better standard of justice. There is a large body of literature which suggests that truth, far from being an absolute, is something which is shaped and constructed by the processes designed to discover it.[21] The traditional English view has been that 'truth is best discovered by powerful statements on both sides of the question'.[22] This sentiment highlights the problem of the imbalance of power before social security appeal tribunals. The unrepresented appellant, lacking resources, experience, and expertise, is unlikely to be able to match the powerful statements made by way of the 'written submission and the oral contributions

[20] At a Legal Action Group conference held in London on 17 March 1990, a representative of the Lord Chancellor's Department indicated that this was the position being taken within Government in response to Genn and Genn's findings.

[21] See, for example, Sanders (1987), where this perspective is adopted in analysing how the police construct files for use in the prosecution process.

[22] *Ex parte Lloyd* (1822) Mont. 70, 72 n., *per* Lord Eldon LC

of the presenting officer. Not surprisingly, the training pro-grammes for presenting officers discourage them from playing an adversarial role, and chairmen are exhorted to act as active inquisitors rather than as neutral umpires. But chairmen doing so run the risk of becoming partial, and not necessarily in favour of the appellant, for by descending into the arena an adjudi-cator's vision is liable to be 'clouded by the dust of conflict'.[23] As Ganz (1974) warns, 'nothing would be gained if for an unequal contest there were substituted an accusatory inquisition' (p. 35).

More generally, one has to be wary about making the false assumption that, because tribunals adopt an inquisitorial approach, they are therefore more likely to be sympathetic to the appellants who come before them. Even under the steward-ship of legal chairmen, a minority of tribunals we observed were still prone to act as if their peculiar view of a claimant's deserts was a more important issue than the claimant's entitlements. Tribunals are not immune from cultural bias or from social stereo-typing, although legal chairmen may be better able to keep in check their personal prejudices. However, the temptation to sit in judgement on the person rather than on the appeal derives not just from cultural and social influences but from the legisla-tion itself. Under the old supplementary benefit scheme, the availability of single payments and additional requirements gave claimants considerable scope to use the appeals system in a pro-active way as a means of securing a higher award of benefit. Take up campaigns organized by welfare rights groups encour-aged claimants to pursue such possibilities, and periodic upsurges in the number of appeals heard by tribunals were testi-mony to their success. The income support legislation, by con-trast, lays down fixed benefit rates which allow little latitude in taking account of individual circumstances, and the nature of social security appeals has undergone a significant shift accordingly.

A striking feature of our sample of 337 cases was the proportion of appeals—38 per cent—brought by claimants as a reaction to decisions to reduce or terminate their entitlement to benefit, or else to recover money paid out in error to them. In essence,

[23] *Yuill* v. *Yuill* [1945] 1 All ER 183, *per* Lord Greene MR.

appeals against such decisions are defensive in nature on the claimant's part. The issues in such cases centre not on the needs but on the actions of the appellant. For example, a claimant can be disqualified from receiving unemployment benefit for up to twenty-six weeks if an adjudication officer decides that the claimant became unemployed through leaving a job voluntarily without just cause or through being dismissed for misconduct.[24] This provision smacks of punishment, and the penal undertones of such regulations can permeate appeal hearings and even be amplified by tribunal members. One case we observed is worth discussing in some detail to illustrate this point, although we stress that this was one of the most extreme examples we encountered of such an approach.

The case in question concerned an Asian shopworker who was appealing against being disqualified from receiving unemployment benefit for twenty-six weeks for leaving his employment voluntarily. The appellant's case was that he had been unfairly dismissed. The chairman made no attempt to put him at his ease and conducted the case in a forceful and domineering style. She fired question after question at the appellant and would not allow his representative to present the case in the way he wished. Although appearing self-confident, she misunderstood the legal issues in the case and had to be corrected on the law on more than one occasion by the representative. The latter was backed up at key points by the presenting officer from the Department who proved to be very fair-minded. Both members followed their chairman's lead and adopted an inappropriately aggressive approach. The woman member's manner was accusatory—at one time she jabbed her finger at the appellant as she tried to ram home a point, and, on another occasion, she accompanied the repetition of a question with the banging of her knuckles on the table. Both members exuded confidence although in fact they were often wrong about the facts or the law, or missed the point. It was as if the members and chairman saw themselves as prosecuting barristers conducting a cross-examination in a Crown Court trial of a suspicious character prone to lying and concealment. The appellant was not evasive and his story was coherent and believable, and it was hard to

---

[24] See the discussion by Ogus and Barendt (1988) at pp. 97–110.

see why the panel conducted itself in the way that it did. The representative had to fight for the right to put his client's case. He managed to stay calm although his exasperation with the tribunal showed once or twice when he wearily dropped his head.

The case illustrates the importance of expert representation in ensuring that an appellant's interests are properly protected. In the absence of the tacit alliance formed by the presenting officer and representative in this case, an injustice would have been much more likely. In the event, the appellant won his case and no disqualification was imposed. This and cases like it drive one to the conclusion that it is unsatisfactory to assume that the best interests of the unrepresented appellant will invariably be served by the members of the tribunal. It is not just a question of the odd tribunal member behaving in an aberrational fashion (a feature which any legal system must tolerate), but a problem which is endemic inasmuch as tribunals must pursue a variety of goals and will not always give precedence to assisting appellants.[25] The inquisitorial approach represents only one of a number of important techniques employed by tribunals in their work, and tribunals perform a range of functions in addition to the most obvious one of determining the case that comes before them. This point is best explored through a closer examination of the way in which appeal hearings are conducted.

The conduct of appeal hearings

It is clear from observing social security appeal tribunals in action that the tone of the hearing is dictated by the style and approach of the chairman. The wing members, the presenting officer, the appellant and any representative all tend to take their cue from this key actor in the hearing. The hearings we attended involved a great variety of individuals, legal issues, social circumstances and personalities. All represented, in some measure, a test of the chairman's competence, and it is fair to record that we were in general impressed by the quality of the chairmen we observed.

[25] Sympathetic treatment is not very likely if, for example, in their inquisitorial search for the truth, a tribunal forms the view that an appellant is lying.

As part of our observations of tribunal hearings, we were interested to discover how full an introduction chairmen gave at the outset of the hearing; whether the parts played by the various people in the tribunal room were adequately explained; whether the independence of the tribunal was emphasized, and whether an explanation was given as to the procedure to be followed in the hearing. We also noted how far the tribunal succeeded in putting the appellant at ease and the extent to which the chairman involved the appellant, presenting officer, and wing members during the course of the hearing. Another area of interest was the amount of questioning undertaken by the chairman, as this is the central element in the inquisitorial approach which tribunals are meant to adopt. Finally, we noted whether chairmen explained the outcome of the hearing clearly to appellants or left them confused about what would happen next.

On the basis of these assessments, we concluded that the chairman's handling of a case was good or excellent in 57 per cent of the hearings we attended, and, in a further quarter of the hearings, the chairman's conduct was assessed as adequate. In about one in every six hearings, however, the chairman's conduct of the case was in our view open to serious criticism. The best chairmen we observed did not make a great show of giving other participants an opportunity to speak, but instead created such a relaxed atmosphere that it was easy for all concerned to say whatever they wanted at any point in the hearing. Hearings conducted by such chairmen did not become formless since control was retained with a deft and light touch. These chairmen could properly be described as fulfilling the enabling role envisaged by Bell.

This kind of atmosphere was achieved in a number of ways. A full explanation at the outset of the hearing of the roles of those present, the independence of the tribunal, the procedure to be followed and the like, seemed effective in putting appellants at their ease and, if skilfully done, removed much of the initial tension from the hearing. Some degree of sympathy for the appellant's grievance also seemed an important component, since the atmosphere of a hearing can quickly become soured where a claimant feels that the tribunal lacks concern. Even so, the most important quality that appellants seek at a hearing is thoroughness, with chairmen disinclined to rely on the summary of facts and law as contained in the appeal papers prepared by the Department. They want someone who will first verify the factual details afresh by drawing them out of the appellant and the presenting officer and then go on to check the legal position with the latter by discussing the applicable regulations.

This is, in our view, what is meant by the inquisitorial role, yet it must be stressed that it often achieves little in pure legal terms. Indeed, in well-run hearings, the bare reality of the limited power of the tribunal is fully exposed. Under these conditions one cannot attribute the dismissal of an appeal to an incompetent chairman, nor to the presence of a dogmatic and adversarial presenting officer, sullenly defending the Department's corner, nor to the wing members remaining mute. The simple truth is that the appellants in many cases lose because the rules predetermine that result.

In other cases a fair and inquisitorial hearing may be crucial in ensuring that a meritorious appeal is upheld. Even in hopeless cases, it is important that the appellant considers the appeal process to have been fair. They need to be able to distinguish between a grievance caused by the nature of the legislation and a grievance due to the handling of the case on the part of the Department or the tribunal. It became clear to us, however, as we observed hearings in different parts of the country, that some chairmen play this inquisitorial role much more naturally and effectively than do others.

We found that some chairmen were able to adopt it in a sensitive and expert manner, skilfully eliciting information from claimants and encouraging them to participate fully in the discussion. Other chairmen experienced evident unease in descending into the fray in this way and reverted to adversarial type at the first opportunity. Still others did not strive to play it at all. It is worthwhile examining the wide variations in approach we observed in the light of the field notes that we made at the time. The following quotes from these notes start with those chairmen who seemed to us to be the most adept at playing an inquisitorial role:

Courteous, sympathetic and clear. She was good at ascertaining the facts and then applying the regulations. The CAB worker was asked to explain why an overpayment of child benefit should not be recoverable by the Department. The representative talked instead about how the appellant had agreed to foster children and what difficult children she had taken on. This seemed to be intended to establish the appellant as 'deserving'. The representative tailed off inconclusively and the chairman asked, 'What is your argument under the regulations?' Through careful questioning, the chairman extracted from the representative the main points of the legal argument required to be put on the appellant's behalf. Later she invited contributions from her members who clearly felt at ease with her. She was also good on the law. A first class chairman. (Comments on case 64, Midlands)

The chairman attempted gently to coax the full story out of the appellant. The procedure was informal with both parties talking and answering questions at the chairman's invitation. No fixed procedure was adopted but, by the end of the hearing, the facts seemed to have been well established. The chairman adopted a truly inquisitorial role and allowed each of the parties to have their say. It was very informal but not disorganized. The chairman was clearly sensitive and sympathetic to the appellant, and this came across clearly at the hearing. (Comments on case 233, Wales and South West)

The chairman explained the role of the tribunal well but referred to it on occasion as a 'court'. In his introduction, he gave a full outline of what seemed a highly structured procedure: 'What I usually do is get the presenting officer to start by going through the summary of facts and allow you to challenge those facts. Then I ask you to present your case and give the presenting officer the chance to ask you questions. Then she presents the Department's case and you put your questions. Then I give both of you a last chance to speak. All right?' Without giving the appellant any choice, he asked the presenting officer to start. The procedure adhered to made the hearing seem adversarial—asking each side to present a case and then face a virtual cross-examination. Despite this, a friendly tone was maintained throughout, and the chairman was at pains to ensure the appellant understood why he was going to lose his case. (Comments on case 86, Midlands)

The chairman was accusatory in approach, and he seemed already to have made up his mind that the appellant was in the wrong. When the claimant explained how he made a mistake on the form, the chairman said, 'Well, that's a mistake you may live to regret.' He put the appellant in an 'us and them' position by talking a lot to the presenting officer and wing members, and addressing himself sternly to the appellant. He spoke in terms of the appellant's 'guilt'. (Comments on case 327, Scotland)

This chairman was very concerned to give a full introduction to the case but gave the impression that he was preparing the appellant for a negative decision. During the hearing he was too dominant and gave the impression that only his view was valid, cutting other contributions short if he considered them to be off the legal point. He did not invite either member to contribute. He treated appellants, in this and other cases observed, as if they were legally qualified experienced representatives. He made little or no allowance for the fact that they were lacking in training, expertise and experience. He placed totally unrealistic expectations on appellants to address the legal points and keep to the legal issues throughout. (Comments on case 95, Midlands)

The chairman maintained a severe, stern tone of voice throughout and displayed no sympathy at all to the appellant or his representative. She made no attempt to put the appellant at his ease or to explain the tribunal's function and procedure. Indeed, she showed some irritation that the appellant had pursued his appeal after previously indicating that he wished to withdraw it. The hearing was conducted according to her personal whim without there being any discernible procedure. She did not invite the appellant or his representative to put their case, let alone ask whether they had any questions for the presenting officer. Her conduct of the hearing was very poor indeed. (Comments on case 52, Midlands)

As these comments indicate, the way that chairmen run the hearings varies enormously. Some are patient and sympathetic, facilitating the difficult task that appellants and other parties face in getting across the essentials of their case. Other chairmen perform these tasks much less satisfactorily. Some of the explanation for such variations lies in the differing personalities involved, but underlying this is a more important factor—the nature of the tribunal's central task and the contradictions involved in its performance. This is highlighted by the official guide to tribunal procedure which declares that:

The claimant should be allowed to put any points he may wish to make in his own way and air any relevant real or imagined grievance, so that nobody can reasonably say that he did not have a fair hearing. The desire for informality should not, however, be allowed to defeat the primary objective of establishing the true facts so that the tribunal may come to a correct decision in accordance with the relevant statutory provisions. The chairman must therefore be prepared to intervene impartially, when necessary, in order to ensure that the proceedings are orderly or to curb lengthy speeches which are obviously irrelevant to the questions at issue.[26]

Chairmen, then, are enjoined both to allow appellants to air imagined grievances in their own way, and to intervene to ensure that proceedings remain orderly and irrelevant contributions are curtailed. Yet in a system that has become ever more tightly

[26] Office of the President of Social Security Appeal Tribunals (1988) at para. 46.

regulated, it is apparent that what claimants have to say at tribunals about their level of need and personal circumstances has become increasingly irrelevant in a legal sense. Chairmen and members, whatever level of sympathy and compassion they might express to claimants, are obliged to apply the law and the elaborate body of legal regulations. It is easy, then, to see why some chairmen find that adopting a traditional, adversarial approach comes more naturally to them. The body of law with which these tribunals deal is both technical and complex, and it was perhaps remarkable that chairmen were prepared to allow arguments to be developed which could only cloud the legal issues to the extent that they did.

A member in London neatly summed up the way that some claimants throw themselves upon the mercy of the tribunal, unconcerned about the legal merits of an appeal. He told us that the grounds of appeal in many cases run along the lines, 'The decision must be wrong because I can't manage.' We observed for ourselves how claimants often rely on a common-sense or intuitive notion of what is right or just, in ignorance of the legal merits of their appeal. In reality this means that many cases are in a strict legal sense flimsy, indeed often doomed from the outset. What is a good chairman to do in such a situation? It is in our view desirable that these cases be dealt with sympathetically but without disingenuousness or equivocation.

It is surely a misguided chairman who seeks to offer a hand to develop arguments which have no merit in law, knowing full well that in the end the appeal must be dismissed. It is small consolation to unsuccessful claimants to see that their executioner has a smile on his face and is ready to raise their hopes, if only temporarily. In consequence, it seems that chairmen need to tailor their approach to the exigencies of the circumstances with which they are dealing. Furthermore, the tribunals simply do not have the time to allow appellants to develop at their own pace arguments which will inevitably fail, still less to encourage them to do so. This is one reason why most chairmen and members prefer to have a competent representative so that the key arguments can be identified and presented clearly to the tribunal.[27] This enables chairmen to adopt a more robust

---

[27] See the discussion on this point by Genn and Genn (1989) at pp. 168–9.

approach so that cases can be disposed of more expeditiously. Where no representative is present, or the representative is of limited competence, there is a need for chairmen to maintain a reasonably tight rein on hearings, otherwise cases may drag on interminably and the list will not be completed on time.

Yet it has to be recognized that the unrepresented appellant rarely has a case so well prepared that the facts have been carefully marshalled for presentation to the tribunal, and it may be necessary for the chairman to draw out details of the case in order to test the facts on which the Department has based its decision. This can be a time-consuming exercise which, as we saw for ourselves, often gets bogged down in a welter of detail about the appellant's work record, the difficulties of making ends meet, wartime experiences and the like. But appellants' perceptions of the fairness of hearings are likely to be influenced by the treatment they receive from the chairman and by whether such details (however irrelevant in a strict legal sense) were considered courteously. It is easily forgotten that an appeal hearing represents for most appellants the first chance to talk to anyone in authority about their needs and grievances. The administration of social security at the local office level, as we noted earlier, has become a highly impersonal business. Adjudication officers rarely come into contact with claimants and, generally speaking, claimants are restricted to talking to junior staff at the reception desk and to filling in official forms. The appeal hearing therefore offers appellants a valuable opportunity to unburden themselves and give vent to any frustration that might have built up as a result of dealing with officialdom.[28]

Many appellants come to the tribunal with grievances which they wish to voice over and above any strictly legal issues that their appeal might raise. These grievances tend to fall into two main categories. The first concern the Department's handling of their case, whether this relates to the behaviour of staff or the administrative procedures followed. Such complaints are bound to be raised in a system which encourages appellants to say their piece. Some tribunals react by forestalling any digressions of this sort, but, more usually, while legal irrelevan-

---

[28] See Christie (1977) who argues powerfully that litigants' perceptions of the important issues at stake in a hearing should be given precedence over a narrower legalistic perspective.

cies are not encouraged, neither are they stifled. Instead the panel simply does not respond to such tirades, and this lack of reaction seems effective in keeping the proceedings moving and reasonably to the point. The other type of grievance concerns the appellants' strong sense that the rules have operated so unfairly against them that they must be wrong—a perception that can even infect the approach of an experienced representative. In this situation, one of the important roles played by the tribunal may be to explain that the decision of the adjudication officer is in law correct and that it is the rules laid down by Parliament, not the Department's implementation of those rules, which are responsible.

We often observed tribunals to go further than this, however, particularly when they found that they were themselves out of sympathy with the hard and fast rules they were duty bound to apply. Typically, they would look for a way around the rules, but usually without success. The next step would be to investigate whether there was any chance of the appellant receiving some other benefit from the Department. Even when this broad approach had been taken to an appeal, the tribunal frequently found itself powerless to assist. Even so, panels on occasion sought to offer advice on other sources of help, such as a local charity, or suggested that the appellant's Member of Parliament be contacted. This wide interpretation of the tribunal's function is surely to be welcomed.[29] Many appeals could be avoided if all claimants were to receive such attention and advice when they first came in contact with the benefits system.

It follows from this discussion that to attempt to characterize tribunal hearings as either adversarial or inqusitorial would be too simplistic, as chairmen and members themselves recognized. We were able to explore in interviews with both chairmen and members the way that they viewed their roles, and, we were particularly interested in finding out how far chairmen and members had absorbed Judge Byrt's philosophy that tribunals should be inquisitorial rather than adversarial in nature. Only about one-third of the chairmen we interviewed saw their role predominantly in these terms. Most chairmen saw their role in quite different terms altogether. Whilst often referring to the inquisit-

[29] See Baldwin and Hill (1987) where comparable steps taken by other types of tribunal are discussed.

orial function of the tribunal (although seldom using this precise terminology), they also saw their own role as defining the issues, guiding the procedure and generally controlling the conduct of the hearing. Chairmen frequently emphasized the central importance of explaining the adjudication officer's decision to an appellant, particularly in those cases where there was no real prospect of success in the appeal, or of simply allowing claimants to have 'their day in court'.

Some indication of the complexities in the chairman's role is given in the following quotes from chairmen explaining how they saw it:

There is a difference between what my role ought to be and what my role is in fact. My role ought to be to ensure that everybody has a fair hearing, that everybody has plenty of time to say what they want to say or ask questions which they want to ask, direct members on the law, and to make everybody feel comfortable and happy. In fact, my role is very much in the nature of an inquisitor. I tend to ask questions, particularly of the presenting officer and of the appellant, if the appellant is here, to try to get to the bottom of the case as quickly as possible. I fear that tends to leave the members out in the cold sometimes, and it may come across as far as the presenting officer is concerned as antagonistic. I'm sorry for that, but it's the only way I can do it in order to get on. Otherwise the thing just carries on endlessly without getting to the real root of the issue. Other appellants waiting outside will get angry if they've turned up at 10.20 and their case isn't heard until 12.30. But I do accept that its function also is to ensure that people feel that they've had a fair hearing and I think that's true of any court. So it has a dual function, to make decisions and to make people feel that they've had a fair hearing. (Interview 17, London North)

I see my role as making the appellant feel at ease, to start with, so that they don't feel daunted by the procedure to such an extent that we can't get to the bottom of the matter. I see my role as being to make very sure that the appellant says everything that they want to say and doesn't leave feeling that they'd wished they'd said something else, because very often they seem to feel that they haven't had the chance up to now to say what is worrying them. And also in many instances I see my role very much as explaining the law in layman's terms. It's so often the case that appellants simply haven't understood why a decision was made because no one's taken the time to explain. I see my role as bringing in the members as much as possible and generally making sure that everybody has their say. It's my role too to explain the law to the members when we come to make our decision. And making sure that the proceeding doesn't become untidy, that it's informal enough to be relaxing; formal enough to be tidy. You can't let it degenerate into a chat, but it has to be a fairly relaxed atmosphere. That's quite a tight line to keep but I do try to do that. (Interview 24, London South)

Social security appeal tribunals are clearly recognized by chairmen as performing more than one function, and chairmen differ in performing the various aspects of their multi-faceted task: enquiring, enabling, explaining, listening, informing, advising, and controlling. In a minority of hearings we observed, the chairman demonstrably failed to reconcile the competing aims of deciding a legal case in a reasonably efficient manner and ensuring that the appellant perceived the hearing to be fair. At both ends of the spectrum, there are obvious problems. Some chairmen focus far too narrowly on the strict legal issues in a case and refuse point blank to allow the appellant to stray from the confines of the law: others adopt such a relaxed approach at the appeal hearing that the proceedings become disordered and the legal point at issue is in danger of being lost.

Conclusion

In this chapter our concern has been to elucidate the main features of hearings before social security appeal tribunals. Perhaps the most striking feature of these hearings is the low rate of attendance, with barely one in two appellants turning up for their hearing. This phenomenon will be explored more fully in Chapter 6, and it has been discussed here as explaining why tribunals often eschew their official inquisitorial role in favour of a more adversarial approach. The inflexibility of much of the body of law which the tribunal administers also makes the exercise of enquiring carefully into the appellant's needs seem rather pointless. On the other hand the low rate of expert representation before the tribunal is clearly seen by chairmen as placing a duty upon them to help appellants make out their cases as best as they can. Most do this skilfully, coping well with the contradictions inherent in the many functions a tribunal is obliged to perform.

Striking the right balance between the primary objective of establishing the legal merits of the case and ensuring that the appellant perceives the hearing to be fair is no easy matter. That this balance is achieved in a majority of hearings is evidence of how far social security tribunals have progressed since the early 1970s when supplementary benefit appeal tribunals were described as 'the slum of the English tribunal system'.[30] Social security appeal tribunals, for the most part, maintain impressively high standards of procedural fairness in adjudication, and it is right that the great strides that have been taken since the Bell report be acknowledged.[31]

In a minority of hearings, however, the chairman's conduct of the proceedings leaves much to be desired. In particular, some chairmen and members incorrectly jump to the conclusion that, in the absence of the appellant, there is nothing to enquire about and simply accept the Department's case without demur. The written submission is not scrutinized, the law is not checked, and the presenting officer is not questioned or challenged. It is an attitude that ought be discouraged since it so clearly conflicts with the inquisitorial philosophy which is meant to underpin the work of the tribunal. At root the problem is structural in that an inquisitorial approach has been grafted on to an essentially adversarial framework. It should come as no surprise, therefore, when this underlying reality surfaces in tribunal hearings.

It would seem to follow that, no matter how good the chairman, an appellant's interests (and often the tribunal's interests too) are best served by the use of expert representatives. There is a price to be paid for introducing representatives into appeal hearings in terms of reducing an appellant's involvement in the proceedings, and the overemphasis on the purely legal points at issue which tends to result. In the light of the findings discussed in this chapter, we would argue that the price is well worth paying.

---

[30] Rose (1975) at p. 150.

[31] The overall high standards of the part-time chairmen we observed suggest that little would be gained by moving towards a greater reliance on their full-time counterparts.

5

The Chairmen and Members

THIS chapter focuses on the decision makers in social security appeal tribunals: the chairmen and two wing members. The discussion covers both the backgrounds of tribunal personnel and the part they play in appeal hearings. Fulbrook (1978) has noted that, 'The number three seems to have acquired almost mystical proportions in many kinds of judicial forums as a number best representing a check on individual bias and idiosyncracy' (p. 208). The extent to which such a check is achieved depends on assembling a reasonable mix of people on the tribunal panel, and the backgrounds of those who sit on tribunals will be explored in the first half of this chapter. It is also important to consider the dynamics of an appeal hearing and the contribution made by each panel member, for, if wing members play only a minor role, their differing backgrounds would be of little real significance. Hence the central concern of the second half of this chapter will be to examine the interrelationship between the legal chairman and the two lay members and the way that this manifests itself at tribunal hearings. In our analysis, we shall use the material collected from interviews carried out with fifty chairmen and ninety-seven lay members of the tribunals we visited in different parts of the country, and draw upon our own observations of the tribunals in action.

One of the main arguments in this chapter will be that legal chairmen play a predominant role in tribunals, leaving their lay members very much on the sidelines. We have of course little direct evidence of that part of the hearing when the tribunal deliberates on its decision, since we were able to observe the deliberations in only five cases.[1] In 21 per cent of the cases observed, there were no formal deliberations because the tribunal reached its decision in the course of the hearing, and, in a further 37 per cent of the cases, the deliberations were concluded within five minutes. In all, only one-fifth of the cases occupied the tribunal at this stage for more than ten minutes, and it is likely that some of this time was used in writing the decision rather than in discussing it. These findings reflect the cut-and-dried nature of many of the cases coming before social security appeal tribunals. Thus, even if it were the case that members played an active (but unseen) part in the deliberations the importance of that stage of the process should not be overstated. It seems more plausible, however, to suppose that only the minority of members who take a full part in the public stage of the hearing will do likewise during the deliberations, and this hypothesis was supported by the material collected from a number of the chairmen we interviewed.

The tribunal personnel

The creation of the social security appeal tribunals by the merger of national insurance local tribunals with supplementary benefit appeal tribunals resulted in three important changes to the principles governing tribunal membership. First, social security appeal tribunal chairmen were required to be lawyers; secondly, the trade unions' right to nominate lay members to the tribunals was abolished; and, thirdly, responsibility for the appointment of lay members and for the administration of the system as a whole was transferred from the Department of Health and Social Security to the independent President of the

---

[1] We encountered much confusion about whether, having attended the hearing, we could remain for the deliberations with the consent of the parties. Some chairmen agreed that this was quite in order, but were effectively 'overruled' by their clerks who insisted that we be excluded. We were reluctant to argue the point since we were dependent on the goodwill of chairmen and clerks in carrying out other important aspects of the research.

Social Security Appeal Tribunals. It will be helpful to consider the significance of each of these three reforms in turn.

(i) The appointment of legal chairmen

The chairman of a social security appeal tribunal must be a barrister or solicitor of at least five years' standing.[2] This requirement has formalized the practice in the old national insurance local tribunals where it was viewed as desirable that chairmen be legally qualified because of the existence of a large body of national insurance legislation and case law, and because of the need for tribunal procedures to conform to the rules of natural justice.[3] The position was quite different in supplementary benefit appeal tribunals. These were traditionally chaired by lay people, the justification being that their hearings were more in the nature of an assessment or case committee 'taking a further look at the facts and in some cases arriving at a fresh decision on the extent of need'.[4] This approach became increasingly unrealistic after 1966 (and even more so after 1980) as supplementary benefit acquired a detailed, legislative basis.

The move towards legally qualified chairmen began in earnest with the publication of the Bell report (1975) which identified the use of lay chairmen as the main reason for the poor quality of adjudication in supplementary benefit appeal tribunals. Lay chairmen, according to Bell, were more likely to fail to appreciate the distinction between the law and Supplementary Benefits Commission policy, to misunderstand the law itself, and to be generally less competent in dealing with procedural and evidential questions. Bell concluded that 'the superior quality of the legal chairmen stood out from amongst their colleagues' (p. 6), and she strongly recommended that more lawyers be appointed to chair these tribunals. The gradual implementation of this pro-

---

[2] Section 97(2)(e) of the Social Security Act 1975, as substituted by section 16 of the Health and Social Security Act 1984. The Lord Chancellor's Department also operates a non-statutory rule that chairmen should not be appointed under the age of 35.

[3] This was not a statutory requirement but the practice arose following undertakings given in Parliament for reasons given in the text. Per Sir Eric Bowyer, Franks (1957b) at p. 35.

[4] See Franks (1957a) at para. 182, referring to the national assistance appeal tribunals, later renamed supplementary benefit appeal tribunals.

posal meant that the proportion of chairmen who were legally qualified on the supplementary benefit side rose from 6 per cent in 1973 to 40 per cent by 1983.[5]

By that time, the need to improve the quality of both substantive and procedural justice provided by supplementary benefit appeal tribunals was not in doubt. The question was whether this would be achieved by making a legal qualification a prerequisite of appointment or whether there was still a place for some lay chairmen in the system. The arguments on each side were finely balanced.[6] Judging by the experience of national insurance local tribunals, legal chairmen offered the prospect of an immediate improvement in standards of adjudication. But legal qualifications are no guarantee of a knowledge of social security law, let alone an understanding of the problems of claimants. Critics of the Government's plans were particularly concerned that the appointment of legal chairmen would result in hearings becoming unduly formal, thereby discouraging claimants from putting their case. Kenneth Clarke, the then Minister of State, assured the House of Commons that:

the intention is not to make the hearings more legalistic or formal in any way. However, lawyers will be better able to cope with the detailed supplementary benefit regulations. Hon. Members will know that 'detailed' is something of an understatement. In conducting the hearings they will also be able to ensure a better standard of hearing for claimants.[7]

In the event, the Government's only concession was to allow lay chairmen to continue to preside over supplementary benefit appeals for a transitional period of five years. This period ended in April 1989 when the fieldwork for the research described in this book was just starting. The Government's insistence on legal qualifications undoubtedly meant the loss of some experienced and competent lay chairmen, a consequence regretted by the Council on Tribunals.[8] Yet this was the price to be paid for the commitment to raise the overall standards of adjudication.

[5] See Harris (1983), p. 215 and *per* Mr K. Clarke, Standing Committee B, col. 638 (19 April 1983).

[6] An alternative strategy, advocated in particular by Frank Field, MP, was the creation of a corps of career tribunal clerks to advise lay chairmen on points of law, following the model of magistrates' courts.

[7] H.C. Debs., Vol. 37, col. 497 (17 Feb. 1983).

[8] Council on Tribunals (1983), para. 3. 36.

From our interviews with chairmen and members, it was apparent that both groups have now largely accepted that the sacrifice of lay chairmen was worthwhile. Eighty-two per cent of chairmen and 78 per cent of members described the requirement for chairmen to be legally qualified as definitely desirable. As several of the chairmen conceded, self-interest alone might account for this high level of support amongst their ranks, but members were almost as enthusiastic. Indeed, only a small minority of members (13 per cent) could be said to have serious reservations about the phasing out of lay chairmen.[9]

The vast majority of both chairmen and members took the view that legal chairmanship has now become an indispensable feature of social security appeal tribunals. The main reason for this was seen as being the increasing complexity of social security law. Some argued that the Government probably had it in mind from the outset that the introduction of legal chairmen would ensure uniform application of its policies as expressed through technical regulations. Ministers could thus achieve policy ends by means of ever more obscure and complex regulations, confident that the tribunals would toe the line required by law.

Other respondents argued that legal chairmanship could offer significant advantages to the appellant, particularly in view of the non-discretionary character of many of the cases now coming before tribunals. If the only way to find for the appellant is to determine that an adjudication officer has erred in law, (say, by wrongly applying the burden of proof), then the appellant is likely to be better served by someone familiar with legal concepts than by a well-meaning but inexpert lay chairman. The range of views of chairmen and members on legal chairmanship is well illustrated by the following quotes drawn from our interviews:

I don't understand how those who weren't legally qualified could in fact have coped in the past. The regulations are horrendously dense and complicated, even the modern ones, the income support regulations. I think they've been amended on five occasions already. It's diffi-

---

[9] There was some support, amongst this minority of members, for the idea that the tribunal clerk be made the legal adviser to the tribunal. Others argued that there should still be a place for experienced lay members with a good understanding of the legislation to be appointed as chairmen.

cult to imagine how someone who hasn't been trained to read statutes can actually cope. (Interview 12, Chairman, Midlands)

When it came to the completion of the AT3 [the official written record of the hearing] and the increasing demands as to the fullness of that document, the non-legally qualified chairmen were falling short. No doubt this is one of the reasons why the requirement was introduced. There were too many appeals for a long time. Very often a decision formulated by a chairman would fail for error of law as being inadequate. (Interview 34, Chairman, Wales and South West)

We are bound by the regulations and have very little discretion, but wing members don't always understand this. There is a tendency on the part of the members to look for a way round, which is just not the object of the exercise. The object of the exercise is, is this person entitled within the regulations or is he not? And I do think they need direction on that. Some of the things the members say sometimes chill me, and that's what makes me feel that you must have a legally qualified person as chairman. (Interview 48, Chairman, Scotland)

I'm all for it. When I first started, there were many chairmen who were not solicitors and I found the older ones rather judgemental, taking the attitude, 'We didn't have this in our day', and turning it into an 'us and them' situation. Chairmen nowadays tend to be more objective. That is what the legal training is for, to enable them to form an impartial view. (Interview 74, Member, Midlands)

It is a great advantage to have a legal chairman who knows the law. We rely on him quite heavily on the legal background now much more than before. The Government probably knew well in advance that it was going to bring in all these rules and regulations and tighten up on them. To prepare the tribunals for that situation, they obviously couldn't have lay members who weren't as well up on the law as legal people. So it was that which must have prompted them to bring in chairpersons who had a more legal background than the old chairmen. (Interview 80, Member, London North)

In the old days, when social security law wasn't so tight, there was much more scope for discretion to play a part and non-legally qualified chairmen were probably a lot more understanding than legally qualified chairmen would have been and exercised discretion in a far more sensible way. Now there's so little discretion left to tribunals, and, in most cases, all you can do is try and find mistakes made by the adjudication officer. That is something that a legally qualified chairmen is much better at doing because he knows what other paragraphs to look at in the law, to refute something that's been said by the AO. So I think they are necessary. (Interview 95, Member, London South)

Nearly all tribunal chairmen are appointed on a part-time basis and so are able to continue in private practice. It should be emphasized that prior expertise in social security law is not a precondition of appointment as chairman of a social security appeal tribunal. Social security is far from being a lucrative area of business for practising lawyers, and those with expertise in this field are a rarity.[10] In our survey of fifty tribunal chairmen, only a handful could claim to have any expertise in the area when appointed. Fully half of our sample described themselves either as general legal practitioners or as working in areas of traditional legal practice such as family or criminal law. A further one-fifth described themselves as specialists in an area of law far removed from social security, such as intellectual property or customs and excise.[11] Futhermore, chairmen rarely had even a theoretical grounding in the subject since the training of most lawyers pays little attention to social security law. The absence of a prior knowledge of social security law is not necessarily a major handicap, however, as the techniques involved in its application are in principle no different from other areas of legal practice. As one chairman explained:

The valuable thing is not that the chairman knows about social security law, but that he's got a mind which is trained to read through and absorb the complicated, legalistic jargon and rubbish which appears in the regulations. They are quite appalling, some of these regulations. That's the important thing, that one should be well versed in finding your way around complicated parliamentary draftsmen's jargon. The less discretion there is in the system, and there is much less nowadays, the more important it is to have someone who can understand the legislation. (Interview 15, Midlands)

If chairmen do not usually start with any expertise in social security law, it is obviously important that those appointed be committed to the job and receive adequate training. Nearly half of the chairmen to whom we spoke said that their interest in the work was their principal motivation for accepting the post of part-time chairman, and a further one-fifth emphasized their wish to play a socially valuable role. Some 38 per cent had

[10] During the debates on the 1983 Act, the Opposition unsuccessfully sought to insert a provision requiring that chairmen be expert in social security law. The Government pointed out that it was doubtful whether there would be enough lawyers with the required years of experience to meet this criterion, with the exception of the Department's own lawyers. *Per* Mr T. Newton, Standing Committee B, col. 653 (19 April 1983).

[11] Fourteen per cent of the sample were academic lawyers and a number of others were women returning to work.

actually put themselves forward for appointment.[12] Most said that they spent a considerable amount of time preparing for hearings by checking the law in works of reference and annotating the appeal papers on the issues to be clarified and pursued. Our own observations tended to confirm that chairmen were, by the day of the hearing, generally well versed in the legal issues that were raised by the appeal submission. It does seem then that there is a high degree of commitment amongst tribunal chairmen to the work. The separate issue of the adequacy of their training is considered below when examining the role of the Office of the President of Social Security Appeal Tribunals.

Having considered the legal background of the chairmen, other important findings on their characteristics may be summarized. Nearly half of the chairmen (48 per cent) were in their fifties; a quarter were under 50 and a further quarter aged 60 or more. This contrasts with the position of members, the great majority of whom (63 per cent) were beyond retirement age. One quarter of the chairmen were female, indicating that there has been some success in appointing a larger number of women to such posts. (The comparable figures for 1971 and 1982 were 15 per cent and 17 per cent respectively.)[13] Nearly two-thirds of the chairmen had been appointed within the previous five years, and had not therefore served under the old dual system. Only one in seven had more than ten years' experience, whereas three times as many lay members (44 per cent) had served for this length of time. As we shall see, this has important implications for the perspectives adopted by the two groups as to the proper function of the tribunal.

(ii) *The appointment of members*

The shift from lay to legal chairmen inevitably means that at least one-third of any tribunal panel comes from a professional

---

[12] Two respondents admitted that the fee they would receive was their prime motivating factor in accepting the appointment, and two others said the work 'filled in time'. A somewhat greater number saw their application to become a chairman as a way of furthering other career ambitions, and it was notable that one-fifth of the chairmen combined their social security post with some other judicial office.

[13] See Wraith and Hutchesson (1973) at p. 11 and Harris (1983) at p. 216 where the proportion of female chairmen in 1982 is given as 17 per cent for England and 22 per cent for Scotland.

background, often with no direct experience of the kind of problems faced by appellants. This makes it all the more important, given the aim of achieving some kind of social balance on a panel, that the people recruited as lay members on the tribunal be drawn from a range of backgrounds. A host of earlier studies were critical of the lack of representativeness of those appointed to serve as wing members on social security tribunals.[14] The average panel member has been depicted as a white, rather elderly, middle-class male, with a consequential under-representation of women, younger people and members of ethnic minority groups. As one MP acidly put it, 'what we get is people who are comfortably off coming to decisions about the incomes and futures of people who are uncomfortably off'.[15]

A contentious change connected with the merger of supplementary benefit appeal tribunals and national insurance local tribunals concerned the methods for appointing lay members. The members of each social security appeal tribunal are drawn from a single list, whereas the old tribunals operated a two panel system. In national insurance local tribunals, there were separate lists for employees and employers, with the members nominated by trades councils and business, commercial and industrial bodies respectively. This composition reflected the role of both sides of industry in contributing to the national insurance fund. The lay members were not appointed to represent sectional interests: rather they were to bring to the tribunal 'a worldly experience of business and industry and a knowledge of life on the factory floor to complement the legal expertise of the chairman.'[16]

Supplementary benefit appeal tribunals were constituted rather differently. One member, called the Secretary of State's member, was meant to have knowledge or experience of conditions in the area concerned and of the problems of people living on low incomes. The other, the Trades Council member, was drawn from a panel representing work people. This system was undoubtedly defective and in practice the Secretary of

[14] See for example Cavenagh and Newton (1970, 1971); Bell *et al.* (1974); Lister (1974); Flockhart (1975); Fulbrook (1978); Becker, MacPherson, and Silburn (1983); Wikeley (1985); and Jones and Adler (1990). For an early and largely uncritical study, see McCorquodale (1962).

[15] *Per* Mr F. Dobson, Standing Committee A, col. 470 (6 March 1984).

[16] Brown (1982) at p. 631.

State's members were generally persons of some standing in the local community with little direct contact with poor people.[17] Moreover, whilst Trades Council nominees might have had more immediate experience of the problems of living on low incomes, they were by no means immune to social stereotyping of claimants into the 'deserving' and 'undeserving' poor. Furthermore, few supplementary benefit claimants were likely to be in employment or members of trade unions.

The Bill leading to the 1983 Act originally included a clause providing for a single panel for the new social security appeal tribunal, so ending the automatic right of trade unions to nominate members. Coming so soon after the Government's controversial employment legislation of the early 1980s, it was no surprise that Labour MPs perceived this as a further attempt to reduce the influence of trade unions in public life.[18] Indeed, such was the opposition to this clause that it was dropped by the Government in order to secure the passage of the Bill as a whole before the 1983 General Election. After its return to office, the Government nevertheless successfully reintroduced the measure as part of the Health and Social Security Act 1984, arguing that a single list would provide a more representative base for the tribunals' membership. As one Minister put it:

Our existing system does not give sufficient weight to single parents and the disabled who may frequently have to appear before appeal tribunals ... it would be right to have a broader range of nominating bodies to include local branches of the Disablement Income Group, the CPAG, the local mental handicap society and MIND.[19]

The Government also pointed to the practical difficulties of constituting panels along the existing lines. It was said that in some parts of the country trade unions were struggling to find enough people to nominate, and Ministers conceded that there were problems in finding Secretary of State's members with sufficient knowledge or experience of the problems of people on low

---

[17] Regarding the Secretary of State's members, one Opposition spokesman and former Minister cynically observed: 'At the Home Office we had a list of the great and the good at national level. I suppose that at local level it would be a list of the mediocre and the moderate', *Per* Mr B. John, H.C. Debs., Vol. 37, col. 552 (17 February 1983).

[18] *Per* Mr A. Bennett, H.C. Debs., Vol. 37, col. 541 (17 Feb. 1983).

[19] *Per* Mr T. Newton, Standing Committee B, col. 626 (19 April 1983).

incomes.[20] Under the single panel system, it was to be left to the President of the social security appeal tribunals to ensure that members had 'knowledge or experience of conditions in the area' of the tribunal, and were 'representative of persons living or working in the area'.[21]

Notwithstanding the hopes and fears expressed at the time of the merger, it seems that in practice the creation of a single panel has made little difference to the composition of tribunals. The interviews we conducted with members from all parts of the country showed that by far the largest single group had been nominated by trade unions: 37 per cent of the total, almost twice as many as fell into the next largest category, those nominated by somebody within the tribunal system itself (20 per cent). These trade union nominees were also amongst the most experienced members of the tribunals, two-thirds of them having served for between five and fifteen years.

The social characteristics of the lay members differed in important respects from those of the chairmen whom we interviewed. Thirty eight per cent were women and considerably more than half were over 60 years of age (55 per cent were in their sixties, and a further 8 per cent were over 70). The proportion of elderly members was even higher than earlier studies have revealed.[22] One reason for this may be that we concentrated in our study on those who sit frequently, since we approached members whom we had observed at tribunal hearings rather than contact-

[20] As Mr T. Newton put it: 'I am advised that, in practice, what has tended to happen is that to fulfil this existing requirement appointments have been made usually of academic sociologists. I am not sure what view the Opposition take of academic sociologists, and I shall not be unwise enough to express any views of my own, but in my experience they are not people living on low incomes' (Standing Committee A, col. 481, 18 March 1984).

[21] See Social Security Act 1975, s. 97(2A) and Sched. 10 para. 1(2), amended by Health and Social Security Act 1984, s. 16. One particular problem emerged during the course of our study. Most of the inner London tribunals have been centralized at tribunal suites in central London: claimants from Stepney, for example, have their appeals heard at Whittington House, just off Tottenham Court Road. The members hearing their case are as likely to come from Chelsea or Mayfair as the East End. This clearly undermines the notion that members should be aware of conditions in the relevant locality.

[22] Lister (1974) interviewed 55 lay members out of 184 approached by a supplementary benefit appeal tribunal clerk and found that 44 per cent were aged 60 or over. Becker, MacPherson, and Silburn (1983) surveyed 171 lay members in the East Midlands and East Anglia and found that 39 per cent were aged over 60.

ing a random sample of all members.[23] The significance of this is that we found that tribunal administrators, when seeking a member to sit at short notice, commonly contact retired members because they are much more likely to be available. (One member past retirement age related how he could get a call during breakfast and be sitting by 10 a.m.) In consequence, retired members tend to sit more frequently than do younger working members.[24] This practice leads to an over-representation of elderly members at tribunal hearings in general.

It is quite clear that large numbers of long-serving members have stayed on under the single panel system with little new blood being introduced. It would be inaccurate, however, to depict members as solidly middle class, since just under a third of members past retirement age had previously worked in manual jobs (although only 8 per cent of members were currently working in such occupations). We came across only one member who described himself as unemployed. More than half of the members were involved in some form of charitable, community or church work. Nineteen per cent were also active in some other form of judicial service, in most cases sitting as magistrates. Given the network of social, political, and charitable agencies to which a majority of members belong, it is appropriate to refer to them as belonging to the same kind of 'local squirearchy' as noted in earlier research.[25] It appears that this continues to be a main recruiting ground for lay appointments to all kinds of judicial bodies.

Overall our findings suggest that the tribunal system has failed to build up a broader base of lay membership to reflect in some

[23] There were in our view good reasons for selecting the sample in this way. First, we did not want large numbers of relatively inactive members in the sample. Secondly, we wanted to be able to observe those members whom we interviewed in order to be able to compare their views about a range of matters with their actual behaviour in hearings. Thirdly, it enabled us to make more efficient use of research resources, since interviewing could take place on the same days we observed hearings.

[24] This had been identified as a problem on national assistance appeal tribunals: see Franks (1957b) at p. 530.

[25] As Bell *et al.* (1974) observed: '. . . the people who serve on tribunals . . . come from a 'local squirearchy' involved in a wide range of community activities, including welfare, church, education and training organisations, local politics, trade unions and professional associations. Depending on one's point of view, this might be regarded as one of the strengths of tribunals or one of their weaknesses' (p. 315). See also Baldwin and Hill (1987) and Jones and Adler (1990).

measure the range of people that appear as appellants. It is still the case that most appellants find themselves facing a row of white, rather elderly faces across the tribunal table, and one must therefore question how far the check on bias and prejudice said to be created by the presence of three decision makers can be effective. If there is nobody on the panel who has much in common with the appellant, there may be a lack of understanding of the appellant's situation, and by the same token less willingness to accept the appellant's evidence.

It must be said, however, that chairmen and members themselves were generally unconcerned about this issue. In the interviews we conducted, over 60 per cent of both groups made no criticisms at all of the composition of the panels. None the less this left a sizeable minority who felt that the panels were insufficiently representative. Some felt that this was inevitable and that it was unrealistic to expect the tribunals to be any more broadly based, while others expressed their criticisms more trenchantly. The views of those members who had doubts about the social mix of tribunal panels are illustrated in the following quotes:

I don't think that working class people, or people who have some understanding of the way in which many claimants live, are sufficiently represented. I think the quality of questioning and the quality of understanding people's lives is limited. On some council estates, the assumption is that you'll get your washing stolen if you hang it out, so claimants would come here seeking money for a drier, and they'd be asked in a patronizing way, 'Why don't you hang your washing out?' If a claimant said they'd had the washing stolen off the line, nine times out of ten they wouldn't be believed because people from middle class homes won't believe that sort of thing. There is cultural bias, 'anti scrounger', anti people on social security really. (Member, Interview 57, North East)

The membership in the Birmingham area is comprised of more middle-class people. I think basically the members speak a different language to that the claimant does. And the claimant doesn't seem to get through to them. If he could get through to someone of his own class, then the outlook would probably be different to him, and it could be explained to him also differently, in his own language. The communication between the claimant and the panel is not good. I would definitely like to see more working class members. (Member, Interview 66, Midlands)

It does seem on the whole to be representative. There is always this quandary. I suppose it would be said that we are mainly middle-class people just like the magistracy, but on the other hand the people appointed have still got to be literate, numerate and be able to remain objective. You have to strike a balance somehow between having people who are intelligent enough to understand the regulations and having a reasonable cross-section of the population. (Member, Interview 74, Midlands)

It isn't representative—certainly in terms of race and probably in terms of class. But I mean that's the nature of the British judicial system that the people who get appointed to these sorts of things like the magistracy and all the rest of it are likely to be middle class people. But that should be compensated for as far as race is concerned. I think it's a bad thing that there are so few black people sitting. I think also we could do with a bit more youth—we seem to take the view that you have to be nearing middle age before you're capable of taking sensible decisions. (Member, Interview 128, North West)

But are the members seen by the chairmen as the right kind of people for the job? Most chairmen seem broadly satisfied with only a minority openly critical of certain members. However, our observations of tribunal hearings tended to support the views of the more critical chairmen, so it is appropriate that we focus here on their concerns. The serious reservations they expressed about the calibre of some of their lay colleagues are reflected in the following quotations:

There is such a variety of members: it is like everything, some you think they are really on the ball and very good. A lot of those who are union reps are very good, the younger ones. Some of the older members on the panel, quite frankly, I feel they are just there to spend the morning filling their time up. (Chairman, Interview 6, North East)

They vary enormously in quality. Some are really first class, quite a lot of magistrates and quite a lot of other high-powered people. Others are frankly pretty hopeless, in the sense that they don't follow the proceedings in any great detail or have a great deal to contribute to it. My frank answer is that some are superb and some are very much of the opposite extreme. (Chairman, Interview 12, Midlands)

They are too old, they are too white, they are too male. They tend to share the same views about some of the issues that we have to deal with. I wouldn't say it was prejudiced, but it is a fairly narrow view. (Chairman, Interview 17, London North)

I think they could appoint more young people. The people who I have come across are mostly retired, and I find that they are sometimes out of touch with new social developments. I find it somewhat curious because I am told that we who are qualified to chair tribunals ought to have some sort of information from the lay members about local conditions, and, if some of them don't know what the conditions are, they can't help us. (Chairman, Interview 26, London South)

As noted above, elderly members sit more frequently than do younger members, but it is also clear that the vast majority of members do not sit often enough. Many members told us of how they used to sit several days a week to help clear the backlog of appeals that built up at the time of the abolition of single payments, and they lamented the dramatic reduction in work for members under the new income support regime. Fully 40 per cent of the members wanted to sit more frequently and only one member wanted to attend hearings less often. At the time of our study, 58 per cent sat no more than once a month, with many sitting on only a handful of occasions each year. In contrast the chairmen sat far more often: 82 per cent sat at least fortnightly compared with only 28 per cent of members.

This striking difference obviously makes it more difficult for members to keep in touch with developments and to contribute effectively to proceedings. There is a strong argument for requiring members to commit themselves to a minimum number of sittings each year, as is the case, for example, with lay magistrates who are obliged to sit for at least twenty-six half days a year. But with the current workload, there is no prospect of there being enough hearings to allow the existing members to sit as frequently as this. Given the relatively low volume of appeals since the 1988 changes, the system is in practice overburdened with members.[26] As one member observed:

I think there is less need for our members since the new regulations came in. Some days it's just not worthwhile having a panel because under the new regulations there is nothing you can do. The Secretary of State has got it sewn up completely. So I don't think we'll be recruiting new members. In fact I think we are going to have less members. The

---

[26] This is not the first time that a tribunal system has been overburdened with members. A striking example is provided by the unemployment assistance tribunals. In 1935 there were about 7,500 people nominated to the panels of workpeople's representatives for these tribunals. Members were called up so infrequently that they did not acquire sufficient experience of the workings of tribunals. The Unemployment Assistance Board made representations to the Minister as a result of which the size of panels was reduced in 1937. See Lach (1950) at pp. 47 and 58.

case load has gone right down, because there's just no point in appealing now. (Interview 147, Scotland).

If the tribunal system were expanding, one could envisage the Regional Chairmen inviting applications from a wider range of organizations and from the general public at large. In a contracting system, this option is largely foreclosed and a rather less palatable course may have to be contemplated. While a large pool of members was invaluable at the time of the explosive increase in appeals which accompanied the phasing out of single payments, the boom times have come to an end as the number of appeals has slumped. Our observations suggest that many members have aged to the point of ineffectiveness and have become essentially redundant. Savage pruning to achieve a smaller, more active, and better balanced panel may be necessary in order to guarantee healthy growth in the future.

If members are to play a full part in hearings which have become increasingly technical and legalistic, it is also important that they receive proper training. As we discuss below, current levels of training amongst members are far from satisfactory.

(iii) *The Office of the President of Social Security Appeal Tribunals*

The third major feature of the merger legislation was an important structural innovation, the creation of the Office of the President of Social Security Appeal Tribunals (OPSSAT). The introduction of OPSSAT was intended to demonstrate the independence of the new tribunals from the Department, with the President and the chairmen at all levels being appointed by the Lord Chancellor. The President himself is responsible for the appointment of lay members, the general administration of the system, and arranging such meetings and training for chairmen and members as he considers appropriate. It was clear from the interviews we conducted with chairmen and members that, before the creation of OPSSAT, little training had been provided. In a few areas, training had been organized through local initiatives on an *ad hoc* basis, but for the great majority of long-serving members their initial training amounted to little more than a chat with the manager of the local DHSS office and the observation of a couple of hearings.

OPSSAT has devised a national training programme for chairmen involving two residential weekend courses. An induction course is run for newly appointed chairmen, and a refresher course is provided for experienced chairmen to remind them of the fundamental principles underpinning the work of the tribunal. In addition, one day seminars are organized on a regional basis, usually with the assistance of local higher education institutions. The training of members is the responsibility of the Regional Chairmen, and the normal pattern is to offer each member the opportunity of a one day meeting every two years. In addition, the Regional Chairmen occasionally sit to hear cases with members and they also observe hearings in order to monitor standards.[27]

There remains a disparity between the training offered to chairmen and lay members, and our study confirmed that chairmen generally receive the more extensive training. It was noticeable that the chairmen were far more enthusiastic about the training they had received: over half described it as good or very good, compared with less than a quarter of the lay members. Members, particularly those with the greatest length of service, tended to be dismissive about the value of training, preferring to lay emphasis on the value of experience they acquired whilst actually attending hearings. Thirteen per cent had not attended any of the one day courses put on annually by regional chairmen, and they spoke much more commonly than did chairmen about relying upon 'common sense', 'native wit', and the like. It seemed to us that those who needed the training most were those who were least likely to volunteer for it.

The absence of adequate induction training was a matter of concern to many newly appointed members who had been surprised to find themselves thrown in at the deep end so quickly. Members are provided with comprehensive annotated guides to the social security legislation[28] but these are rather indigestible for a beginner. While it would be a good idea to issue members with more readable texts, such as the two Child Poverty Action Group guides to welfare benefits and non-means tested benefits, the more important implication of these findings is that training

---

[27] See Partington (1986) at pp. 176–7. For a critical analysis of OPSSAT training arrangements, see Jones and Adler (1990), pp. 24–9.

[28] The principal guides are Mesher (1991) and Bonner *et al.* (1991), both produced annually.

should be compulsory for all chairmen and members, regardless of their length of service.

One difficulty in pursuing this course lies in the fact that members do tribunal work on an entirely voluntary basis. Unlike the chairmen, they receive no fee for hearing cases and can claim only modest expenses. In addition, the current methods of appointment provide little guarantee that they will have sufficient enthusiasm for the work to undertake extensive training or a commitment to sit a set number of times a year. It is common for chairmen to apply for a tribunal post, or else to have been nominated by someone within the tribunal system. By contrast, most members have been nominated either by their employer or trades union. In either case the nominating body will rarely have had much idea of what tribunal work entailed. Indeed, the nomination may well have had more to do with who was willing to have their name put forward than their suitability for the job. One member, when asked why he had agreed to become a member, replied 'probably because I was asked to do it'. As another explained:

I was sponsored by the NFU and they were looking for someone to do the job and nobody was very keen. So I said, 'Okay, I'll have a go.' We'd had a member on for several years but he'd packed up. That's how I got involved. (Interview 78, Midlands)

Notwithstanding the abolition of the two panel system and the transferring of responsiblity for recruitment from the Department of Health and Social Security to OPSSAT, the selection of members seems to have remained a hit-and-miss business.[29] In view of the increasing judicialization of the social security appeal tribunals, it would still seem essential for lay members to have far more training than they currently receive and for them to sit on a more regular basis. If it is thought unrealistic to attach these requirements to a voluntary post, then the question of paying a fee to lay members should be looked at seriously. Becker, MacPherson, and Silburn (1983) have argued that:

We should constantly bear in mind that serving on appeal tribunals is, for lay-members, an entirely voluntary activity. It is an increasingly demanding form of public service, but one which, if well done, offers an important protection to some of Society's poorest, weakest and most vulnerable members (p. iv).

[29] See Jones and Adler (1990), pp. 6–24.

The demands of this form of public service have now increased to the point where the job is unlikely to be done well if it remains an entirely voluntary activity. We may already have reached the stage where the goodwill of members can no longer be relied upon. Nowadays they are largely denied the opportunity to exercise their common sense or discretion, yet are expected to absorb complex legal issues and to contribute sensibly to proceedings. If they are also to be placed under an obligation to undergo further training and sit more frequently, the job may lose its attraction unless some financial incentive is offered.[30] This might seem an expensive option, but the alternative is to render wing members increasingly marginal as law becomes ever more intrusive and technical in tribunal adjudication.

The 'marginalization' of the wing members

As part of the inquisitorial and enabling approach, chairmen are expected to encourage their members to play a full part in appeal hearings. Particularly influential in the development of this aspect of the tribunal's philosophy was Bell's (1982) summary of the views of appellants on the role of members:

They felt strongly that lay members should *actively* assist the chairman during the hearing; that they should play an *enabling* role towards the appellant by listening carefully, understanding the problem and asking relevant questions, thus drawing him out and enabling him to sort out his case and make his points (p. 145).

The official guide to procedure at social security appeal tribunals cites this argument, and calls upon lay members 'to be interested, alert, knowledgeable, active, questioning and helpful'.[31] But there are a number of factors which inhibit members from playing such a participative role. Chief amongst these is the context in which tribunal adjudication takes place. In an arena where an ability to understand and apply a complex body of law has become of paramount importance, chairmen enjoy numerous advantages over lay members: superior training, a legal back-

[30] Lay members serving on industrial tribunals receive a fee for attending hearings, although the legally qualified chairmen are paid at a higher rate. See Dickens *et al.* (1985), p. 65.
[31] See Office of the President of Social Security Appeal Tribunals (1988) at para. 14. See also para. 47.

ground, and expertise built up through their more frequent attendance at hearings. Observation of tribunal hearings quickly shows how chairmen are marginalizing their members by assuming a dominant role at appeal hearings.

We saw in Chapter 4 how chairmen have by and large accepted the requirement that they play an inquisitorial role in tribunal hearings even if the scope for them to do so is now more circumscribed than was once the case. Members were much less likely to view the chairman's role as being inquisitorial, and it emerged clearly from our interviews that most had no real understanding of what the concept means. Less than one-quarter of members spoke in terms of an enabling or inquisitorial function, and almost a half described the chairman's part as the 'leader' or 'referee' of the tribunal. A further one-fifth of the members viewed the chairman in strictly legalistic terms. As one put it, 'they are there to ensure that the legal aspects are taken care of and that the members don't go haywire'. The greater emphasis placed by members on the chairman's directing role is doubtless indicative of their own experiences whilst sitting. The following members' views on the chairman's job illustrate the point:

To make sure the lay members keep within the law, I think. When all's said and done, the solicitors are trained really to follow an argument through logically. I think they're a bit better at it than we are, although lay members sometimes come up with a thought that the chairman hasn't thought of and then it can be silly or not, according to the law. But they will put it right as far as the law is concerned. (Interview 55, North East)

Basically to conduct the hearing as a whole and the fact that he has all the legal background means he should be able to guide us on procedural points. Sometimes members, including myself, tend to be too emotional and tend to be swayed by the appellant's background, but at the same time we've got to be realistic. You can't just give everybody what they want just because they've appealed. There's got to be a reason, and they've got to comply with the law, the regulations. I think the chairman enforces that; he makes sure that people are not just carried away with sentiments. (Interview 120, Wales and South West)

The training provided by OPSSAT encourages chairmen to think of their members as equal partners, and a large number of them appeared to accept this in principle. Still more argued, however, that the principle of equality was difficult to achieve in practice. Most saw their role in part as controlling their lay members, preventing them from pursuing irrelevancies in the hearing and ensuring that they concentrated on the material points in deliberations. Many chairmen made the point in interview that they often found themselves forced into playing a dominant controlling role, as in the following quotes:

Ideally, in a perfect tribunal (which isn't usual) the members will have read the papers thoroughly, thought about it carefully and come prepared with specific questions to ask. More frequently it's the case that the members make some sort of feeble attempt to read the papers, or sometimes won't have done. They won't have understood them properly, they'll be relying to some extent on folklore, attitudes, prejudices. An example was seen today where a member said 'Why should we support someone?', when what she meant was 'Why should we as taxpayers pay a social security benefit to somebody in these particular circumstances?' They don't understand the issues, and when it comes to making findings of fact, they don't really understand what's involved in that, and they don't understand the issues, no matter how much one tries to guide them. And I'm afraid it does tend to be the elderly, white, male members who are doing the job as a retirement job who are the worst. (Interview 17, London North)

A great deal depends honestly on the personalities of the wing members. Some days I carry it through myself; they just sit dumb and don't take part. But if I've got a reasonably active interested couple of wing members, I very much see my role as to make sure the more difficult legal aspects are considered and to balance any conflicting views within the wing members. I also see it as my role, whether they are active or inactive wing members, to make sure that they are looking at it properly. I mean some wing members have a very much palm tree justice approach, and they may take a very simplistic view of what they think is fair, quite regardless of what the legal position might be and regardless of what an analytical consideration of the evidence may point to. Really, my role is one of correcting them and keeping them on the right lines. Whereas if they are the dumb wing members, my role then is to run the whole show, to elicit evidence, to assess it and reach the decision myself. Where you've got wing members who just won't contribute, no matter how much you prod them into saying something, they just follow what you say in the deliberations. Some wing members, it is extraordinary, you'll say to them, 'Well, Mr X, what do you think about it, do you think A or B?', and they just won't throw anything into the discussion at all. When you've got two like that, it rather leaves you high and dry. (Interview 43, North West)

It's essentially a fact finding exercise and I do see myself as leading the questioning. Sometimes I am conscious of hogging the questioning to the extent that, by the time I say to the members, 'Do you have any questions?', they'll say 'No, you've asked them all', which is not really the impression that should be given to the claimant. In a sense it doesn't matter who asks the questions, but it maybe doesn't give the claimant the feeling that this is a three person tribunal, rather than a one person one. I do see my role in a sense also as controlling the members. If they do go way off beam, and start talking irrelevancies, it is my function to get them back on. In one case the appellant said she couldn't manage on her benefit, and a member started asking if she knew how to make economies. Well, it's simply not our function to give advice, to lecture, or to judge how a person conducts themselves. (Interview 48, Scotland)

It is evident to any observer of tribunal hearings that few of the members say very much. In part this is attributable to the widespread view amongst members that, in those cases where the appellant is not present at the hearing (around half of the total), there is nothing they can do other than rely on the submission of the presenting officer. We have already suggested that this is a questionable assumption and it provides only a partial explanation of the passivity of members. Even when appellants attend their appeal hearings, members generally fail to make their presence felt. In all, we found that less than one-fifth of the members made more than a limited contribution to the proceedings that we observed—indeed almost a half were entirely silent throughout.[32] We recognized that members, despite not saying a word, may help put appellants at their ease by behaving in a positive fashion—by, for example, smiling or nodding or demonstrably paying close attention to the case. About two-thirds of those members who remained silent were entirely passive, however, and a few behaved in a distinctly offputting manner—such as by yawning or looking bored. One actually fell asleep during the hearing. This strongly suggested to us that, even if it would be unfair to characterize them as 'stuffed dummies' (as some appellants described them to us),

[32] Jackson, Stewart, and Bland's (1987) study of Scottish tribunals offers a more positive appraisal of the members inasmuch as a majority were found to make a contribution to the public part of the hearing. The study was conducted when lay chairmen were still sitting and suggested that legal chairmen were more likely than lay chairmen to inhibit the contributions of members. The authors concluded that 'the increasing legalisation of the . . . system makes it more difficult for members to contribute fully' (p. 251). Our own findings suggest that the marginalization of lay members has increased significantly in the four years since this Scottish study was carried out, and this is consistent with the view that this marginalization is inextricably linked to the legalization of the tribunal.

then at least many of them can be said to have given the appearance of being seriously out of their depth.

The relative non-involvement of the tribunal members should, however, come as no great surprise. A competent legal chairman almost inevitably dominates any hearing in which the issues raised are largely matters of straight law. At best the members can only play a subsidiary role to the lawyer who usually has the advantage. Where, as in one hearing in London we attended, the chairman talks about 'calling evidence' and uses terms like 'fetter', 'nexus', *'simpliciter'*, and 'quasi-legal privilege', it is obvious that it is not just the appellant who may need a helping hand. While this is an extreme case, it does serve to illustrate the general proposition that, whatever the legal theory and however benignly chairmen may view the members with whom they sit, the legal chairman is not the *primus inter pares* but is the pre-eminent adjudicator in most cases.

The material collected in interviews and in observations of hearings demonstrates that Mesher's concern that the introduction of legally qualified chairmen would reinforce the dominance of chairmen and the passivity of members was well founded.[33] Furthermore, our interviews with chairmen and members suggest that frequently members fail to participate actively in the deliberations following a hearing. Certainly they rarely dissent from the decision considered correct by the chairman. In 331 cases out of our sample of 337, the decision was unanimous, and, in the six where there was disagreement, the chairman was in the majority. In other words, there was not a single case in which the chairman was outvoted by the lay members.

Members are themselves aware of the way they have become marginalized, and only 10 per cent described themselves as being full participants in tribunal hearings. Over a half saw their role as limited to introducing 'a bit of common sense' or to the asking of a few supplementary questions. Some members tended to place the responsibility for their lack of involvement on the shift from lay to legal chairmen. As they put it in interview:

I think some chairmen know before they come in what they are going to say in certain cases. With some chairmen I recognize that we're just an appendage. Some try to finish in record time, which I don't think

[33] See Mesher (1983) at p. 139.

is quite right. But I wouldn't dare say anything—they are the lawyers. (Interview 52, North East)

If I had the choice, I would go for the old chairmen that used to do it, rather than the legality side of it which we have today. I think there was more family spirit in the old chairmen and chairwomen than there is in the legalities today. Today it's too set. The atmosphere, there is a great deal of difference than in the way it used to be. It was easier to work as a team before. (Interview 66, Midlands)

To a great extent it's down to the chairmen, some of whom still don't accept that the members are an essential part of it. Their attitude is that they're the legally qualified ones. I think it's very important that the members are given the chance to contribute. But if you ask all the questions as chairman, as a lot do, and then turn to the members and say, 'Have you got any questions?', well, you'll have used them all up. It makes the panel feel useless, and, to the appellant, look useless. Also there are still some chairmen who write up the decisions after the hearing when the members aren't there, which is quite wrong. Indeed, that is laid down at every chairman's meeting, but there are still people doing it. (Interview 90, London North)

Our own observations confirm the view that chairmen commonly dominate the questioning. Some do not even bother to ask members if they have supplementary questions to put. But the question is whether it is realistic to expect chairmen to behave differently, given the calibre of many of the members with whom they are working. The members often appear to be confused about their role, and this is illustrated by the disparate views they expressed on this point in interview:

Politics comes into it a little bit. I consider myself a spokesman for the Union. The trade union still enters into it at the back of my mind. Sticking up for the underdog if they've got a true case. I try to put my concern for the underdog in practice by seeing how far we can get round the regulations. (Interview 68, Midlands)

We rely heavily on the chairman to deal with the legal side. Although the President of the tribunals would like all the members to be *au fait* with the law, I think most of us take the view that, after all, the chairmen are well enough paid for doing their job. We're just volunteers; we're just there to see that common sense and justice is done as far as possible. I think one is there to apply common sense with a broad brush approach as far as one can, given the cloistering effect of the law. If we're thwarted by the law, then the chairman should tell us. And to try and make sure that people understand that they have had a fair opportunity to put their case. In other words, it is largely a public relations exercise. (Interview 95, London South)

I see the role as getting all the information, thoroughly understanding the situation, deciding what sort of natural justice is in the case—if there's a real need, is it a need which one would think on the face of it should be met by the system? And then to refine that into what you think the outcome should be, within the limits of the Social Security Acts of course. (Interview 104, London South)

I follow the case and I turn on a bit of psychology. I take a good look at the claimant from head to toe, what they're wearing, what quality it is and so on, and I listen carefully for if they're lying. As a teacher, you know the scalliwags, and, if you ask them a few questions, you begin to know if they're lying or not. That's my contribution rather than the legal aspects. (Interview 107, Wales)

Do you want me to be honest? Waste of bloody time! At one time we had discretion. We'd say, 'It's 50/50, let's give them half of it', and everyone was happy. But now there is no bloody discretion. I may not always be right legally, but I think that, in applying myself in life, I use a lot of common sense and that can be important here. (Interview 134, North West)

As far as I am concerned, at the tribunal the Department have everything going for them. They have all the majesty of the law and a huge Department behind them, and we have a little appellant there who knows nothing. To that extent my job is to assist and make sure that this person has been justly treated. (Interview 142, Scotland)

Members most commonly see their job in terms of looking after the interests of the claimant. This reflects a considerable divergence of view between chairmen and members as to the proper role for members to play at the tribunal. Not one chairman to whom we spoke saw the members' job as being to safeguard claimants' interests, and it is arguable that the attitude of the members is indicative of ambivalence on their part as to their appropriate function. Few saw their task in judicial terms—to be impartial and to apply the law. Indeed, the views expressed by members suggest that the spirit of the old discretionary and paternalistic system hangs over the tribunal and, though times have changed, continues to haunt social security adjudication. It is a ghost from the past which has not been exorcized.

The application of common sense and the lay person's 'benevolent' approach are not what are required at social security appeal tribunal hearings nowadays: it is rather the clinical and impartial application of the law, combined with an objective assessment of evidence.[34] It is in this sense that the lay members have become marginalized—one might almost say rendered redundant—by the ever tightening legal regulation of social security provision and by the appointment of lawyers as chairmen. As Genn and Genn (1989) rightly argue, none of the assumed benefits of tribunal adjudication (informality, procedural flexibility and the like) 'negates the necessity of the appellant bringing his case within the regulations or the statute, and proving his factual situation with evidence' (p. 112). Given this essential truth about tribunal adjudication, it is unrealistic and misguided to regard the contribution that members can make as being more than modest. The issues raised in most social security appeals are too legal, too technical, and too complex to allow the average lay member much scope to make a significant contribution.

There are of course some extremely competent members sitting on social security appeal tribunals. But these days the definition of a good member has to include a sound grasp of the statutes, regulations, and the legal issues raised by appeals. Few appellants are likely to be impressed by a member expressing sympathy for their plight if the member is manifestly ignorant of the legal points raised by the case. Chairmen themselves can often be seen to be uneasy where a member's intervention causes the proceedings to stray off the point or take on a moralistic tone. One chairman neatly summed up the underlying attitude of chairmen to their members as follows:

There are days when I can look at the list of the tribunal members and think that today is the day of the real legal experts. The chairman can almost sit back because the other two know their law so well. One or two of them are trained CAB personnel who really are very keen and very much up-to-date with changes in the law. Very helpful. There are others who are not so good and perhaps don't take such an interest in the intricacies of social security law and practice. But for the most part now they keep quiet, relatively quiet, and accept advice very readily. I don't have any difficulties with members at all. (Interview 15, Midlands)

That some members are regarded as effective and useful by chairmen suggests that the potential remains for them to play an important part at tribunal hearings. Unfortunately, many

---

[34] See Commissioner Mitchell in *R(SB) 2/82* noting that there is 'a legislative labyrinth through which the appeal tribunal must pick its path with consummate care' (para. 5).

members have retained their own peculiar and idiosyncratic approaches to social security adjudication. The attitudes of long-serving members, in particular, reflect an era when the tribunal was able to 'do justice' as it saw fit. The members have not accepted, indeed perhaps have not understood, the changed role the tribunal is meant to play. They have failed to master what Becker, McPherson, and Silburn (1983) refer to as the 'major alterations in both content and style' which the 1980s have witnessed (p. iii). The 1980 legislative changes are described as being 'very significant indeed, with profound implications for the procedure and conduct of the tribunals, requiring tribunal members to master a complex new set of laws and regulations, [and] to exercise their function in a new spirit . . .' (p. i). The further legislative changes since 1980 serve to underline this observation about the fundamental recasting of the tribunal's role in the last decade. The relatively low level of training that members receive has proved insufficient to equip them for the task of adjudicating on a complex body of law. The Presidential system seems to have been far more successful in persuading chairmen of the merits of its philosophy, and chairmen have proved more adept at working within the confines of a tightly regulated system. While the members are clearly struggling to come to terms with their much reduced role, chairmen have accepted the political reality and have knuckled down to the central task of ensuring that the regulations are being applied correctly.

Conclusion

Many members are plainly uncomfortable with the new regime of social security adjudication, and their failure to adapt to new demands and changed circumstances means that they have become in large part legal and historical anachronisms. It is all too evident that the member's role has been effectively sidelined by the increased legalization of social security appeal tribunals. This does not necessarily mean that members should be phased out of the system altogether. There would be little support amongst chairmen for such a move, and it is important to recognize the strong arguments of principle which support the retention of three member panels. Members offer the prospect of a more socially representative panel and a better standard of justice for the appellant. It is unrealistic to expect a chairman, who is often busy keeping a note of the evidence at hearings, to follow every point made by an appellant or presenting officer. Members can act as useful back-stops, asking supplementary questions and picking up points that are missed. There remain types of case where a lay person's experience and considered judgement of evidence may be more relevant than the chairman's expert knowledge of the law, as, for instance, where the issue is whether someone has 'just cause' for voluntarily leaving a job.

Moreover, while the scope for the application of sympathy and local knowledge in hearings has been much reduced, it has not been eliminated altogether. In particular, where the tribunal is unable to uphold an appeal but is reluctant to turn the appellant away empty handed, lay members may be able to draw upon their local knowledge and experience to suggest sources of help outside the social security system. Nor must it be forgotten that, if chairmen sat alone, they would be deprived of the opportunity to discuss their view of the case before taking a decision. The presence of two lay members, who are able to outvote a chairman on the decision, can also be seen as injecting a democratic element into the system, providing a check against bad or autocratic chairmanship.[35]

Yet if members are to be retained, attention needs to be paid to their numbers, recruitment, and training. Panels remain unrepresentative of the wider community, and, because members are denied adequate training and the opportunity to sit regularly, they are not well placed to identify the really salient issues raised at hearings or to ask sensible supplementary questions or to contribute effectively to deliberations. Where chairmen consider that they are duty bound to control their members, the extent of the marginalization of members becomes apparent. The chairmen sit more frequently, are younger, are more recently appointed, better acquainted with the legal issues and with the

[35] In our travels around the country, we encountered only one maverick chairman who took a highly irregular approach to tribunal adjudication. As he put it in interview, 'to be blunt, if we think the justice of a man's case decides it, we don't hesitate to ignore the regulations'. Observations of hearings chaired by this respondent indicated that the lay members at this tribunal had a better grasp of the law than the chairman and were providing an invaluable check against his *laissez-faire* attitude.

appropriate functions of the tribunal, and they are better trained than their lay colleagues. Urgent action is needed to redress this imbalance if members are to contribute effectively to social security adjudication.

6

The Appellant

SOCIAL security claimants are a disgruntled group, and in truth they have much about which to feel aggrieved. The throw of the dice in life has been cruel for many of them. They are frequently afflicted by a constellation of social ills—bad housing, unemployment, chronic illness, and the like. Many of them share the view that they have been let down by the social security system. Very few of the appellants we interviewed regarded a visit to a social security appeal tribunal as an agreeable or interesting day out: for most it was an unnerving or traumatic experience to be endured in the hope that it might bring about some improvement in their situation. It is indeed an indication of the desperation that many claimants feel that they are prepared to enter the unfamiliar arena of an appeal hearing. Most of them approach the tribunal in a spirit of hope rather than expectation. Their experiences of dealing with officials have engendered a certain fatalism, and it is perhaps surprising that they retain any optimism at all about their prospects. But many express some confidence that any independent, fair-minded tribunal will be bound to see the intrinsic merit of their claim, whatever the law might say.

We regarded it as a central part of our study to find out what claimants made of their appearance before social security appeal tribunals. The so-called consumer's perspective is valuable in assessing the performance of institutions such as courts or tribunals. One can argue that, however impartially the law may be applied and however refined the procedures adopted might be, searching questions need to be asked about the operation of the system if ordinary citizens remain dissatisfied about the way their appeal has been handled.

A reading of the early research on social security tribunals does not encourage high hopes on this score. The surveys conducted in the 1970s provided a consistent catalogue of complaints about the failure of tribunal personnel and procedures to enable ordinary citizens to put up a reasonable showing at a hearing.[1] The studies suggested that the ideology of informality and accessibility operated merely as a smokescreen in practice, obscuring sloppiness in procedure and arbitrariness in decision making. Study after study demonstrated that the hearings before supplementary benefit appeal tribunals were seen as frustrating and humiliating for claimants, and tribunal chairmen and members were portrayed as playing a philanthropic role, doling out state bounty to those regarded as morally deserving. The picture in short was of charity and paternalism, with the application of legal principle coming a poor second.[2] Researchers saw claimants as powerless and alienated, no match for the powerful government bureaucracy against which they were pitted.

It was in large part because of this body of critical literature that social security tribunals were restructured in the early 1980s. As we have discussed in earlier chapters of this book, the new regime has swept away many of the old (and potentially broad) discretionary powers and replaced them with a much firmer and narrower basis of legal entitlement. This means that a tribunal, whether or not it likes the look of a claimant, is obliged to apply the letter of the law without favour. Our own observations and interviews have convinced us that this is a fundamental change of substance: it is no mere tinkering with the old system. Consequently the typical tribunal appearance is nowadays a quite different experience from what it used to be. The pendulum has swung, and the key question is whether it has swung too far.

We attended the hearings of 337 appellants and we sought to conduct interviews with the 181 (54 per cent) who turned up

---

[1] This literature is discussed in greater detail above in Chapter 1 and in Baldwin and Hill (1988) at pp. 107–9.

[2] There were results from research that ran counter to this general picture. Bell *et al.* (1974, 1975), for instance, found that a majority of appellants could adequately follow the proceedings and had no serious complaints about the opportunity they were given to put their case. Whether this reflected satisfaction or a grim resignation among claimants has been the subject of some debate: see Fulbrook (1978) at p. 227, and Dean (1991) at p. 150.

to them. Eleven (6 per cent) declined to take part,[3] and virtually
all of the people whom we interviewed agreed to the interview
being tape recorded.[4] The discussion in this chapter is based
principally on these interviews and explores three main themes:
first, the extent to which appellants understand the nature of
the appeals process which they initiate and whether lack of
understanding is related to non-attendance at the tribunal hearing; secondly, the issue of delays in the hearing of appeals, and
finally, the perceptions of those appellants who attend their
appeal hearings.

Appellants' understanding of the appeals process

For most of the appellants we interviewed, this was their first
experience of appealing to a social security appeal tribunal.
About 80 per cent had never appealed to any type of tribunal
before, and many evidently regarded the hearing with some tre-
pidation. As one claimant tellingly put it, 'I've never, never,
never been in trouble in my life.' Seventeen per cent had
appealed to a social security tribunal before, yet, like Bell (1975),
we found no evidence that people were treating their rights of
appeal lightly or irresponsibly, or that appellants persistently
appealed as part of a vendetta against the Department.[5]

The typical appellant was, therefore, a one-shotter rather than
a repeat-player, using Galanter's (1974) typology, and this made

[3] These were not necessarily refusals in the strict sense of the word, since
some of them left the tribunal building before we had had chance to approach
them. For reasons of confidentiality, we were not given addresses to enable
us to contact them by other means.

[4] We approached claimants, wherever possible, in the waiting room before
the start of hearings, to explain the purpose of our research and to seek a short
interview with them immediately after the hearing. We hoped to be able to
conduct the interviews before the decision in the case had been announced.
This proved much more difficult than we had anticipated, however, and in many
cases the decision was announced immediately without the panel retiring to
deliberate. We were successful in achieving our original objective in only a minority of cases, and we concede that it was inevitable that, in the remainder, knowledge of the outcome will have coloured to some degree appellants' views on
the fairness of hearings: on this, see further Milton (1975). Since more appellants
lose than win at the tribunal, the levels of satisfaction with the fairness of the
hearing that we report in this chapter are all the more remarkable.

[5] As Bell (1975) put it, 'on the contrary, for many people the whole business
was a significant experience in their lives' (p. 14).

it particularly important to find out how claimants had become aware of the possibility of appealing against an adverse decision made by an official, and what advice, if any, they had sought about it. The existence of a right of appeal is stated on all the standard official letters which notify benefit decisions, and it was no surprise to find that 52 per cent of those interviewed gave an official letter as the source of their knowledge about the right of appeal. A further 16 per cent had been told by a departmental officer. In some of these latter cases, staff were being genuinely helpful, but in others it seemed more a strategy to deal with dissatisfied and aggressive claimants. As one appellant admitted to us: 'I finally swore at somebody at the unemployment benefit office and they said I should appeal in that case.' The fact that the appeals system is sometimes used as a defensive tactic by staff may account for the lodging of some of the appeals which can fairly be characterized as hopeless in point of law. This gatekeeping function was recognized by many of the adjudication officers that we interviewed. As one commented:

If someone hasn't understood a decision in their case, the benefits officers simply give them the appeals form. I spend an awful lot of time trying to get through to some of the benefits officers that they could save a lot of time and money if they explained things to claimants when they come into the office to complain about decisions. Some officers are very good at that, but you can't get through to some of the other officers. They just throw appeals forms at them. (Interview 98, Unemployment Benefit Adjudication Officer)

While 67 per cent of respondents said that they had been notified of their right of appeal through official channels, this left a substantial minority who did not attribute their knowledge of appeal rights to departmental sources. The most commonly stated source of information for this group was a Citizens Advice Bureau or similar agency. This suggests that advice and representation services have an important role in alerting people to the possibility of exercising their rights in the first place as well as in assisting them once an appeal has been lodged.

The extent to which appellants understand the tribunal papers sent to them inevitably affects their ability to participate fully in the hearing. Appellants were asked whether they understood the adjudication officer's written submission setting out the facts and the law applicable to their case. Interpreting the responses to such a question is problematic as some people are reluctant to admit to having had difficulties in comprehension, and others may wrongly believe that they have grasped the essentials of the papers. Forty per cent of the sample stated that they had experienced no difficulties at all in understanding the documentation. We have no doubt from the general tenor of their answers that this was indeed an accurate assessment by many of these appellants, though for others this was less so (including some with serious literacy problems). A further third of appellants said that they had understood most or at least some of the submission, whilst nearly a quarter frankly admitted to having understood little or nothing at all.[6]

It seems, then, that there has been no real improvement since Bell (1975) reported that 22 per cent of her sample had difficulty in understanding the papers.[7] This perhaps suggests that improvements in the layout of submissions over recent years have been outweighed by the increased complexity of the law involved. The problems faced by appellants in seeking to understand what are often highly technical, legal documents are typified by the following quotations:

I didn't really understand them. When they start saying section this and section that, and everything else, you're lost. Then they quote the Social Security Act, and this other Social Security Act. And then look at this nonsense: 'R(U) 24/85' etc. What's the point of sending me that? I can't look these up. I wouldn't know where to look anyway. (Case 54, Midlands).

I didn't really understand the papers, no. They baffle you with figures. This first page here, I could understand that and I understand what I'd written. But then there are all those pages of figures and saying what they said happened, which is totally confusing. How can somebody in my position remember that far back, when I haven't got files to remind me? They have got files. But the papers you are sent are a load of rubbish for all you can understand them. (Case 72, Midlands)

No, not at all, not at all. I felt like either I'm stupid or they're not explaining it properly. They use a lot of sections like section four some-

---

[6] As Mashaw (1983) points out, there are bound to be difficulties in 'communicating to an audience that has modest interpretive skills and a strong incentive to feel aggrieved' (p. 141).

[7] At p. 15; see also Kay (1984), pp. 40–2.

thing or other and you're thinking, 'What's that section, then?' You can't get that information; it's only allocated to them which I think is totally unfair. (Case 171, London South)

Given the difficulties which a substantial proportion of appellants have in understanding the appeal papers, we were interested to discover whether they had sought any advice or assistance, and, if not, why not. The obvious source of advice might seem to be the Department itself, and it was noticeable in interviews with local office staff that many adjudication officers rather resented the fact that claimants seek advice from outside agencies instead of asking the Department for an explanation. Yet, when asked whether they knew where to seek further advice about their appeal, only two appellants mentioned the Department itself.

There have undoubtedly been some improvements in the provision of departmental information services,[8] but, once an appeal is lodged, little further assistance is forthcoming. Appeals officers were, it seems, wary of being thought to be seeking to persuade claimants to withdraw their appeals, although some said that they were prepared to explain decisions to appellants by telephone if asked to do so. This *ad hoc* approach, however, is a poor substitute for a more organized and constructive response which would include the giving of oral explanations of decisions on a routine basis together with information about the appeals system.[9]

At present the Secretary of State is merely obliged to make copies of the income support and family credit schemes available for public inspection at local offices without charge,[10] but in itself this does little to redress the claimant's lack of power. One claimant graphically described the kind of problems that are commonly encountered:

I rang up—I wanted to find clarification of some point and I rang up the DSS because they had quoted some document in the papers that

---

[8] The Freeline telephone service is one example.
[9] Such a service would need skilled staff who could explain the reasons for a decision without giving the impression that the Department was incapable of making mistakes. See further Mashaw (1983), pp. 141–2.
[10] Social Security Act 1986, s. 20(2); see also Kay (1984), pp. 44 and 61.

they sent me quoting subsection 1 of Article 1 of something else. Well, I had no idea what those were. I would have liked to have seen them but they said I would have to go into the office and ask to be shown them. But obviously nobody would explain and I thought they would probably be similarly worded and I wouldn't really understand them anyhow. She said they couldn't photocopy it and send me a copy so, if I wanted to do it, it was up to me to go in and ask to be shown this massive tome. So I just didn't bother proceeding any further. (Case 7, North East)

In this discussion we should not lose sight of the fact that only a half of all appellants attend their hearing before a social security appeal tribunal.[11] Bell (1975) explored the reasons claimants failed to attend their hearings, and found that 80 per cent gave practical reasons such as job commitments, family circumstances, ill health, travel problems, and shortage of money or of suitable clothes in which to appear. Almost one-third, however, mentioned factors which related to their perception of what would happen at the hearing, including many who regarded the outcome of the appeal as a foregone conclusion after having seen the tribunal papers.

A more recent survey of non-attenders was carried out by Farrelly (1989).[12] A thousand questionnaires were distributed to non-attenders, 43 per cent of whom responded. Seventy-three interviews were later conducted at the homes of non-attenders. Farrelly found the same kind of practical reasons as Bell had identified ten years earlier. One-quarter of his sample had not attended because of illness, and a further tenth were unable to attend because they were caring for a member of their family. He also identified a number of other reasons for non-attendance: 7 per cent had had alternative appointments such as visiting hospital or attending court, and 4 per cent had language problems.[13] Eight per cent claimed not even to have received the

---

[11] We decided not to seek to interview non-attenders. A major study on this issue had been completed by Farrelly (1989), and it seemed sensible to concentrate our resources on other aspects of the system, especially given the great difficulties involved in obtaining a representative sample of non-attenders. In addition, the Department of Social Security made it clear that assisting with such a study would be problematic given the duty of confidentiality it owes to claimants.

[12] Ibid., chs. 6–8.

[13] Farrelly conceded that this probably understated the extent of the problem since the figure was based on a postal survey.

tribunal documents informing them when their appeal was to be heard. More generally, Farrelly's interviews suggested that worry and the inability to find a representative were common reasons for non-attendance.

Both Bell and Farrelly uncovered considerable misunderstanding or ignorance about the appeals system which influenced the likelihood of attendance. Farrelly's interviews revealed that only 10 per cent of non-attenders were confident that a tribunal would give them an impartial decision, and no more than 4 per cent had a clear perception of the tribunal's role. His conclusion that nearly two-thirds did not realize that they would have to attend a hearing when they first lodged their appeal closely paralleled Bell's earlier findings. Non-attenders, even more than appellants who attend, seemed confused by the tribunal papers. Ten per cent of those Farrelly interviewed assumed from reading the documentation that the decision had already been made. The receipt of the tribunal papers was therefore identified as a critical stage in the appeals process in that it increased levels of anxiety, resulting in nearly 60 per cent deciding at that point not to attend.

The material from the interviews which we conducted with those appellants who attended their hearings may be usefully contrasted with these earlier studies. Seventy-two per cent of the appellants in our sample stated that they were aware at the outset that they would be required to attend a hearing. This suggests that those who understand the nature of the process which they are setting in train by appealing are more likely to attend the tribunal. It can further be argued that such appellants are more likely to seek to overcome any practical problems associated with attendance at the tribunal, such as the need to rearrange other commitments or to find someone to look after their children. Conversely, those who are less well informed about the appeals system are more easily put off attending by such practical considerations. Since official communications play an important part in shaping appellants' understanding of the nature of the appeals process, it is likely that any deficiencies in content or clarity will be reflected in lower attendance rates.

It is significant that we found that appellants who attended their hearings were generally well informed about the possible non-departmental sources of advice available to them. Forty-one per cent mentioned Citizens Advice Bureaux as a possibility, and a further 18 per cent cited other similar advice agencies. Five per cent regarded going to see a solicitor as an option, and 17 per cent referred to some combination of these three sources of independent advice. Only 7 per cent said that they had no idea at all about where to go for advice.

We were also interested to find out how appellants knew about these various organizations. The two most common sources of information about advice agencies were the details provided by the local office in its letter of decision and by OPSSAT with the appeal papers. It seems that the policy adopted in 1989 of distributing lists of voluntary sector agencies to appellants has had some success in increasing appellants' awareness of the avenues open to them. Sixty-eight per cent of our sample had succeeded in obtaining some advice, and only 3 per cent had been unable to obtain advice despite trying to do so. Notwithstanding the generally high level of awareness of sources of advice, 29 per cent of the sample did not try to get any help with their case. Most of these claimants assumed that they had a strong, straightforward case and that therefore it was unnecessary to seek advice. Only a handful of appellants were so pessimistic about their prospects of success that they saw no point in seeking advice about the hearing. Of the 110 appellants who had obtained advice, seventy-eight described it as helpful or very helpful, with less than one-fifth describing it as unhelpful.

Delays and their effect on attendance rates

Another important consideration to be examined in explaining the high rate of non-attendance at social security appeal tribunals is the question of delays in hearing cases. The prompt hearing of cases has traditionally been seen as one of the advantages of tribunals over the ordinary courts, indeed almost as their *raison d'être*. Yet delays in hearing social security appeals have become increasingly lengthy. In the first quarter of 1984, for example, the average time from lodging a supplementary benefit appeal to the hearing was 10.5 weeks.[14] This was regarded at

---

[14] Council on Tribunals (1985), para. 26.

the time as unacceptable, and the Government expressed the hope that the reforms of the adjudication system would improve matters.[15] Yet delays had increased to an average of twenty-three weeks by 1990.[16]

In an attempt to gain a clearer picture of the points at which delays occurred, we collected data on the delays in the cases in our sample at two distinct stages: from the date of the appeal being lodged to receipt by OPSSAT of the departmental submission, and from submission to hearing date.[17] More than half of the appellants in the sample lodged their appeal within four weeks of the original decision and only 6 per cent sought dispensation to lodge appeals outside the time limit of three months. It would seem then that appellants react quite quickly to an adjudication officer's decision. The same cannot be said of the Department's response to any appeal. The first column of Table 9 shows the length of time it takes the adjudication officer or appeals officer to prepare and forward the written submission on the case to OPSSAT, and this indicates that most submissions took between one and three months to prepare. Despite the official departmental target of fifteen days for submissions to be cleared, the target was achieved in only 16 per cent of cases in the sample. It is a matter for concern that fully 61 per cent of the cases took more than a month to prepare, and that over a fifth took in excess of three months. These delays were reflected in a mean time of sixty-six days' delay, well outside the departmental target. These figures are even more disturbing than those presented in the Chief Adjudication Officer's Annual Report for the same period.[18] One explanation for this discrepancy is that

[15] *Per* Mr K. Clarke, H.C. Debs., Vol. 37, col. 497 (17 Feb. 1983).

[16] H.C. Debs., Vol. 186, col. 26 (written answer, 18 Feb. 1991).

[17] We are grateful to the OPSSAT staff in the seven Regional Offices who assisted us in collecting data on delays and on the outcome of the cases observed in this study. We also wish to express our thanks to Mrs A. Heal of OPSSAT for liaising with Regional Offices on our behalf. Information on delays was not available in eighteen of our total sample of 337 cases.

[18] The report shows that 60 per cent of income support and supplementary benefit appeals were cleared within fifteen days, whilst another 27 per cent were completed within thirty days. The corresponding figures for appeals relating to other benefits dealt with by local offices of the Department of Social Security were 48 per cent and 30 per cent respectively: Chief Adjudication Officer (1991), Appendices 17 and 19.

our sample included unemployment benefit[19] and family credit appeals where the longest delays were experienced.[20]

Further analysis revealed marked differences in the delays at this stage depending on the type of case involved. Overall 39 per cent of submissions were completed within a month. The figures for income support and supplementary benefit cases (excluding overpayments cases) were 56 per cent and 30 per cent respectively, suggesting that the more streamlined income support scheme has helped to reduce delays at this stage.[21]

The second stage at which delay occurs is between receipt

TABLE 9: *Delays at each stage of the appeal process*

Length of time	Delay between date of appeal and submission		Delay between date of submission and hearing	
	No.	%	No.	%
2 weeks or less	48	15.7	12	3.8
2–4 weeks	70	22.9	65	20.4
1–3 months	120	39.2	145	45.5
3–6 months	45	14.7	60	18.8
6–12 months	20	6.5	33	10.3
Over a year	3	1.0	4	1.2
	306	100.0	319	100.0

Note: the total of 319 cases in the second column includes thirteen references. These were cases referred by an adjudication officer for the tribunal to make the initial decision, so are excluded from the first column.

[19] The unemployment benefit category included all those cases involving an issue of voluntary unemployment such as disqualification from benefit by reason of dismissal for misconduct, leaving without just cause, or non-availability for work.

[20] Submissions were completed within a month in only one-fifth of these cases. The Chief Adjudication Officer has also criticized the poor quality of decisions and delays in these areas: see Chief Adjudication Officer (1991), paras. 5. 24–5. 31. A further possible explanation of the differences is that our sample is confined to submissions in cases which proceeded to a hearing, whereas the official figures include all submissions, even though the appeal may subsequently have been withdrawn.

[21] The comparable figure for overpayments cases (where delay may arguably be of less concern to appellants) was 35 per cent.

of the submission by OPSSAT and the hearing date itself. The official average clearance time for this stage was eight weeks in the first quarter of 1989.[22] The official statistics, however, are based on the time which elapses before the first hearing. Since hearings are often adjourned to a later date, it makes more sense to measure the delay between the receipt of the submission and the date on which the tribunal disposes of the case by making its decision. On this basis, the figures derived from our own sample suggest that the official data considerably underestimate the scale of the problem.[23] Table 9 shows that only a quarter of cases were heard within a month of receipt of the submission, and that 30 per cent of appeals took over three months to be listed for a final hearing.[24]

Overall these figures show that only 23 per cent of appellants had their cases disposed of within two months of their appeals having been lodged, and a further third within four months. The remaining 45 per cent waited for more than four months for their appeal to be listed, one-sixth of whom waited for over a year. In keeping with the findings concerning delays in preparing submissions, the delays were most pronounced in respect of the old supplementary benefit cases and unemployment benefit appeals (77 per cent and 59 per cent respectively taking more than four months).

It has always been assumed that lengthy delays in hearing cases are a major contributory factor in non-attendance at tribunals. Bell (1975), for example, argued that most appellants want a speedy hearing of their appeal, and that, if this is achieved, a higher attendance rate is likely to result.[25] Our own findings, however, cast some doubt on this conclusion. We hypothesized that the longer it took for a case to be heard after the appeal was lodged, the less likely it would be for the appellant to attend.

[22] House of Commons Social Services Committee (1989), p. 54.

[23] Our figures somewhat understate the length of delays as, for the purpose of calculations, we have treated hearings where the tribunal adjourned the case part-heard (7 per cent of the sample) as the final disposal of the case.

[24] The data did not cover the delay from the hearing date to written notification of the decision. In 1989 this varied from an average of ten days (North West Region) to three and a half weeks (London South): H.C. Debs., Vol. 178, col. 671 (written answer, 1 Nov. 1990).

[25] Bell (1975), p. 15. Bell found that two-thirds of cases were heard within five weeks of lodging the appeal.

In fact, as Table 10 shows, we found no significant increase in non-attendance rates with lengthier delays.

TABLE 10: *Attendance rates and delays in hearing cases*

Delay in hearing case	Appellant, assistant or representative present No.	No attendance by or on behalf of appellant No.	Attendance rate %
2 months or less	40	29	58
2–4 months	55	45	55
4–6 months	28	22	56
6–9 months	25	20	56
9–12 months	10	10	50
Over 12 months	9	13	38
	167	139	55

The attendance rate was slightly higher in those cases which were listed promptly, but it remained at 50 per cent or above for up to twelve months. It was only after delays of over twelve months that the non-attenders formed a majority. Although these findings must be treated with some caution, given the sample size, the data suggest that delays are not the prime reason for non-attendance. A much more significant factor, as we argued earlier, is the appellant's understanding both of the written submission and of the appeals system as a whole. Whilst we do not underestimate the importance to appellants of prompt hearings, it seems that attendance rates will only improve if more attention is devoted to enhancing appellants' awareness of what an appeal involves.

Appellants' perception of the appeal hearing

Having considered why it is that around half of those appealing to a tribunal fail to appear at their hearing, we turn now to focus on those who do attend. The interviews we conducted with this group also explored the practical problems associated with attending tribunal hearings. As far as the accessibility of tribunal centres and travel arrangements were concerned, it seemed that most attenders encountered no serious difficulties. Despite the move towards centralizing tribunal centres, most appellants' journeys were relatively short, with just over half taking thirty minutes or less. For one in five appellants, however, the journey took more than an hour, and four appellants spent more than two hours travelling to the hearing.[26]

The typical social security appeal tribunal is housed in a government office, Town Hall or private office block. The smaller tribunals, which sit at most once a fortnight, use premises hired for the day, such as church halls, hotels, or even, on one occasion, a Masonic Lodge. The desirability of emphasizing the independence of tribunals by locating them away from social security offices has been a recurrent theme of the Annual Reports of the Council on Tribunals.[27] We came across only one tribunal in the sample which could be said to have been seriously compromised by its position. This was at Oxford where the tribunal is situated in a large complex of government offices, most of which were housed in wartime Nissan huts. The Unemployment Benefit Office was next door to the tribunal hut, and a local Department of Social Security pensions section was actually in the same hut as the tribunal, although access was through a locked door. There were other tribunals which, although not located near social security offices, nevertheless exuded the air of a government office. Some of the worst tribunals were distinctly unwelcoming. Our field notes described one Scottish tribunal as follows: 'Atmosphere of a DSS office: long corridor with room numbers, hard to see where people go, who they

---

[26] A majority arrived at the tribunal by bus (40 per cent) or car (39 per cent). The latter category includes some who were given lifts by their relatives, friends or representatives. Seven per cent walked and the same number came by taxi. (Fares are reimbursed for those unfit to travel by public transport.) These findings are consistent with earlier studies which have shown that most attenders experience little difficulty in getting to the hearing: Bell (1975), p. 6, and Kay (1984), p. 34.

[27] See, for example, Council on Tribunals (1988), pp. 3–4. See also Baldwin and Hill (1988), pp. 114–15.

should see. Very unfriendly building—a long corridor of closed doors.'

Only about one in ten appellants experienced major difficulties in finding the tribunal itself. These problems were largely confined to a small number of tribunals since all but four of the twenty-eight tribunals visited were in central locations, and most tribunal offices send appellants a map showing the tribunal's location.[28] Even where the tribunals were centrally located, however, the signposting both inside and outside the building was often inadequate. We experienced some of the same uncertainty and confusion as appellants, wondering if we were in the right place for the hearings we wanted to observe. In only ten of the twenty-eight centres was there a receptionist or anyone else on the door to deal with queries.[29] In ten others, there were merely written instructions, such as 'Please take a seat and wait until the clerk comes to see you'. At eight tribunals there was no assistance whatsoever. For appellants who arrived tense and nervous, this uncertainty served merely to increase their sense of unease.

The tribunal clerk is usually the first person to see the appellant, and an important part of his or her role is to put appellants at ease on their arrival. The standard practice is for the clerk to sit with the appellant and explain briefly the nature of the tribunal and the proceedings. Some clerks we observed were adept at doing this; others perhaps lacked the necessary social and communicative skills, with the purported explanation assuming the form of a series of hurried and ritualistic statements. One clerk's swift setpiece on the tribunal's role always ended with an emphatic 'The tribunal is entirely independent of the Department whatsoever.'

The clerk's main functions, however, include ushering and dealing with administrative queries and appellants' travelling expenses, as well as being present at least at the beginning and end of each hearing. We found that tribunal clerks on the whole

[28] Twenty-one out of the twenty-eight centres sent appellants a map.

[29] This point is of concern to disabled appellants, particularly as we found that half of the tribunals presented problems of access at the entrance to the premises. Access difficulties inside the tribunal building were less marked, although there was no lift in two of the seventeen centres in which the tribunal suite was above the ground floor.

did a good job in often difficult circumstances, although in many cases more could have been done to explain matters to appellants. The worst type of practice was illustrated at one tribunal where a clerk with a distinctly offhand manner attended the waiting area only intermittently. On arrival, appellants were left to their own devices for up to twenty minutes, becoming increasingly perplexed as time passed. To compound their disorientation, there were no signs at all to indicate that they were in the right place. The tribunal was held in a Town Hall, and appellants were seen being shown into the wrong committee room (a public inquiry full of lawyers) by well-meaning Council staff.[30]

The facilities on offer at different tribunals vary enormously. The larger tribunals usually have a waiting room, one or more tribunal rooms, a room each for the clerk and the presenting officer, and possibly a private room for appellants to consult with their representatives. The smaller tribunals are more cramped although they are frequently in more accessible and neutral venues. Most of the public areas have the feel of a rather drab and depressing doctor's waiting room, with scruffy furniture and little if any literature or useful information on display. At the other extreme, there are much more imposing venues in town halls, complete with portraits of former mayors, which create an air of grandeur and formality off-putting to appellants. A few waiting rooms showed what could be done with some imagination. Manchester, for example, had a clean, bright, spacious waiting room with fresh flowers and a range of reading matter, and was the only one we observed with welfare rights literature available. Cardiff had some toys for children to play with while waiting. Such thoughtfulness, however, was rarely evident.

The arrival of the appellant at the tribunal centre before the hearing of an appeal represents an opportunity for appellants to be put at ease and for matters of procedure to be explained. Our conclusion, based on observations of tribunal waiting rooms, is that this opportunity is being missed. If anything, the anxiety that appellants display on arrival at a tribunal is exacer-

---

[30] On the importance of the clerk's role, see further Bell (1975), p. 10.

bated by their initial treatment while they wait for their case to be heard. To many the waiting is all too familiar from their experiences of visiting departmental offices. This increases the burden on the tribunal chairman of ensuring that appellants feel sufficiently at ease to present a case effectively in the hearing.

It is all the more remarkable to report, then, that the most striking point to emerge from the interviews we conducted with appellants was that, whatever the nature of their grievances, few complaints focused upon the tribunal hearing itself. However we approached the question, it was apparent that most claimants thought that the tribunal had dealt fairly with their appeals. Eighty-one per cent, for example, said that they had been able to understand all or most of the hearing; 80 per cent thought that they had been given full opportunity to put their case; 82 per cent said that they had been given a fair hearing; 81 per cent thought that the chairmen had done all that could reasonably be expected to put them at their ease, and no fewer than 87 per cent said that they had no serious criticisms of tribunal procedures. These figures represent impressive testimony to the efforts made in recent years to create a more professional approach in social security adjudication, and they indicate that the legal chairmen have made considerable headway in ensuring that appellants perceive their hearing to be fair. In these respects, they are evidently having greater success than did their predecessors. It is worth pausing to consider how these high levels of satisfaction were reflected in the interviews we conducted with appellants:

The chairman was a nice lady. I think having a woman was better for me. I think that women are more understanding. It was quite informal. I didn't feel nervous. I've got no criticisms of the procedure. (Case 67, Midlands)

He seemed like a very good chairman actually. He was trying to make me feel confident in the room, and I think it's good that you can project yourself across to people. He understood what I was saying to him. I have been given a fair hearing. He was very understanding in the circumstances. (Case 171, London South)

I definitely felt I had a fair hearing. I was so worried about the case. I was so tight inside and worried; there was such a lot at stake for me. But the chairman did everything he possibly could to make me feel at ease. Very much so. He was a very sensible man. I think they pick the right kind of people to run these tribunals. I would have no criticisms at all about the procedures. (Case 232, South West)

I understood completely. I was very pleased about that. I've generally been disgusted with the DSS approach to everything. I was really pleasantly surprised to come here because I could see from the reaction of the people involved that they weren't pleased with the way we'd been treated either. But it was good, given the treatment that we've become used to. It's nice not to be talked down to. It was very fair. (Case 286, North West)

Whilst there is no doubt that these findings bear witness to the success of the Presidential system in improving tribunal adjudication, caution must be urged in their interpretation. Appellants may perceive hearings to be fair, but in certain respects they are not well placed to judge. Appellants have only a fleeting acquaintance with tribunal procedures, and their assessment is almost invariably based upon a single, often traumatic, experience when too much is at stake for them to form an objective view of what has taken place. Presenting officers, by contrast, have considerable experience of both attended and non-attended hearings, spanning months, if not years. It is noteworthy, then, that when we asked the officers involved in the hearings we observed whether they thought the tribunal had been conducted fairly, most responded as favourably as did appellants. But some serious reservations were nevertheless voiced by presenting officers about certain aspects of the hearings.

For example, we were often taken aback by the vehemence with which officers criticized the quality or comprehensibility of the Department's written submissions. In virtually half of all cases the presenting officer expressed doubts about how far an appellant could be expected to understand the papers. The word, 'gobbledegook', cropped up again and again in interviews, and 'waffle' and even 'crap' were chosen in other interviews as the appropriate epithets. Problems in making sense of the appeals papers were seen as hampering in turn appellants' ability to understand the hearing itself. 'How can you say he's had a fair hearing,' a presenting officer in the North East observed in one case, 'if he doesn't understand what points are in issue?' In over a quarter of the cases, presenting officers seriously doubted whether appellants had genuinely grasped the issues in the case, and, in a further fifth of the cases, some doubts were expressed on this matter.[31]

It is also worth noting that a large proportion of appellants expressed reservations about the level of formality at the appeal hearing. It is perhaps helpful to visualize the standard arrangement of the tribunal room. The three members of the tribunal sit along one side of a large table, with the appellant (and any representative) and the presenting officer facing them. The clerk sits to one side, either at the same table or at a separate desk. Tribunal layouts have therefore been largely standardized,[32] and we found no instances of cases where presenting officers were seated in such a way as to jeopardize the independence of the tribunal in the appellant's eyes.[33]

Tribunal chairmen and lay members tended to view the seating arrangements as informal, a perception inevitably moulded by their social and professional backgrounds. Legally qualified chairmen are accustomed to court procedures, and, as we have seen, many of the lay members also have experience sitting as magistrates. Only half of the appellants, however, viewed the setting as informal, and the remainder saw it in varying degrees as formal. It was common for these appellants to see the tribunal in terms of a court of law as in the following examples:

Feeling like you were a criminal in a court case—that's what I felt like. I felt like I was in the Crown Court in front of the judge waiting to be sentenced. I was very intimidated. I felt like I had done something wrong because I had appealed against not getting unemployment benefit. It should be more informal—not like being in the County Court. (Case 12, North East)

It was like a criminal court in a way. The lady who was representing the DHSS is the prosecution and the three tribunal members were like

---

[31] While 81 per cent of appellants told us that they had understood all or most of the hearing, some of these may have been reluctant to admit to a lack of comprehension and others may have been mistaken in thinking they had grasped the essentials of the case.

[32] In twenty-four of the venues visited, the tribunal layout was in this standard format. The four other venues adopted minor variations on this arrangement.

[33] On this see Rose (1975), pp. 144–5, Fulbrook (1978), p. 253, and Kay (1984) pp. 27–9. Dean (1991), however, drawing on Donzelot's (1980) work on juvenile justice, describes the seating arrangements as bringing about the 'encirclement' of the appellant (p. 161).

magistrates with me stating my own case. It was formal—it could have been more informal, much more informal. (Case 53, Midlands)

It's more like a magistrates' court, isn't it? They dictate to you what you are allowed to say and what you are allowed to do most of the time. (Case 144, London North)

I'd say it was formal. It doesn't matter how many times you call something 'informal', you're sitting in front of three people armed with regulations. They can call it informal but it feels formal. We feel nervous. That means it's formal. (Case 147, London South)

It emerged clearly from our observations of hearings and from interviews with appellants that they often failed to grasp the importance of representation. The literature that they are sent by the Department, stressing as it does the informality of hearings, probably encourages them in this view.[34] In consequence, some appellants get a nasty shock when they find that the informal hearing they have been promised turns out to be a relatively formal confrontation.

Few appellants are accustomed to expressing themselves in such a structured environment. When observing the tribunals in action, we sought to assess the extent to which appellants participated in the hearing of their appeal. Evaluation of such behaviour is necessarily subjective, but the importance attached to the tribunal's enabling function means that the issue cannot be avoided. Our observations at hearings indicated a surprisingly high level of participation by appellants. Nearly 20 per cent of the 174 attenders were judged to have undertaken a full part in the hearing, and a further 36 per cent were thought to have played a substantial part, by, for example, giving detailed answers to questions put to them. Thirty per cent were involved to only a minor extent whilst a mere 14 per cent adopted an entirely passive stance. Where appellants were represented by professionals, such as welfare rights or Citizens Advice Bureau workers, the level of participation tended to be lower than when they appeared unaided. The chairman's responsibility to assist appellants is lightened when a competent representative is handling the case, and most appeals can then be dealt with in a more expeditious and business-like manner. Exchanges between chairmen and representatives are often couched in formal, lega-

---

[34] See Genn and Genn (1989), p. 222.

listic language which reduces the scope for appellants to become involved in the hearing.[35]

It can be argued that the main function of the tribunal—to determine whether an appellant is legally entitled to benefit—is essentially formal in nature. For while tribunal chairmen and members are on the whole humane and sympathetic as individuals, they are none the less constrained to operate within a fixed framework of rules and regulations. At every stage of our enquiry, we have been obliged to recognize this essential truth. Yet it is not easy for lay people to grasp the distinction—at root one between law and justice. They ask how an independent and apparently sympathetic tribunal can ignore their plight in favour of the mechanical application of laws that the tribunal itself might acknowledge are unjust in the circumstances. Without a representative, appellants quickly discover the disadvantages under which they labour in getting to grips with technical regulations. One-third of those without a representative said that they would have preferred to have had one, and none of those who were represented thought that they would have been better off without one. Given the essentially legalistic framework within which the tribunals operate and the complexity of the law they administer, the benefits of such representation seem to us to be almost self-evident.

We noted in Chapter 4 how even the most solicitous chairman, skilfully playing the inquisitorial role he or she is now expected to adopt, must somehow restrict the presentation of facts and arguments to those that have some legal validity. To do otherwise is merely to encourage appellants to introduce legal irrelevances. Hearings cannot be allowed to become unduly protracted, and it does no good to mislead appellants into believing that they have a case when in reality it is groundless in law. This tension runs through the whole of social security adjudication, and chairmen have to find a way of striking a balance between allowing appellants fully to have their say and at the same time steering proceedings along the course that the present law requires. This

---

[35] Of the eighty-six appellants who attended without any form of representation or assistance, twenty-nine (34 per cent) played a full role and thirty-six (42 per cent) a substantial role. The reason for this could be that these appellants were naturally more confident and articulate, or it may point to the success of the enabling philosophy in engaging appellants in participation.

is no easy task, and it is remarkable that chairmen achieve it to the evident satisfaction of so many appellants.

Yet in interview after interview, appellants drew a distinction between the agreeable way that chairmen dealt with them and the objectionable nature of the law that was being applied. Many left the tribunal dissatisfied with the decision finally reached. Appellants make this point forcefully and eloquently in the following quotes:

They did no more than the Social Security. It was just someone with a little bit more authority quoting the same rules. The people are nice enough but they told me just as much as everyone else, and the rules can't be changed. I just think that the rules are unfair. (Case 56, Midlands)

They just go by the law, and that's it. There's no flexibility in the law, it's rigid. There's no compassion built in. They were all sorry, they were genuinely sorry. The form they give you tells you that you can appeal. This to me seems a bit stupid, that you can appeal when there's no chance of you winning the appeal. This to me is a waste of their time and a waste of my time. It's like putting you in a race that you can never win. They slightly raise your hopes, then dash them again. It makes it seem like a sham. It's a sham trial almost. But I'm greatly disappointed. There should be a chink. There shouldn't be a steel wall that doesn't allow for any extenuating circumstances. (Case 68, Midlands)

I don't really think the tribunal's a lot of good because, if they're only going to quote the law that the DSS have set down, then it's a waste of time them being there, because the DSS go by the book when they send you the stuff anyway. When the chairman said right at the beginning that they had to abide by the criteria set down by the DSS, I might as well have got up and gone then. It's pointless having tribunals because the DSS aren't going to make mistakes. So it's just wasting taxpayers' money really. (Case 143, London North)

The tribunal may be independent but they are influenced by a set of rules made by the Social Security and they only follow that set of rules. What's the point in having the tribunal if everybody follows the same rules? (Case 236, South West)

Yes, I thought it was a fair hearing. But they couldn't do anything about it. I couldn't see why they agreed in the first place to let me come to the tribunal because all the facts are there on paper, and they knew very well before we have even started that there was nothing they could do about it. They say it's such-and-such regulation and that it's not applicable. As the regulations stand, there's no leeway at all for different cases. (Case 247, North West)

I got the impression I was a hopeless case. I got the impression from the man that he was saying, 'You are here, we are going to listen to you but there is not much we can do—it's not in our hands.' It felt hopeless before you opened you mouth. You felt, 'Wait a minute, this is a waste of time.' (Case 305, Scotland)

Those on the receiving end tend to view social security appeal tribunals as hide-bound by statute and legal regulation. At the extreme, appellants see the tribunal hearing merely as a charade, as an added humiliation in their prolonged dealings with uncaring officialdom. As the quotations above illustrate, some of these appellants felt that their expectations had been raised by being told that they had a right of appeal only to be dashed at the hearing itself. It is certainly more common for tribunals to confirm than overturn earlier decisions, and, however sincere might be their hand-wringing, they often find themselves powerless to intervene when justice seems to cry out for them to do so. These tensions are strikingly illustrated by our observation notes on one of the hearings we observed:

The appellant claimed one parent benefit because she was bringing up her son alone. Her husband was paralysed by a stroke three years ago and has been in hospital ever since. The presenting officer explained that the legislation provides that married claimants cannot receive one parent benefit for a week in which they reside with their spouse, and they are treated as residing with their spouse even if the latter is in hospital, whether temporarily or otherwise. The chairman intervening, stated, 'This case bothers us a lot. What is the purpose of the legislation?' The presenting officer was unable to assist. The appellant observed, 'Looking at it from my point of view, I'm a single parent. ... I'm not divorced and as my husband is technically alive I'm not a widow. I don't slot into the normal run of the mill case.' After listening carefully to the appellant's account, and having with great circumspection indicated that a divorce might be the only answer, the chairman summed up by indicating that they were sympathetic but were bound by the regulations: 'It seems that there is nothing we can do, so a formal decision will follow.' The tribunal encouraged the appellant to see her MP to pursue the matter. (Case 67, Midlands)

There are, however, a minority of appeals which are successful in that earlier decisions by adjudication officers are changed or the tribunal looks again at matters and reaches a fresh determination. The reports of the Chief Adjudication Officer make it clear enough that mistakes are often made by adjudication officers and these are not always rectified as a result of internal departmental reviews. There is often a genuine discretion or judgement to be exercised and in these areas adjudication by a tribunal provides a useful safety net. In all, the claimant's appeal was upheld in 26 per cent of the cases we observed, and appellants succeeded in part at least in a further 6 per cent.

Yet whilst it is clear that not everybody leaves the tribunal disgruntled with the decision, this remains the most common reaction of appellants. This is all the more frustrating for them given the length of their trek through the appeals system. As we have seen, few appellants have their cases dealt with swiftly, and nearly half of those in our sample waited for over four months for a resolution of their appeal.

It is clearly critical to establish what delays of this order mean to those on the receiving end. It was no surprise to find that appellants expressed great dissatisfaction about them. There were varying degrees of frustration, with 37 per cent expressing anger at the length of time their appeal had taken.[36] Some of those who had had to wait a long time for their hearing experienced great financial hardship as a result, as in the following quotes:

When people go to these things, they need what they're asking for, generally, straight away. They need help with their situation right then, at the time. There needs to be a resolution, for people who are refused by the DHSS, within a few weeks at the most. ... It makes it seem odd when you get the money, like how I did today, when my situation has changed and I don't really need the money any more. So when I needed it, I couldn't get it and now I don't need it they give it to me. (Case 53, Midlands)

I think they left me far too long. It's been four and a half months, and I've had absolutely no money since then until I got my present job a month ago. So when it's quite desperate like that, it's not right that it takes so long. (Case 56, Midlands)

I've waited nine months since I first claimed to get here. I waited to get this day ever such a long time. It's put me in debt because I've waited so long. It's very difficult to live on one income, especially part-time. (Case 78, Midlands)

The only thing I didn't understand is why they couldn't have given

[36] In some instances this resentment was fuelled by the practice of certain chairmen of notifying appellants of the decision by post, rather than on the day, and by tribunals adjourning cases for no reason understandable to the appellant.

me the decision here, why I've got to hang about now. This has been hanging over me now since 1986 or 1987 and I think the time lapse is absolutely disgusting. Surely when I can produce a letter saying I am not guilty, surely I'm entitled to my money backdated on the day. (Case 179, London South)

It took a very long time for this to come around. We're talking over a year now. It's a ridiculously long time to wait because you obviously forget some things. It would have been better if it was a bit closer to the time when it actually happened. (Case 182, London South)

It was three months to get the first date. Then that had to be changed and it's been another two months to get here. That's too long definitely as I've not been paid a penny for five months. (Case 332, Scotland)

Even in overpayments cases, where delay might be thought to work to the advantage of the appellant (since no repayment will be required unless and until the appeal is lost), the levels of dissatisfaction were just as high. No one, it seems, likes to have cases hanging over them for the length of time that is common for social security appeals.

There will always be a tension between the speed and accuracy of decision making, and we have already seen how this exists at the initial stage of the adjudication process in the local office. Speed in disposing of appeals may be to the advantage of the tribunal system in terms of reducing the backlog of cases, but will be at the appellant's expense if the quality of decision making deteriorates. Genn and Genn (1989) demonstrate how cases inevitably take longer to process if the appellant seeks advice or representation. Although Genn and Genn find a positive correlation with success rates, they none the less concede that 'it takes longer to win a social security appeal than to lose' (p. 149).

The major sources of delay, however, are to be located within the social security system itself. The sheer volume of work in local offices means that adjudication officers often have to make decisions in the absence of all the necessary information. This in turn causes delay if an appeal is subsequently received because further enquiries need to be made. Pressures of other work, staff absences and delays in typing all contribute to the problem. At the appeal stage proper, OPSSAT has had to cope with booms and slumps in its workload whilst its staffing complements are fixed in advance on the basis of predictions as to the volume of appeals. The first President was understandably reluctant to recruit large numbers of extra chairmen and members one year 'only to dump them the next'.[37] Ultimately, however, the efficiency of the system is constrained by political choices as to the allocation of resources. The fact is that, especially in local offices, appeals work is not generally seen as a high priority.

Conclusion

The nature of the cases dealt with by social security appeal tribunals varies greatly. Some appeals concern relatively small sums of money; in others (especially overpayments cases) thousands of pounds are at stake. Regardless of the sums involved, the outcomes can well have a critical bearing on the lives of appellants and their families. These are not people who exercise their right of appeal lightly; nor do many find it easy to face a tribunal appearance. Confronted with a technically worded submission from an adjudication officer, it is no real surprise that a high proportion of claimants fail to attend the hearing.

Hearings are an ordeal for most appellants—so much so that in some cases we saw them break down in tears in the course of the hearing. It was remarkable, therefore, to note that very few of them (only about 5 per cent) said afterwards in interview that they would have preferred to have been spared a hearing and instead had their appeal dealt with on the basis of the papers. This provides some indication of the importance that the appellants who attend attach to the hearing, whatever the outcome might be.

Tribunal chairmen do for the most part succeed in satisfying appellants about the fairness of hearings. On the basis of our own observations of hearings, we can state that chairmen have not on the whole descended into unthinking routines, nor can they be said to deal superficially or brusquely with appellants. The experiences of most appellants, as we have described them in this chapter, suggest that social security appeal tribunals in the great majority of circumstances operate in an even-handed and humane manner. Whether they are in a position also to do justice is of course an entirely different question.

[37] House of Commons Social Services Committee (1989), p. 41.

7

The Presenting Officer at the Appeal Hearing

AT hearings before social security appeal tribunals, an adjudication officer is entitled to be present, to be heard, and to call and question witnesses.[1] This officer need not be the one who took the original decision which is the subject of appeal, and practices vary according to the type of benefit in question. Income support adjudication officers do not appear before tribunals, and in these cases specialist appeals officers responsible for processing the appeal in the local office attend the hearing instead. On the other hand, most contributory benefit and unemployment benefit adjudication officers appear at tribunals, sometimes presenting their own decisions, sometimes those of colleagues. When carrying out this function, adjudication and appeals officers are known as presenting officers. In Chapter 3 we discussed how the tribunal exerts, through the mediating role of the presenting officer, a significant influence on initial decision making and on the internal review process within local offices. This chapter is concerned with the role played by presenting officers at appeal hearings and the factors which influence or constrain their behaviour.

To investigate these matters, we interviewed a total of 178 presenting officers, ninety-three at the tribunal and eighty-five within local offices.[2] It was usual at most tribunals for one officer to deal with a batch of cases at each hearing, and it was our practice to conduct a single interview with the officer at the end

[1] Social Security (Adjudication) Regulations 1986, S.I. 1986 No. 2218, reg. 4(5) and 4(9).
[2] The sample in local offices comprised those adjudication and appeal officers, interviewed as part of our investigation of initial decision making, who also appeared before tribunals to present cases.

of the session when there was sufficient time to discuss each case in turn.[3] As with other respondents, we were able to tape-record the vast majority of these interviews. The interviews covered a total of 314 appeals heard at tribunals throughout the country.[4] In those cases where we interviewed presenting officers at the tribunal, we were therefore able to compare their perceptions of their role with their actual behaviour before the tribunal. We also obtained information about their reactions to the way the tribunal had handled each case in which they had been involved. When interviewing officers within local offices, the emphasis was rather different inasmuch as we were restricted to asking about their general impressions of how well tribunals had dealt with cases, although the questions about how officers perceived their own role before the tribunal were common to both groups of respondents. This chapter is based mainly on the interviews we conducted with presenting officers and our own observations of hearings, although material derived from interviews with chairmen, members and appellants is used to illustrate certain points.

The role of the presenting officer: theory and practice

In the preceding chapter, we saw how the great majority of appellants are 'one-shotters' in that they are appearing before a tribunal for the first time. By contrast, the presenting officers in our sample were experienced 'repeat players'. On average, those presenting contributory benefit or unemployment benefit cases appear before tribunals at least once a month, while those presenting income support appeals appear two to three times a month.[5] They normally have easy access to the adjudication

---

[3]   This had the disadvantage that, by the end of the session, presenting officers knew the result of most cases, and this may have affected their view of the fairness of the hearing. It was often not possible to contact officers between hearings because of the speed at which decisions were given.

[4]   In ten of the 337 cases observed, no presenting officer attended the hearing, and in a further thirteen cases we were unable to obtain an interview with the officer because of lack of time or other practical problems.

[5]   Although income support appeals officers appeared more frequently, they were generally less experienced than their contributory benefit colleagues: 28 per cent of the latter group had been presenting for more than five years, compared to only 2 per cent of income support appeals officers.

officer who made the decision, the legal regulations, the Adjudication Officers' Guide, Commissioners' decisions, and files of relevant correspondence. Many will have painstakingly prepared the appeals submission for the tribunal. In short, they are in a much more powerful position than the appellant when it comes to the appeal hearing.

Given that most appellants are unrepresented, or do not appear at all, the contest between the presenting officer and the appellant would be a most unequal one if the tribunal operated on strictly adversarial lines. We saw in Chapter 4 how the tribunal attempts to redress this imbalance through adopting an inquisitorial approach at hearings. Further redress is intended to be achieved by discouraging presenting officers from acting as advocates for the Department. The formal legal position is well established. For example, in a case under the industrial injuries scheme, Diplock LJ observed that:

Insurance tribunals form part of the statutory machinery for investigating claims, that is, for ascertaining whether the claimant has satisfied the statutory requirements which entitle him to be paid benefit out of the fund. In such an investigation neither the insurance officer nor the Minister (both of whom are entitled to be represented before the insurance tribunal) is a party adverse to the claimant. If an analogy be sought in ordinary litigious procedure, their functions most closely resemble those of *amici curiae*.[6]

This perspective is adopted and elaborated upon in all the official guidance to departmental staff, and the Adjudication Officers' Guide offers the following succinct explanation. The presenting officer's role is described as:

most closely analogous to that of *amicus curiae* (i.e. 'friend of the court') and not as an advocate. The AO should not put questions to any claimant or witness in a hostile manner, and it is entirely inappropriate for the AO to think in terms of 'winning' the case. The objective of the AO should be to assist the tribunal to assess correctly the facts, relevant law and case law relating to the case. This can best be achieved by the AO highlighting the question(s) to be decided and by clarity in the presentation of evidence, argument and advice to the tribunal (Vol. 1, para. 05287).

[6] *R* v. *Deputy Industrial Injuries Commissioner, ex p. Moore* [1965] 1 Q.B. 456 at p. 486. See also *R* v. *Medical Appeal Tribunal, ex p. Hubble* [1958] 2 Q.B. 228 at p. 240.

Presenting officers are therefore directed to deal with any points put forward by the appellant, even if they only seem to be vaguely relevant to the issue, and to give proper emphasis to points in the appellant's favour.[7] The Social Security Commissioners have also stressed this aspect of the presenting officer's role. For example, in one reported case, the presenting officer was rebuked for disclosing only part of the relevant correspondence to the tribunal, this being 'inconsistent with the objectivity expected of benefit officers presenting cases to tribunals'.[8]

Early studies of social security tribunals revealed many instances of presenting officers failing to act according to this prescription. Elcock (1969), for example, reported that national insurance officers were on occasions argumentative and 'definitely aggressive' (p. 75), and Rose (1975) noted the subtle tendency of presenting officers to upstage appellants by sliding to the end of the table so as to reaffirm their identification with the tribunal rather than as someone of equal status with the appellant (p. 145). Similarly, Frost and Howard (1977) depicted many presenting officers as straight advocates for the Department, sometimes openly antagonistic towards appellants.[9]

Bell (1975), by contrast, found 'no evidence of the overbearing rather intimidating manner and attitude which has been referred to in some publications on S.B.A.T.s. The common style was rather low key—courteous and reasonable'.[10] Bell none the less viewed the role of *amicus curiae* as unrealistic in that it placed the presenting officer in an impossible dilemma, particularly in unattended cases where there was very little that an officer could do to fulfil this function. She also stressed that presenting officers needed to be of high calibre if they were to cope with their conflicting duties to the Department and the tribunal.[11] Bell

[7] *Adjudication Officers' Guide*, vol. 1, para. 05168.

[8] *R(SB) 18/83* at para. 11. See also *R(U) 6/88*.

[9] At p. 45. See also Lister (1974), p. 14 who found tribunal members to be heavily reliant upon the presenting officer for guidance.

[10] At p. 10. Fulbrook (1978) argued that the differing conclusions drawn by Bell might be explicable on the basis that neither she nor her colleagues were lawyers, and the significance of legally prejudicial commentary may therefore have been overlooked (p. 242).

[11] At the time Bell was writing, supplementary benefit presenting officers were specialists drawn from the higher executive officer grade whereas presenting is now carried out in income support cases by appeals officers, who are ordinary executive officers.

concluded that the solution was not to seek to purge presenting officers of bias but to strengthen the tribunals so that they adopted a genuinely inquisitorial approach. The introduction of legally qualified chairmen was the key to this improvement, and we consider the impact which this has had on the role played by presenting officers later in this chapter.

In their more recent study, Genn and Genn (1989) found that most presenting officers described their function as being to assist the tribunal, and none claimed that their role was adversarial in nature. In their observations of hearings, however, Genn and Genn noted that 'despite the views expressed in interviews . . . many Presenting Officers were seen to argue their cases forcefully and to display pleasure when their decision was ultimately confirmed' (p. 161).

We sought to examine in some detail the extent to which presenting officers understood and accepted the officially sanctioned role. We found that, in the interviews we conducted with them, no fewer than 58 per cent described themselves as a 'friend of the court'.[12] Others saw themselves in more neutral terms as presenters of the adjudication officer's decision (23 per cent), but only 8 per cent admitted to regarding their function as being to act as advocates for the Department. It seemed to us that the training received by presenting officers had been effective in the sense that most of those we interviewed seemed to have a reasonable grasp of the concept of the *amicus curiae* (although often unfamiliar with the term itself) as the following quotes illustrate:

My role is purely as friend of the court. I'm not there to win. I'm there to listen to what the appellant says, and you've got to think on your feet. If an appellant comes up with something that isn't in the appeal papers, I should apply the law to that and perhaps ask for an adjournment. But I'm purely there to answer the chairman's questions if he's not certain about some aspect of the law. But I'm not there to win. And I'm not there for the Department. I'm a friend of the court. (Interview 162, Presenting Officer, North East)

My job's to make sure that the tribunal and the claimant understand what's in the papers. If you find anything to the claimant's advantage,

[12] When we asked presenting officers specifically whether they saw themselves as fulfilling the role of an *amicus curiae*, this proportion then rose to 75 per cent. This increase perhaps reflects an awareness that this is the answer that ought to be given since both the training programme and the official guidance for presenting officers emphasize this role.

you tell the tribunal. It's not just to defend the AO's decision, come what may. If they're entitled to the money within the law, then I would say so, even if the AO had made a mistake in the papers. It's to make sure the law is applied properly. It doesn't matter whether the Department wins or loses. (Interview 177, Presenting Officer, Midlands)

We are all in it to ensure that the claimant gets the benefit to which he or she is entitled. The one difference between my role and the tribunal's and any reps who might come is that I'm also going to make sure that they don't get benefit to which they are not entitled. Generally I'm there to help the tribunal, and I'm not there, as many people think, as prosecution counsel. (Interview 215, Presenting Officer, Wales and South West)

Most presenting officers are aware, then, of what their role is in principle, but the important question is how this translates into practice. In each of the 337 hearings which we observed in this study, we made notes on the presenting officer's role. We were particularly interested to see whether presenting officers commonly adopt an *amicus* role or whether they take up an adversarial stance. What these assessments clearly revealed is that most of the time presenting officers fall somewhere between these two extremes. In only one in five hearings did the presenting officer appear to us to be adopting the full role of an *amicus curiae*, and in only 8 per cent of the hearings was an adversarial position taken. It was far more common for presenting officers to be essentially passive, merely answering one or two questions or reading out a brief summary of facts or reciting what was written down in the submission. We assessed their role in these terms in 45 per cent of the cases. In a further 20 per cent of cases, the presenting officer took a more active role, explaining the adjudication officer's decision, without either defending it or suggesting that another way of looking at the matter was possible.

In practice the role adopted most often by presenting officers can best be described as neutral and reactive. The presenting officer rarely takes on a crude adversarial position, but the adoption of the *amicus* role is far from being the norm. It is unusual for a presenting officer to take the initiative and make points in favour of the appellant or to suggest an interpretation of the law that differs from that in the submission. It is true that on occasion the presenting officer intervened at the very start of a hearing in effect to concede the appeal. But there were other instances where the presenting officer, despite having apparently concluded that the original decision was incorrect, refrained from indicating this to the tribunal, or did so only elliptically. It is much commoner for it be left to the tribunal to look for deficiencies in the submission, with the presenting officer merely acquiescing in this exercise. There were cases in our sample where seemingly courteous and helpful presenting officers admitted to us afterwards that they had held back vital information from the tribunal. It was not uncommon for them to make comments such as, 'If they'd have pressed me, I'd have had to admit that I had my doubts too.' Particular discomfort seemed to be experienced by presenting officers if the tribunal asked them for their personal view about the correctness of a decision. The following series of quotes exemplify such attitudes:

I don't take sides. A lot of the decisions that are made by adjudication officers are a bit iffy, but I can't go in there sort of giving the impression that it's a load of rubbish. I present it, like I say, as a neutral person really. (Interview 164, Presenting Officer, North East)

In the second case today, there wasn't really much for me to argue about. All I could do was just present the official view. But at the end of the day, if they'd really pressed me on it, I'd have said that I couldn't defend it any further. I don't want to prolong their time over something where you are flogging a dead horse. (Interview 176, Presenting Officer, Midlands)

Really we are only there for answering questions, perhaps to give some background information if they want it, padding out a little bit. Quite often you're glad when it's reversed because you don't think the adjudication officer's view is the proper answer anyway. Sometimes you don't agree with the officer's opinion so you wouldn't push it. We have a little system. If we agree with the submission we'd say, 'I think that . . .', and, if we don't, then we say, 'The adjudication officer thinks that . . .' And a lot of the chairmen realize what we are doing. (Interview 182, Presenting Officer, Midlands)

The chairman adjourned that last one this morning part-heard so that the appellant could get some advice on his case. But if he'd have pressed me, there were all sorts of dodgy things about that case. I think it was one complete cock-up from start to finish, and we could have been taken to task over it. Perhaps the case could have been allowed without an adjournment if we'd have gone into it. I think that the chairman has just looked at it on paper and thought it looks pretty bleak. Personally I don't see it as being as bleak as he does, because I think we've made a right mess of it. There's an awful lot of factors which, if I'm pushed, I will have to reveal. But sometimes things that I think will come up don't come up. I wouldn't actually say it myself because that could get us into a very nasty grey area where I might find that I was backed up against the wall. (Interview 239, Presenting Officer, Wales and South West)

Sometimes tribunals forget that you're there merely to present. You're put on the spot too much or you're asked to make judgements or comments on the adjudication officer's decision and you're caught between the two. Obviously you're wanting to remain loyal to them. They're not there to give their argument so you've got to try and not prejudice the adjudication officer's decision unfairly. Sometimes the chairman or a member will say, 'Well, what do you think?', which I think is a bit unfair. (Interview 246, Presenting Officer, North West)

These findings suggest, then, that presenting officers do not always practice what they preach. Whereas most claim to play the role of an *amicus curiae*, the role is adopted in only a relatively small minority of hearings. They pay lip service to the principle, but, when it comes to the hearing, they tend to be passive and neutral, neither fighting for the decision to be upheld, nor actively assisting the tribunal in its consideration of the appeal.

This gap between the presenting officer's ideology and their practice requires some explanation. A number of factors may be identified: the near impossibility for departmental employees to act with the independence and objectivity which the *amicus* role requires; the reliance placed on the written appeals submission; the problem of unattended hearings; the shift away from discretion in social security law, and the introduction of legal chairmen. It is important to examine these points in turn to illuminate how the dynamics of an appeal hearing affect (and are affected by) the position taken by the presenting officer.

(i) *Problems inherent in the* amicus curiae *role*

In seeking to understand the behaviour of presenting officers in appeal hearings, it is vital to appreciate the constraints under which they work and which lead to them taking up the passive or reactive role we have described. When we asked those officers who claimed to see their role as that of an *amicus curiae* whether they found it difficult to adopt this role in practice, around half conceded that it was indeed a difficult role to play. It should be made clear that we uncovered no evidence to suggest that office managers sought to undermine this role by encouraging a more adversarial frame of mind amongst their staff. As presenting officers explained to us in interview:

I don't feel under any pressure to win cases. The pressure I get is to write and process appeals very quickly. What's coming down from line management is, 'Just get the cases cleared, it doesn't matter whether you think there's a right or a wrong or what the result is, we're not interested. We just don't want all these cases showing as uncleared on our statistics.' So you can see that we're not under pressure to defend decisions, because the Department doesn't care what the decisions are anyway. (Interview 218, Wales and South West)

We find that people who are new to it feel it's a matter of pride that they win the case. But we are encouraged not to think of it in that way, and it doesn't really matter. Nobody checks on what decision the tribunal's given so they don't bring out any stats to say that such a person's lost so many cases or won so many cases. So it doesn't really matter. (Interview 228, North West)

While there is no overt pressure exerted by line management to 'win' cases, this is not to say that the fact that presenting officers are based in the Department has no influence on the role they play at tribunals. It was certainly evident that many felt a conflict of loyalties between backing up the adjudication officer before the tribunal and offering so much assistance to the tribunal that it might lead to the overturning of a colleague's decision. Others were adamant that they stuck to their official role but conceded that colleagues often expected them to defend their decisions. Similarly, some contributory benefit and unemployment benefit adjudication officers admitted to being 'psychologically' committed to their own decisions, finding it difficult to present these in an objective way. 'I feel that it is my decision that is on trial' is how one officer put it.

It was as a rule apparent that the presenting officer's personal view of the merits of an appeal (and of an appellant), often shaped by an awareness of the appellant's previous dealings with the Department, affected the level of commitment to playing the role of the *amicus*. The essential dilemma for presenting officers, illustrated in the following quotes, is that they are so steeped in departmental practices, procedures and ways of thinking that it is impossible for them to be truly detached.

It's always there nagging at the back of your mind that you're working for the Department, and this is the Department's view. When I write the submission, I'm supposed to be doing it on behalf of the adjudication officer, and, let's be honest, when all's said and done, I still work for the Department. Even though you might not agree with something, you've got that loyalty. I've been in the Department for eighteen years. It's a difficult role to get yourself out of, because I'm Department-orientated at the end of the day. (Interview 124, Presenting Officer, Midlands)

I'm told in my instructions that I'm there as a friend of the court to help them arrive at a proper decision and to present facts both for the claimant and the Department. It is difficult to do that even in the run of the mill case. Obviously my feelings come into it. I have certain inbuilt prejudices when I go into the tribunal, having read through the papers, as to whether Mr X has been fiddling the system or deliberately made himself unemployed or whatever. I try to overcome these feelings but it's not always easy, simply because I work in this office with the people who have made the decision. You're paid by the Department and you work for the Department. You've done the same job as the adjudication officers whose decisions you are presenting and you know how they work. So it makes it that much more difficult to be independent of them and to distance yourself from them. (Interview 144, Presenting Officer, Wales and South Western)

It is drummed into you that you are the friend of the court, that you are only representing the Department in order to assist the tribunal. But you can't help leaning towards the Department, because you're associated with the Department. It's the old cliché of, 'What was the score? How many did we win?' That's not what it's really about, but you can't get away from that. (Interview 151, Presenting Officer, North West)

My official role is that of presenting officer, to present the Department's case. And this bit that appellants are supposed to come away with, that it's supposed to be independent of the Department, I think is totally artificial. In no way can it be independent of the Department. I work there every day and only come here once a week. But I certainly don't see myself as here to defend the Department in an antagonistic or adversarial way. If the appellant comes up with more evidence which changes what we know and would enable us to authorize his benefit, then I see no point in pushing on regardless. In a case like that, I'd back off and just accept it. But let me say that it's virtually impossible to stand in here independently of the Department. You just can't do that at all. (Interview 247, Presenting Officer, Scotland)

(ii) *The importance of the written appeals submission*

As we have noted in earlier chapters, the submission, prepared by an adjudication or appeals officer, is sent to the tribunal over a week before the appeal hearing. By the day of the hearing, the chairmen and members should be sufficiently familiar with the position taken by the adjudication officer so that there is no need for the presenting officer to explain the basis for the decision, still less to read out the submission. There may be points that the panel may wish to clarify, but more often it will simply wish to supplement the written material before it. This might involve, for example, asking the presenting officer to express a view on the adequacy of the submission or the significance of any evidence provided by the appellant at the hearing. What is sought, in short, is for the presenting officer to refrain from acting as a mere mouthpiece for the adjudication officer or for the Department.

In Chapter 4 we saw how tribunals sometimes sought to go beyond the points raised by the appeal in an attempt to give some assistance to an appellant, particularly where the appeal seemed doomed to failure. Some presenting officers were clearly aware of this broad approach to appeals and on occasions introduced points themselves about other possible benefits to which the appellant might be entitled. The problem for presenting officers is that the Department does not seek to investigate a person's circumstances and entitlements in this broad fashion. While the tribunal may feel that more ought to be done for a particular claimant, the onus in the current benefits system is upon claimants to do more for themselves. Thus, there can be a clash of expectations between the tribunal and Department. The Department is content to do no more than react to specific claims, whereas the tribunal often wants to see the adoption of a more proactive role. It is the presenting officers who must manage this tension, and the good ones achieve this, to some extent at least, by viewing the appeal in the widest perspective. Accordingly, they have the answers ready when the tribunal asks about benefits beyond those that, strictly speaking, form the subject matter of the appeal. As one explained when asked about his role:

I'm supposed to say *amicus curiae*, and I do see it as that. The people I'm appearing in front of expect that probably. Very frequently they will ask me what else they can do for the claimant. So you've got to be able to say that you will do some liaison with housing benefit or whatever, and advise that perhaps they could claim for these other benefits. It's very much a helping role. (Interview 135, Presenting Officer, London North)

We saw for ourselves the lengths to which certain presenting officers were prepared to go after a hearing in explaining to an appellant in the waiting room other benefits which might be claimed. This was, however, an infrequent occurrence, and most presenting officers were content to play a much more neutral role, presenting information relating specifically to the case without arguing for or against the decision in question. Since most, if not all, of the information considered relevant by the presenting officer has already been presented to the tribunal in the written appeals submission, it follows that such presenting officers see little need to say much in the appeal hearing. As one put it:

I'm there to be asked a question of, and if not, keep my mouth shut, keep my head down and hopefully the submission should do it. I needn't really be there technically, that's our view. If the papers are prepared correctly, there is no need of a presenting officer. But some side issue may come up and then they'd look at me as if to say, 'Oh God, how does that apply to this case?' That's why I'm there. (Interview 164, Presenting Officer, North East)

The gap between tribunals' expectations of the presenting officer's role and the officers' own more modest understanding of their function leads to difficulties when presenting officers fail to attend hearings. This was seen as a matter for concern by tribunal chairmen and members alike even though it happens rarely—in our sample the presenting officer was absent in only ten cases.[13] The general view was that it was highly unsatisfactory for the Department simply to stand by its submission in this way. One member encapsulated these concerns when he observed in interview that 'they ask us to take as gospel what's written down'.

---

[13] A Social Security Commissioner has warned of the 'considerable risk of an injustice being done or at least of the tribunal not being properly informed as to the facts and the law relating to the issues before it' if the tribunal proceeds in the absence of the presenting officer (*CSB/582/1987*). In view of the findings in this chapter, it may be that this statement is based on an unduly optimistic view of the contribution of presenting officers.

(iii) *Unattended hearings*

The submission takes on even greater importance when the appellant does not attend the hearing. In such circumstances the chances of the presenting officer acting as an *amicus curiae* are further diminished. When we asked presenting officers whether their role changed when the appellant was absent, 39 per cent said it made no difference; 43 per cent thought that the hearing became more informal and that there was less for them to do, and only 12 per cent saw a greater need to assist the tribunal in checking the accuracy of the submission. The majority viewpoint was summed up by one officer who told us, 'All I can usually say is, "He's appealed on such and such a ground, and that's the written evidence."'

This reflects the view of most presenting officers that, unless appellants themselves bring new evidence before the tribunal, the adjudication officer's decision should be confirmed. Sometimes this adversarial stance derives from the law itself, as where the burden of proof is formally placed upon an appellant. But more often the attitude seems to be that, whatever the formal legal position, the onus is on the appellant or the tribunal to introduce new material and to raise queries. If this is done, then most presenting officers are quite prepared to accept that a tribunal is entitled to take a different view of the case. But if presenting officers see the essence of the *amicus curiae* role as the duty to respond constructively to new evidence provided by the appellant, as most evidently do, then in roughly half of the cases coming before the tribunal, there is no opportunity to play this role since the appellant is not present and there is nothing to which to respond.

(iv) *The reduction of discretion*

We have repeatedly referred in this book to the reduced role of discretion in the administration of means tested benefits. As we explained in Chapter 3, one result of this has been that obviously meritorious income support appeals are generally weeded out at the internal review stage, leaving only the appeals regarded as weak to go forward to the tribunal. This has in itself made it increasingly unlikely that presenting officers will take a different view of a case from that adopted by an adjudication officer. As two income support presenting officers explained:

Under single payment appeals, which have now more or less finished, the adjudication officers were adamant, 'That's my decision, end of story.' I used to find it difficult to present appeals that I disagreed with. You were sort of sitting there trying to convince the tribunal when you weren't convinced yourself. That doesn't tend to happen any more. I disagree with the way the tribunal goes on some of them, but not the adjudication officer. (Interview 118, North East)

In the old days of Supp. Ben., quite often it was opinion-based, and sometimes one would come in to an appeal tribunal not agreeing with the decision that was in front of you. And that could make life a little bit awkward. But I think these days the role is simply and solely to represent the Department. With Income Support, there's very little opinion-based decisions or discretion, so more often than not it's a straightforward matter of saying, 'Well, this is what we have to do under the law.' I'm just putting forward a decision made by somebody else. (Interview 227, North West)

(v) *The introduction of legal chairmen*

A final important factor which inhibits presenting officers in playing the *amicus curiae* role concerns the phasing out of lay chairmen. Our observations of tribunal hearings and our interviews with the participants have led us to the conclusion that the deployment of lawyer chairmen has radically altered the internal dynamics of the hearing. We have already commented upon the way in which lay members tend to become marginalized, and in a similar way the chairman's dominant role has affected the part played by the presenting officer. A prime feature of the *amicus curiae* role is the ability to offer the tribunal guidance as to the meaning of the legislation. Whilst presenting officers can advise the tribunal as to departmental practices or the adjudication officer's perception of the facts, it is somewhat incongruous to expect a relatively junior civil servant, who has received no formal legal training, to offer the legally qualified chairman advice on a point of law. As one chairman observed, 'They're good within their limits, but they're not lawyers: it's laymen having a go at the law.'

Presenting officers, it is true, build up considerable expertise in certain aspects of social security law, and we observed presenting officers on occasion giving valuable assistance on legal points.

But the extent to which they are able to do so should not be overstated and many presenting officers consider themselves at a distinct disadvantage when legal matters are raised at the tribunal. The presenting officer's discomfort in this respect is accentuated where the tribunal is dealing with a centrally prepared appeal (for example, child benefit or family credit), where the officer may have no more than a cursory knowledge of the legislation at issue. The following two comments by a chairman and a presenting officer indicate the problems:

Although I accept, that within a limited field, the layman may know as much about the law as a lawyer, if not more, it's quite a wide field that they're dealing with and they don't know it all. Their presentation is really an extension of the submission. And you've seen this afternoon that, when the submission isn't very good, they don't improve it by their presentation. (Interview 5, Chairman, North East)

I think some chairmen forget that we are not trained solicitors. Some talk to us as if we were, and it does get very difficult because we don't understand the law in that depth. We know the basic field, but we don't understand the law as a lawyer would. (Interview 210, Presenting Officer, London South)

The adversarial expectations of participants at the tribunal

In the light of these factors, it is no surprise that presenting officers experience great difficulty in playing the role of an *amicus curiae*. Their difficulties are further compounded when other participants in the tribunal hearing treat the procedure as adversarial and confrontational in nature. Notwithstanding the obligation upon the tribunal to follow an inquisitorial approach at hearings, many chairmen, members, appellants and representatives are without doubt influenced by the adversarial model of justice. This is reflected in the views of tribunal members and appellants on the part they expect presenting officers to play.

The views of chairmen are of particular interest in this regard since they occupy a pivotal position in appeal hearings. Somewhat surprisingly, we found in the interviews we conducted with chairmen that only 58 per cent saw the presenting officer's role in terms of an *amicus curiae*. Most of these took the view that presenting officers on the whole fulfilled this role and were prepared to concede a point if the appellant produced fresh evidence,[14] as in the following quotation:

They vary from person to person, but for the most part they do see their role as being the *amicus curiae* role. They don't see themselves as being there to defend the decision of the adjudication officer come hell or high water. Many of them are eminently fair. There are some exceptions. I would support the idea of the *amicus curiae* role. I've always seen the object of the exercise as to get at the truth: it sounds rather hackneyed, but to do justice as between the individual and the state. I certainly don't see it as adversarial. (Interview 12, Chairman, Midlands)

A smaller group of chairmen, however, while accepting the *amicus* principle, expressed a rather less sanguine view of how presenting officers acted in practice. Asked about the presenting officer's role, one chairman replied:

What it should be or what it is? They should be able to explain the Department's case very simply so that the claimant can see what the Department is trying to do. And they should be reasonably *au fait* with Commissioners' decisions that apply and be prepared to discuss the regulations. I think they should be prepared to think that we are trying to help the claimant. Some of them are extremely good at this and they will mention anything that occurs to them that might help the claimant. In practice they vary tremendously. The most irritating ones are the ones who are totally passive, who probably haven't looked at the papers and who say, 'I've nothing to add to the submissions'. They are not helpful at all. They might as well not come. I would think it's about half and half actually. But some of them are absolutely first class. They are very knowledgeable. They've checked over the papers carefully and seen if anything's wrong and some are very good at playing the *amicus* role. (Interview 10, Chairman, Midlands)

Not all chairmen adhered to the conventional understanding of the presenting officer's role. As many as 42 per cent of chairmen saw matters in a different light, including a number who, strongly influenced by their adversarial training, described the presenting officer in terms which were more consistent with traditional court procedures. One of this group stated that he 'would like to see the role of the presenting officer on a much more adversarial basis, presenting more forcefully the case of the Department'. Another chairman argued that it was disingenuous to pretend that the process was anything other than

[14] This view was also expressed by Judge Byrt, the first OPSSAT President, in Chief Adjudication Officer (1990), para. 5. 33.

adversarial. 'It's like a cricket match', he said, 'where you have here two sides banging away at each other. To suggest that one of the batsmen has not really taken sides but has taken up some kind of independent stance is, to most people, manifest nonsense.' He continued:

People say they're independent—I think that's nonsense. They're not independent, they're doing exactly what the name suggests, they're presenting the views, or presenting the decision made by the adjudication officer. To pretend that there's some sort of independence in that is absolute nonsense. There may be some measure of independence in the Department but I think it's simply nonsense to the claimant. . . .To most people, our system here, whether you like it or not, is adversarial, and the whole process is adversarial. (Interview 28, Chairman, London South)

Many presenting officers themselves recognize the difficulty of taking an objective view of a case given their organizational base in the Department. Some went further and accepted that it is simply unrealistic to expect other participants in a tribunal hearing to see the presenting officer as a neutral friend of the court. As one presenting officer put it:

I am there to represent the adjudication officer who made the original decision. You are there to present the Department's side of it, without having an axe to grind personally. But by the whole nature of the process, it's going to look as if you are grinding an axe because you're obviously against what the claimant is saying. I always try to break the ice with the claimant so that they don't feel I'm on a personal vendetta against them. But the whole nature of the job, given that you are representing the Department's position, may give that appearance. (Interview 142, Presenting Officer, Wales and South West)

There is not much doubt either, whatever the legal theory, that most appellants who appear before social security appeal tribunals see the hearing in adversarial terms. They come to the tribunal (with or without a representative) in a confrontational frame of mind. They commonly perceive themselves as having fought tooth and nail against the Department over many months or years to obtain their entitlement and are not likely to regard an employee of the Department as any kind of friend. Their representatives are aware that the conclusions reached in the appeals submission must be challenged if the appeal is to be successful and are, not suprisingly, sceptical about how far a presenting officer will assist in this task.

The natural tendency of appellants to see the hearing in an adversarial light underlines the importance of chairmen taking time to explain the official roles of the various participants in the hearing.[15] In 23 per cent of the hearings where the appellant attended, however, no explanation of the presenting officer's function was given by the chairman. Even when chairmen referred to the presenting officer's role, it was often in a cursory or inadequate way, or else the words used implied that the officer would be taking a confrontational position. One chairman, for instance, described the presenting officer to the appellant as 'the lady here to represent the interests of the Department'.

It must be conceded that the concept of the *amicus curiae* is not easy for a chairman to explain or for an appellant to grasp, particularly when the latter is likely to be agitated or anxious about the hearing. But the consequence is that many appellants are confused by the attendance of the presenting officer, and this confusion was reflected in the interviews we conducted with appellants after the hearing:

I mean, what is that lady? Is she from the Social Services? She's there giving the details out to them [the tribunal]. She's feeding them with what they've got to fight the Social for our benefit, aren't they? Or are they? (Case 21, North East)

I understood everything, except for the lady who was representing the DHSS. I didn't understand exactly what she was doing there and what or who she was representing. What was she doing there? I'm still not clear. I am clear to a certain extent. Her point of view was that I was definitely wrong to have gone to a tribunal. I should have accepted her decision—which is her job. She wasn't there to help me. I understand now what her role is, but to begin with I didn't. She never said who she was representing or what she was doing there. Now obviously she was there to save the DHSS money and I suppose she won. (Case 53, Midlands)

Having that woman from the Social Security sitting right next to you on the same side of the table was daunting. I'd rather have had her at the back where I couldn't have seen her. . . .They shouldn't sit you next to the Social Security, that's who you are fighting against. It's ridiculous to have them sat next to you as if they are your friend. They should be where the clerk is sitting. (Case 72, Midlands)

---

[15] The failure of some chairmen adequately to explain the role of the presenting officer was a frequent cause of complaint amongst presenting officers who favoured the *amicus* role.

There was a big distance between me and the Department of Employment man who turned out to be nice. But there was a chair between us and a big distance. So were we against each other, or what was he there for? I was only told he would be there when I arrived today. I didn't know that someone like that was going to be there. It could be frightening. I'm quite hard to make really nervous so I wasn't frightened. But I was jolly glad to have that cigarette when I came out. (Case 102, London North)

We should emphasize that appellants were by no means all hostile to presenting officers. Where the presenting officer had acted in a true *amicus curiae* role, their efforts were appreciated by appellants, as in the following cases:

The man from the Department was all right, he seemed to want to co-operate for a change. That was rather a surprise. He'd already made a phone call to the Child Benefit people before we'd got there because he saw a discrepancy in the papers. (Case 144, London North)

It was easy to accept the independence of the tribunal because I thought that [the presenting officer] didn't really believe what she was trying to do. I wasn't sure whether she was on their side or our side. I thought that she would be much more determined to resist the appeal and just give the reasons for the Department's decision whereas she was actually giving reasons why the tribunal should allow the decision! That is to the credit of the DSS. She did not come over as someone prosecuting, nor was she defending the decision that had been taken. It was very good that she comes across as more or less an independent person. It was all very fair. (Case 233, Wales and South West).

It is clear, then, that chairmen, members, appellants and representatives bring to the tribunal a range of differing expectations of the presenting officer's role. Most appellants expect to have to fight their corner at the hearing and remain unpersuaded that the presenting officer is there to help them, the more so when the chairman explains the role of the presenting officer in adversarial terms. Even where a chairman favours the *amicus curiae* role of the presenting officer, this may not be evident at the hearing. Criticisms were occasionally expressed by chairmen during hearings that presenting officers seemed uncertain about the facts or the law, but only infrequently were comments directed to the type of role that the presenting officer was seeking to play, whether adversarial, *amicus*, neutral, or passive. Chairmen do not on the whole see it as their function, as one chairman in the Midlands put it, 'to try and restrain a presenting officer who takes the line of doggedly defending the decision of the adjudication officer: I wouldn't see it as part of my role to suggest how they might like to do their job'.

The differing approaches of participants at the tribunal explains why it makes no sense to classify presenting officers in terms of a dichotomy between those acting as adversaries and those as *amici curiae*. It is more realistic to view presenting officers as ranging over a spectrum of types of roles and attitudes, and to recognize that the position at which each presenting officer is placed on this spectrum is rarely fixed. Rather it is negotiable and contingent, shifting from case to case, according to the attitudes of chairmen, members, appellants, representatives, and departmental colleagues, and according to how these attitudes find expression in the dynamics of an appeal hearing.

Some presenting officers come to accept an *amicus curiae* role, not so much through the influence of training, but because of the expectations placed upon them by chairmen. Others, by contrast, find that the behaviour of certain chairmen or appellants turn hearings into adversarial contests in which they feel obliged to act as advocates for the Department. This complex interplay between the participants at the tribunal can be seen in the responses given by presenting officers when asked about the difficulties they encountered in playing their prescribed role:

It's very difficult. One chairman in particular, whether he's trying to bend over backwards in impressing on the claimant that he's independent, doesn't even look at you when you enter the room, sort of kicks you out of the room at the end of the hearing, and he's so nice to the claimant. He doesn't even look at you when he's addressing you, which I find very irritating. He's different if the claimant isn't there, an entirely different person. So I don't know if it's his way of showing the claimant that he's independent. (Interview 24, Wales and South Western)

Representatives tend to be more formal and treat it like a court hearing and this sometimes leads to antagonism. I hope that wouldn't cause me to change my role in any way, but I think, on occasion, it does. If somebody's trying to rubbish what you've said, you do try and defend it. (Interview 100, Midlands)

If they have a rep I would tend to sit back more and think, 'All right, you get on with it, mush. Why should I help you?' (Interview 103, London South)

Some chairmen look at you as performing the role of an adversary. It takes you months to get used to each chairman. One chairman likes me to contribute a lot whereas another, when I say something, makes a snide comment as if I were grinding an axe. So I just don't know where I stand, where I start and when I stop. It's an awfully difficult role to play. (Interview 142, Wales and South Western)

Whether it's difficult to act as a friend of the court depends upon the attitude of the appellant. If the appellant is an angry or arrogant person, your attitude inevitably changes and you do start to be on the defensive and be a little bit more aggressive yourself. (Interview 151, North West)

There are, then, a host of factors which explain the limited contribution that presenting officers make at most appeal hearings. In practice they do not usually fulfil the requirements of the *amicus curiae*. Yet the Department's encouragement of the *amicus* role is more than mere window dressing. Rather, the training and guidance received by presenting officers produce concrete effects in terms of the way in which they carry out their role. They may not live up to the demands of the role and some may not even aspire to do so, but at least most acknowledge that they should not try obdurately to defend decisions. As one officer put it, with disarming frankness, 'I like the role because I'm lazy. If you only have to answer questions now and again, you can sit back. If you wanted to argue the toss, it would be hard work.'

Presenting officers' perceptions of fairness at hearings

Given the differing expectations of the roles they are expected to play, it is important to ask whether presenting officers consider themselves fairly treated in appeal hearings. When asked about their general impressions of the way tribunals handled cases, most presenting officers replied in a qualified, though generally favourable, manner. They tended to say that by and large the right results emerge but most of them identified 'rogue' chairmen who ignore the statutes and regulations to pursue some frolic of their own. It is, however, more important to evaluate tribunal procedures, and the presenting officer's satisfaction with them, with reference to individual cases. When we did this we found that presenting officers expressed overwhelmingly favourable comments about the quality of the hearings in which they had participated. In 87 per cent of cases, for example, they said that they had been given a fair hearing and full opportunity to present their case; in 86 per cent, chairmen and members were thought to have grasped the relevant issues in the case; in 80 per cent, chairmen were viewed as handling the hearing in a helpful manner, and in 83 per cent no criticisms whatever were raised about the procedures adopted at the hearing. The high level of satisfaction expressed by the presenting officers to whom we spoke is evident in the following comments:

The chairman was very helpful, and basically I had to say very little. I thought it was a very fair hearing. I can't really see that he could have done it any better because he took account of what she said and he took account of what I said. (Case 185, London South).

The chairman was very good. Although when I go in there it's fairly informal, I still think that for the claimant it's an ordeal, and I'm very conscious of that. It always depends so much on the chairman. This particular chairman is very good at asking me questions and asking if I have anything else to say. (Case 195, London South).

They grasped the issues, very much so. The tribunal had to question the claimant, and what they asked was relevant. But the chairman didn't just concern himself with the matter and questions at issue. He went a bit further looking at her welfare which is a good thing, and something he doesn't have to do. (Case 305, Scotland).

It could be argued that these high levels of satisfaction merely reflect the fact that tribunals most of the time confirm the original decision. On the other hand, it is true to say that the favourable assessments made by presenting officers related much more to the way the tribunal had handled the case than to the decision reached.

In one sense, the views of presenting officers on tribunal procedures constitute impressive evidence of the care and courtesy that is shown by most tribunals to participants in reaching decisions. But our findings need to be interpreted with caution. For example, the fact that 87 per cent of presenting officers considered themselves to have been given a full opportunity to present their case should not be taken as meaning that this opportunity was taken. Presenting officers anticipate, as we have noted, playing only a limited role at hearings and most are in practice rather passive. This is reflected in answers given to us when we asked whether there had been a chance to present the case properly:

Yes. I mean the chairman just said, 'Do you rest on your submission?' So I said, 'Yes.' You know, 'There's nothing more to add to it.' (Case 24, North East)

There was nothing to say. I mean there was absolutely nothing to add to that submission at all. We only had to process the appeal because he'd said, 'I want to appeal.' So really it was just sort of going through the motions. I think he [the appellant] already knew beforehand that it was hopeless. (Case 44, North East)

By the same token, while the great majority of presenting officers thought that chairmen had grasped the relevant issues in the case, this begs the question of what issues the presenting officer considers to be relevant. While it was apparent that chairmen grasped the issues as laid out in the written appeals submission and highlighted by presenting officers, they were unable to grasp those issues which remained hidden at the hearing because the presenting officer had failed to volunteer some crucial piece of information. We are for our part unable to say with confidence how often this occurs but, as we have seen, presenting officers are in general reluctant to take much initiative in throwing doubt upon an adjudication officer's decision. In consequence, certain matters will not be disclosed unless the adjudication officer is pressed by the tribunal for an opinion about the decision or the relevant legislation or else for further information about the case.

The trouble is that chairmen and members do not often challenge the presenting officer in this way because they are not conscious of the need to do so. Just as most presenting officers have no serious quibble with the way hearings are conducted, so chairmen and members are generally satisfied with the way in which presenting officers carry out their role: 76 per cent of the chairmen and 77 per cent of the lay members described the quality of presentation as good or reasonable, and only a handful had any serious reservations about the adequacy of presenting officers. We argued in earlier chapters that tribunals often jump too quickly to the conclusion that a case is cut-and-dried and that this helps explain why the presenting officer's passivity is tolerated. In such a situation chairmen and members alike appear to accept that the scope for the *amicus curiae* role to be played is marginal.

It is clear, then, that tribunals are generally satisfied with presenting officers and vice versa. But this cannot be taken as showing that tribunals and presenting officers do a good job, but only that they are perceived by each other as doing so. In other words, it is arguable that the high levels of satisfaction expressed by both appellants and presenting officers are based on only a limited understanding of what the tribunal should or could have done in a case. The helpful and neutral tone that officers appear to strike at hearings has a beguiling quality which diverts attention from the fundamental contradictions in their role. And while presentation may be done in a neutral way, what is usually being presented is a one-sided view of a case already committed to writing in the appeals submission and considered to be strong enough to proceed to the tribunal by the adjudication officer who made the initial decision.[16] Thus the presenting officer does not need to argue the case strongly since this has already been done on paper. There is certainly a case for chairmen and members to scrutinize the appeals submission in greater detail and challenge the presenting officer more forcefully than they do at present. Their satisfaction with the way in which cases are presented before them may in that sense reflect no more than an unwarranted complacency.

Conclusion

Presenting officers adopt what they consider to be a helpful approach at tribunal hearings, and are far from conforming to the stereotype of the faceless and uncaring bureaucrat. On the contrary, we found them to be, almost without exception, approachable, thoughtful, and open about their work. They generally expressed strong support for the principle of an independent appeals system: very few had any fundamental criticisms to make of the present arrangements, and most thought it vital that there be a source of redress outside the Department to which claimants could turn when aggrieved by benefit decisions. It was particularly interesting to note that, when we asked presenting officers if they had been given a fair hearing, many thought this was an irrelevant consideration compared

---

[16] See at pp. 103–4 for further discussion of the appeals submission.

to the question of whether the appellant had been dealt with fairly.[17]

The problems we have identified in this chapter should not, then, be attributed to the personal failings of presenting officers: rather they should be seen as defects inherent in the appeals system itself. For a variety of reasons, not least the underlying adversarial nature of the proceedings, the role of the *amicus curiae* is only infrequently played in hearings. The reactive and neutral position adopted by officers is a product of the tensions associated with the function of presentation at the tribunal, and represents something of an uneasy compromise. But because presenting officers refrain from acting openly as advocates for the Department, observers can easily assume that the presenting officer's role in the hearing is unproblematic and that all relevant information will be volunteered. This is far from being the case.

The implications are clear. Just as we have argued that it is mistaken to regard the interests of the appellant as adequately protected by an inquisitorially minded chairman, so too it would be wrong to assume that requiring a Departmental employee to assume the unfamiliar garb of an *amicus curiae* redresses sufficiently the fundamental imbalance between the Department and the claimant. Despite the best intentions of the participants, appellants inevitably remain at a serious disadvantage in a process which remains stubbornly adversarial.

[17] It is also worth recording that some presenting officers strongly attacked the system of internal review initiated for social fund decisions as a wholly inadequate substitute for the right to appeal to an independent body.

8

Conclusion

AN attempt has been made in this book to assess the dramatic and fundamental changes made to the system of social security adjudication in this country in recent years. A number of areas have been explored and we have concentrated in particular on the dynamics of the relationships between the various actors involved in the system. In this final chapter, we seek to identify the broader themes which have emerged from our study and to discuss some of the more important implications.

That social security appeal tribunals have been transformed since Professor Bell's report was published in 1975 is indisputable. The phasing out of lay chairmen has resulted in a more professional approach to the conduct of hearings, and the Presidential system has been instrumental in strengthening the independence of the tribunals and has given chairmen a much clearer sense of purpose and direction. This is not to say that the tribunals are faultless. For instance, there remain too many lay members whose involvement is only peripheral, and there is a strong case for more careful scrutiny of members on reappointment. The performance of tribunals is also likely to be enhanced by training chairmen and members together to emphasize the co-operative nature of their task. Even so, the broad satisfaction with tribunal hearings expressed by presenting officers and claimants alike provides one benchmark by which to judge the success of the reformed tribunal system.

From the claimants' point of view, the appeals process is simple to initiate and ensures that those who challenge decisions have their cases reconsidered at two levels—first, on the basis of the papers (with any new information taken into account), and secondly, if it is determined within the local office that the decision must stand, by a social security appeal tribunal.[1] No complicated forms need be completed and, once the process is set in motion, the appeal generally receives careful attention. The strengths of the social security appeal tribunals have been recognized by policy makers with the creation of disability appeal tribunals along similar lines.[2] These tribunals are integrated into the same Presidential system which oversees the operation not just of social security appeal tribunals but also of medical appeal tribunals and vaccine damage tribunals. This should guarantee a welcome degree of consistency in training, guidance and philosophy across these four tribunals.[3]

Any balanced appraisal of the system for adjudicating social security benefits in local offices must include a recognition of its considerable strengths. The formal independence of adjudication officers from the departments within which they work provides a foundation on which good adjudication practices can be built.[4] The guidance and training provided to adjudication officers do much already to foster this sense of independence, as does the decision by the Department of Employment to distance adjudication officers from the hurly-burly of benefit administration by locating them in specialized adjudication offices. Futhermore, the creation of the Office of the Chief Adjudication Officer has led to the quality of decision making being monitored

---

[1] This may be contrasted with the complicated system for handling housing benefit (administered by housing authorities) under which claimants have to lodge two separate requests before obtaining a review board hearing: see further Sainsbury and Eardley (1991).

[2] Social Security Act 1975, Sched. 10, as amended by Disability Living Allowance and Disability Working Allowance 1991, Sched. 1. These tribunals deal principally with appeals relating to the medical aspects of claims for disability living allowance and attendance allowance. The tribunals are constituted as a variant on social security appeal tribunals in that they consist of a legally qualified chairman, a doctor, and a member experienced in dealing with the needs of the disabled. See also the creation of child support appeal tribunals under the Child Support Act 1991, Sched. 3.

[3] As a result of this expansion, OPSSAT was relaunched with a new corporate logo as ITS, the Independent Tribunal Service, in 1991.

[4] See further Partington (1991), recommending that the Secretary of State's adjudicatory functions be brought within the mainstream of social security adjudication.

in a more systematic fashion and the encouragement of good practice.

Notwithstanding these undoubted strengths, weaknesses persist in initial decision making. The independence of adjudication officers has become, particularly in the Department of Social Security, a chimera. Adjudication is insufficiently differentiated from the overall administrative machinery to permit an independent stance to flourish. In addition to adjudicative duties, adjudication officers have been saddled with various managerial, administrative, and clerical tasks, and their workload is ever more diverse and bureaucratic in nature. And even where specialization has been achieved, as in the Department of Employment's sector adjudication offices, the standard of decision making remains poor. Independence has not come under threat through attempts by line managment to influence particular decisions: it is undermined by the sheer scale of work that has to be processed.

The local offices are so severely under-resourced that poor quality work is now the norm. Corners are cut in routine fashion in local offices as adjudication officers struggle to keep abreast of the workload. Adjudication standards in these offices reflect the reality that this is a system of mass administration—less adjudication by careful assessment of individual claims than processing by rubber stamp. Accuracy in decision making has been sacrificed on the high altar of cost effectiveness.

The implications of the Department of Social Security's structural reorganization, carried through since the fieldwork was conducted for this book, must be considered in this context. In April 1991, as part of the Government's 'Next Steps' strategy, formal responsibility for most of the work of the Department's central and local offices was transferred to a semi-autonomous executive body, the Benefits Agency, under the control of a Chief Executive appointed from outside the Civil Service. The ostensible aim was to devolve more responsibility to managers at district level, to encourage greater flexibility, and to make the service more responsive to the needs of its customers.

The Chief Adjudication Officer has seen in this reorganization an important opportunity to improve adjudication standards. He argues, for example, that it will enable a greater specialization in adjudication and the writing of submissions, and allow staff of the rank of higher executive officers to make monitoring and advice the core of their job.[5] The question is whether this opportunity will be seized. The Chief Adjudication Officer has no power to direct the Benefits Agency's managers to organize their work in a particular way, and the danger is that the Agency will develop its own organizational goals as it seeks to meet the Department's demands on such matters as clearance times. It is likely that the performance indicators established will be directed towards quantitative rather than qualitative criteria. The Chief Adjudication Officer has already expressed his disappointment that the Agency is unlikely to be given a performance indicator aimed at raising adjudication standards.[6]

While social security tribunals have been reformed with a large measure of success, the prognosis for initial decision making remains gloomy. Yet as Griffith argued over thirty years ago, in his celebrated critique of the Franks Report, tribunal procedures have always given much less cause for concern than 'the closed, dark and windowless procedures' which precede them.[7] Tribunals, after all, deal with only a small fraction of the total number of claims decided by adjudication officers. It is arguable, then, that the series of reforms to the tribunals has merely served to lend an air of fairness to an unfair system, and diverted attention from the serious weaknesses of first tier adjudication. As we have argued in this book, however, it is mistaken to view the separate parts of the adjudicative system in isolation. The measures aimed at improving social security tribunals have undoubtedly had a wider impact on the system as a whole.

In particular, the internal review carried out by an adjudication officer on receiving an appeal can be much influenced by the prospect of the case being heard by an independent tribunal. Tribunals perform a useful educative function not only in this

[5] Chief Adjudication Officer (1991), paras. 1. 16–1. 18.

[6] Ibid., at para. 1. 14.

[7] Griffith (1959) writes: 'There is the open side of administration and the closed side. The [Franks] Committee was asked to consider only the open side. Minor improvements can there be made, many of which the Committee recommended. The Committee was told to look at procedures which were predominantly open, fair and impartial and asked to see if they could be made more so. And the Committee answered that they could in a few small ways. But into the closed, dark and windowless procedures the Committee was not asked to let air and light' (p. 127).

sense but also for those adjudication officers who appear as presenting officers at appeal hearings. To some extent at least, the lessons learnt in presenting cases are carried over into the routine business of adjudication and the carrying out of internal reviews. Tribunals serve, then, a valuable function in providing an external and independent point of reference for local offices. The 'closed, dark and windowless procedures' of first-tier adjudication are far from being completely insulated from the outside world. Social security appeal tribunals have opened up procedures to critical scrutiny, shed light on the work of adjudication officers, and blown fresh judicial air into the anonymous corridors of local offices.

Our study has been one of the mainstream system of social security adjudication, but our findings have implications for areas of social security where different arrangements are in place such as housing benefit and discretionary social fund payments. Decisions on housing benefit are made not by adjudication officers but by administrative staff within local authorities. There is no right of appeal to an independent tribunal, and all the claimant can do is ask the authority to review its decision. If still dissatisfied, the claimant must lodge a further request for a hearing before a housing benefit review board, composed of councillors from the same local authority. The housing benefit review system thus lacks the combination of a fresh internal look at the case within the responsible bureaucracy, informed by the prospect and experience of re-examination by a genuinely independent external agency—features identified in this research as crucial to satisfactory adjudication.

Sainsbury and Eardley (1991) have identified wide variations in local authority practices in processing internal reviews, and fundamental weaknesses in the system of review board hearings, such as the poor conduct of hearings, inconsistency in the application of law, a lack of training for members, and a lack of independence. It is just such weaknesses that the reformed system of social security appeal tribunals has been successful in combating. There are strong arguments, then, for bringing housing benefit appeals within the jurisdiction of social security appeal tribunals. A further step would be to bring the monitoring of initial decision making on housing benefit within the remit of the Office of the Chief Adjudication Officer. The most rational course would be to transfer the administration of housing benefit to the Department of Social Security. Only in this way can full advantage be taken of the strengths of the social security adjudication system examined in this book.

The discretionary part of the social fund is another area which lies outside mainstream social security adjudication. Initial decisions on applications for budgeting loans, crisis loans, and community care grants are the responsibility of social fund officers within the Department of Social Security.[8] Despite the fact that these officers are often the same staff who would otherwise be employed as adjudication officers under the income support scheme, their work does not fall within the remit of the Chief Adjudication Officer. The principal means of redress against an unfavourable social fund decision is to seek an internal review. If the matter is not resolved satisfactorily within the local office, the applicant has the right to a further review by a social fund inspector who has only limited powers to interfere in decisions.[9] The social fund system of reviews suffers from the same defect as that for housing benefit: the internal review lacks an independent and external reference point.

Again, the most effective reform of the social fund system would surely be to bring it under the umbrella of the Chief Adjudication Officer and the social security appeal tribunals. It is disingenuous to argue, as the Government has, that tribunals are ill-equipped to deal with the kind of discretionary issues raised by the social fund. Social fund officers are in practice constrained by the same type of detailed directions and guidelines that the tribunals are used to coping with in the form of statutory regulations.[10] What probably lay behind the decision that social fund determinations should not carry a right of appeal was the view that tribunals would not be able to work within a fixed budget, as local offices are now required to do.[11] In the absence of such budgetary constraints, the decisions taken by tribunals might have led to expenditure on the social fund spiralling upwards, an outcome which the Government was clearly

---

[8] Social fund decisions on claims for maternity, funeral, and cold weather payments still carry a right of appeal to a tribunal.

[9] See further Wikeley (1991).

[10] See Drabble and Lynes (1989).

[11] Ibid., 313. See also Bolderson (1988), Mullen (1989), and Mesher (1990).

anxious to avoid. But the fears of policy makers on this point seem exaggerated. Our assessment of social security appeal tribunals is that, under the guidance of their legally qualified chairmen, they exercise discretion in a restrained and judicial fashion. Indeed, we would suggest that chairmen tend to underestimate the degree of discretion which still remains to them within the regulations to be applied.

While attention should be drawn to the great improvements that have been made in social security adjudication over the last fifteen years, it must also be recognized that the reforms have exposed new problems. These cannot be dismissed as mere teething troubles since they represent continuing difficulties in the reformed system of social security adjudication. For at the same time as major procedural reforms have been introduced, the law to be applied in the adjudicatory process has, on balance, become more restrictive, rigid, and harsh in its application to claimants. It has been a recurrent theme of this book that the system for adjudicating social security claims has to be examined within the context of the political and economic forces in which it has developed. The formulation of social security policy is an intensely political activity, and it is naïve and artificial to view adjudication in a political vacuum or to assume that it can operate independently of this context. The reduced scope for discretion and its replacement by an increasingly complex web of legal regulation is the creation of politicians, not of departmental staff or tribunal personnel.

This changed nature of adjudication has fundamental consequences for the various actors involved. We have seen in several chapters of this book how unrealistic expectations and tensions have been generated for them. Not all legal chairmen, for instance, naturally play the inquisitorial role expected of them; lay members have signally failed to adapt to the new regime based on law instead of paternalism; and presenting officers are ill-suited to be *amici curiae* and for the most part adopt feebler alternative roles. The concepts which have been promoted in the 1980s, in part as a reaction to the acknowledged inadequacies of the old system, fit awkwardly into the reformed nature of social security adjudication. Moreover, the attempt to graft inquisitorial elements on to an essentially adversarial process has served to mask the need for a greater availability of advice and representation services for the claimant. Neither the inquisit-orial efforts of chairmen at hearings nor the best intentions of presenting officers can adequately redress the scales for unrepre-sented appellants.

Even when the actors play their roles according to the script, the gains to claimants are for the most part limited. What matters first and foremost to claimants is not whether they were treated in an even-handed and courteous manner but whether their claim is successful or not. Many claimants find themselves living in dire financial circumstances, and they cannot afford the luxury of caring overmuch about social niceties. It is something of a paradox that, as the tribunals have become more professional in approach ('judicialized' in the vernacular), claimants' substan-tive rights have simultaneously been eroded. Tribunals are forced to decide whether the regulations have been correctly applied by officials, not whether justice has been done in the individual case. 'The grid of rules promulgated in the regula-tions,' as Bradley (1985) rightly argues, 'has become too fine a mesh to serve the broader interests of justice' (p. 431).

These difficulties stem in large part from the Government's determination throughout the 1980s to limit the growth of public expenditure. The rapid growth in expenditure on social security payments made it a prime target for cuts. Yet these moves have coincided with the great increase in the numbers of people dependent upon state benefits. Tightly drawn legal entitlements provide a mechanism by which expenditure can be controlled. As we argued in Chapter 1, the main thrust of social security policy in the 1980s (whatever the gloss put upon it) was the concern to cut costs. It was not to improve the rights of claimants. We encountered in the present study many chairmen and mem-bers of tribunals who struggled to ease the plight of claimants, but their efforts were inevitably to a large extent nullified because they were so much hamstrung by the restrictive nature of the legal framework within which they had to operate.

One does not need to be a conspiracy theorist to see the advan-tages for governments in an adjudicatory system operating within a more regulated framework. The days of benevolence and paternalism are over, and massive cash savings for govern-ment are an important by-product. Whatever might be the private views of adjudication officers, chairmen, or lay members, and however sympathetic they may feel towards individual claimants, the legal regulations must be applied correctly. The rallying cry of the 1970s for legal entitlements for individuals in preference to state charity has a hollow ring to it in the 1990s as the consequences for claimants become increasingly apparent.

Bibliography

ADLER, M., and BRADLEY, A. (1975), *Justice, Discretion and Poverty: Supplementary Benefit Appeal Tribunals in Britain* (London: Professional Books).

ATKINS, S., and HOGGETT, B. (1984), *Women and the Law* (Oxford: Basil Blackwell).

ATKINSON, A. B., and MICKLEWRIGHT, J. (1989), 'Turning the screw for the unemployed, 1979–1988', 125–57 in (ed.) ATKINSON, A. B., *Poverty and Social Security* (London: Harvester Wheatsheaf).

BALDWIN, J. (1989), 'The Role of Citizens Advice Bureaux and Law Centres in the Provision of Legal Advice and Assistance', 8, *Civil Justice Quarterly*, 24–44.

—— HILL, S. (1987), 'Tribunal Membership: The Role of Local Politics in Recruitment to Local Valuation Panels in England and Wales', 6, *Civil Justice Quarterly*, 130–41.

—— —— (1988), 'Rating Appeals Heard by Local Valuation Courts in England and Wales', 7, *Civil Justice Quarterly*, 107–24.

BECKER, S., MACPHERSON, S., and SILBURN, R. (1983), *Supplementary Benefit Appeal Tribunal Members* (University of Nottingham: Benefits Research Unit).

BELL, K. (1975), *Research Study on Supplementary Benefit Appeal Tribunals* (London: HMSO).

—— (1982), 'Social Security Tribunals—A General Perspective', 33, *Northern Ireland Legal Quarterly*, 132–47.

BELL, K., COLLISON, P., TURNER, S., and WEBBER, S. (1974), 'National Insurance Local Tribunals', 3, *Journal of Social Policy*, 289–315 (Part II at (1975), 4, *Journal of Social Policy*, 1–24).

BELTRAM, G. (1984), *Testing the Safety Net: An Enquiry into the Reformed Supplementary Benefit Scheme* (London: Bedford Square Press).

BERTHOUD, R. (1987), 'New Means Tests for Old: The Fowler Plan for Social Security', 7–30 in (eds.) BRENTON, M., and UNGERSON, C., *The Year Book of Social Policy 1986–87* (Harlow: Longman).

BEVERIDGE, W. (1930), *Unemployment—A Problem of Industry* (London: Longmans, Green and Co.).

BOLDERSON, H. (1988), 'The Right to Appeal and the Social Fund', 15, *Journal of Law and Society*, 279–92.

Bonner, D., Hooker, I., Smith, P., and White, R. (1991), *Non-Means Tested Benefits; The Legislation* (London: Sweet & Maxwell).

Bradley, A. W. (1976), 'Reform of Supplementary Benefit Tribunals—the Key Issues', 27, *Northern Ireland Legal Quarterly*, 96–119.

—— (1985), 'Recent Reform of Social Security Adjudication in Great Britain', 26, *Les Cahiers de Droit*, 403–49.

Brown, L. N. (1982), 'Formality or Informality: A Case-Study of British National Insurance Local Tribunal Procedure and Practice', 23, *Les Cahiers de Droit*, 625–50.

Bull, D. (1981), 'Adjudicating Public Assistance Decisions: A British Perspective on Practice in an American State', 4, *Urban Law and Policy*, 1–53.

Burkeman, S. (1975), ' "We go by the Law here" ', 91–7 in (eds.) Adler, M., and Bradley, A. (1975).

Cavenagh, W. E., and Newton, D. (1970), 'The Membership of Two Administrative Tribunals', 48, *Public Administration* 449–68.

—— —— (1971), 'Administrative Tribunals: How People Become Members', 49, *Public Administration*, 197–218.

Chief Adjudication Officer (1990), *Annual Report of the Chief Adjudication Officer for 1988/89 on Adjudication Standards* (London: HMSO).

—— (1991), *Annual Report of the Chief Adjudication Officer for 1989/90 on Adjudication Standards* (London: HMSO).

Child Poverty Action Group (1985), *Burying Beveridge* (London: Child Poverty Action Group).

Christie, N. (1977), 'Conflicts as Property', 17, *British Journal of Criminology*, 1–15.

Civil Justice Review (1988), *Report of the Review Body on Civil Justice* (Cm 394) (London: HMSO).

Cole, G. F. (1979), *The American System of Criminal Justice* (Mass: Duxbury).

Coleman, R. J. (1971), *Supplementary benefits and the administrative review of administrative action* (London: Child Poverty Action Group).

Collins, L. (1990), *European Community Law in the United Kingdom* (London: Butterworths).

Cooper, S. (1985), *Observations in Supplementary Benefit Offices* (London: Policy Studies Institute).

Coughlin, R. M. (1988), 'Comment', in (eds.) Nash, G. D., Pugach, N. H., and Tomasson, R. F., *Social Security: The First Half Century* (Albuquerque: University of New Mexico Press).

Council on Tribunals (1983), *The Annual Report of the Council on Tribunals for 1982/83* (HC 129, Session 1983–4).

—— (1985), *The Annual Report of the Council on Tribunals for 1984/85* (HC 54, Session 1985–6).

—— (1988), *The Annual Report of the Council on Tribunals for 1986/87* (HC 234, Session 1987–8).

—— (1989), *The Annual Report of the Council on Tribunals for 1987/88* (HC 102, Session 1988–9).

CRANSTON, R. (1985), *Legal Foundations of the Welfare State* (London: Weidenfeld & Nicolson).

DAVIS, K. C. (1969), *Discretionary Justice; A Preliminary Inquiry* (Chicago: University of Illinois Press).

DEACON A., and BRADSHAW, J. (1983), *Reserved for the Poor: the Means Test in British Social Policy* (Oxford: Blackwell).

DEAN, H. (1991), *Social Security and Social Control* (London: Routledge).

DETMOLD, M. J. (1989), *Courts and Administrators: A Study in Jurisprudence* (London: Weidenfeld & Nicolson).

DHSS (1978), *Social Assistance: A Review of the Supplementary Benefits Scheme in Great Britain* (London: DHSS).

—— (1982), *Social Security Operational Strategy: A Framework for the Future* (London: DHSS).

—— (1985*a*), Green Paper, *Reform of Social Security*, Vols. 1–3 (Cmnd. 9517-19) (London: HMSO).

—— (1985*b*), White Paper, *Reform of Social Security: Programme for Action* (Cmnd. 9691) (London: HMSO).

—— (1987), *Appeals Handling in Local and Central Offices* (London: DHSS).

DICKENS, L., JONES, M., WEEKES, B., and HART, M. (1985), *Dismissed: A Study of Unfair Dismissal and the Industrial Tribunal System* (Oxford: Basil Blackwell).

DIGBY, A. (1989), *British Welfare Policy: Workhouse to Workfare* (London: Faber).

DILNOT, A. W., and WEBB, S. (1988), 'The 1988 Social Security Reforms', 9, *Fiscal Studies*, no. 3, 26–53.

DONZELOT, J. (1980), *The Policing of Families* (London: Hutchinson).

DRABBLE, R., and LYNES, T. (1989), 'The Social Fund—Discretion or Control?', *Public Law*, 297–322.

DSS (1990), *Disability Allowance: Assessment and Adjudication* (consultation paper) (London: DSS).

—— (1991), *Social Security Statistics 1990* (London: HMSO).

ELCOCK, H. J. (1969), *Administrative Justice* (London: Longmans).

FARRELLY, M. (1989), 'The Reasons why Appellants fail to attend their Social Security Appeal Tribunals', unpublished Ph.D. thesis (University of Birmingham).

FLOCKHART, R. (1975), 'Some Aspects of Tribunal Membership', 99–107 in ADLER, M., and BRADLEY A. (1975).

FRANKS (1957*a*), *Report of the Committee on Administrative Tribunals and Enquiries* (Cmd. 218) (London: HMSO).

—— (1957*b*), *Committee on Administrative Tribunals and Enquiries: Minutes of Evidence* (London: HMSO).

FROST, A., and HOWARD, C. (1977), *Representation and Administrative Tribunals* (London: Routledge & Kegan Paul).

FULBROOK, J. (1978), *Administrative Justice and the Unemployed* (London: Mansell).

—— (1989), 'HASSASSA and Judge Byrt—Five Years On' 18, *Industrial Law Journal*, 177–81.

GALANTER, M. (1974), 'Why the "Haves" Come Out Ahead: Speculations on the Limits of Legal Change', 9, *Law and Society Review*, 95–160.

GALLIGAN, D. J. (1986), *Discretionary Powers: A Legal Study of Official Discretion* (Oxford: Clarendon Press).

GANZ, G. (1974) *Administrative Procedures* (London: Sweet & Maxwell).

GENN, H., and GENN, Y. (1989), *The Effectiveness of Representation at Tribunals* (London: Lord Chancellor's Department).

GOODIN, R. (1986), 'Welfare, Rights and Discretion', 6, *Oxford Journal of Legal Studies*, 232–61.

GRIFFITH, J. A. (1959), 'Tribunals and Inquiries', 22, *Modern Law Review*, 125–45.

HARRIS, N. (1983), 'The Reform of the Supplementary Benefit Appeals System', *Journal of Social Welfare Law*, 212–27.

HAYEK, F. A. (1944), *The Road to Serfdom* (London: Routledge & Kegan Paul).

H.M. TREASURY (1991), *The Government's Expenditure Plans 1991–92 to 1993–94: Social Security* (Cm 1514) (London: HMSO).

HERMAN, M. (1972), *Administrative Justice and Supplementary Benefits: A Study of Supplementary Benefit Appeal Tribunals* (London: Bell).

HILL, M. (1969), 'The Exercise of Discretion in the National Assistance Board' 47, *Public Administration*, 75–90.

HOUSE OF COMMONS SOCIAL SERVICES COMMITTEE (1989), *Ninth Report—Social Security; Changes Implemented in April 1988* (HC 437-I, Session 1988-9).

HOUSE OF COMMONS COMMITTEE OF PUBLIC ACCOUNTS (1991), *Eighth Report—The Elderly: Information Requirements for Supporting the Elderly and the Implications of Personal Pensions for the National Insurance Fund* (HC 124, Session 1990-1).

HOWE, L. E. A. (1985), 'The "Deserving" and the "Undeserving": Practice in an Urban Local Social Security Office', 14, *Journal of Social Policy*, 49–72.

HOWELLS, G. G. (1990), 'Social Fund Budgeting Loans—Social and Civil Justice?', 9, *Civil Justice Quarterly*, 118–38.

JACKSON, M., STEWART, H., and BLAND, R. (1987), 'Tribunals Hearing Supplementary Benefit Appeals: the members' role' 15, *Policy and Politics*, 245–51.

JONES, C., and ADLER, M. (1990), *Can Anyone Get on These: A Study of the Systems of Appointment and Training of Justices of the Peace and Members of Social Security Appeal Tribunals and Children's Panels in Scotland* (Glasgow: Scottish Consumer Council).

JOWELL, J. L. (1975), *Law and Bureaucracy: Administrative Discretion and the Limits of Legal Action* (New York: Dunellen Publishing Co.).

KAY, D. (1984), *A Study of Access to Social Security Tribunals in Scotland* (Glasgow: Scottish Consumer Council).

LACH, G. (1950), 'Appeal Tribunals under the National Assistance Act, 1948', 36–66 in (ed.) POLLARD, R. S. W. *Administrative Tribunals at Work* (London: Stevens & Sons).

LESLIE, W. (1985), 'Legalism in Industrial Tribunals?', *Employment Gazette* (September), 357–62.

LEWIS, N. (1973), 'Supplementary Benefit Appeal Tribunals', *Public Law*, 257–84.

LISTER, R. (1974), *Justice for the Claimant* (London: Child Poverty Action Group).

—— (1975) 'SBATs—an urgent case for Reform', 171–82 in (eds.) ADLER, M., and BRADLEY, A. (1975).

—— (1989), 'Social Security', 104–29 in (ed.) McCARTHY, M., *The New Politics of Welfare—An Agenda for the 1990s* (Basingstoke: MacMillan).

LOGIE, J. G., and WATCHMAN, P. Q. (1989), 'Social Security Appeal Tribunals: An Excursus on Evidential Issues', 8, *Civil Justice Quarterly*, 109–28.

McBARNET, D. J. (1978), 'False Dichotomies in Criminal Justice Research', 23–34 in (eds.) BALDWIN, J., and BOTTOMLEY, A. K., *Criminal Justice: Selected Readings* (London: Martin Robertson).

McCONVILLE, M., and BALDWIN, J. (1981), *Courts, Prosecution, and Conviction* (Oxford: Clarendon Press).

McCORQUODALE, S. (1962), 'The Composition of Administrative Tribunals', *Public Law*, 298–326.

MACK, J., and LANSLEY, S. (1985), *Poor Britain* (London: Allen & Unwin).

MARSHALL, T. H. (1950), *Citizenship and Social Class* (Cambridge: Cambridge University Press).

MASHAW, J. L. (1983), *Bureaucratic Justice: Managing Social Security Disability Claims* (New Haven: Yale University Press).

MESHER, J. (1981), 'The 1980 Social Security Legislation: The Great Welfare State Chainsaw Massacre?', 8, *British Journal of Law and Society*, 119–27.

—— (1983), 'The Merging of Social Security Tribunals', 10, *Journal of Law and Society*, 135–42.

—— (1987), 'Social Security Law', 211–17 in (ed.) KIRALFY, A., *The Burden of Proof* (Abingdon: Professional Books).

—— (1990), 'The Legal Structure of the Social Fund', 35–57 in (ed.) FREEMAN, M. D. A., *Critical Issues in Welfare Law* (London: Stevens & Sons).

—— (1991), *CPAG's Income Support, The Social Fund and Family Credit: the Legislation* (London: Sweet & Maxwell).

MICKLETHWAIT, R. (1976), *The National Insurance Commissioners* (London: Stevens).

MILTON, C. (1975), 'Appellants' Perception of the Tribunal Process', 129–41 in (eds.) ADLER, M., and BRADLEY, A. (1975).

MISHRA, R. (1984), *The Welfare State in Crisis: Social Thought and Social Change* (Brighton: Wheatsheaf Books).

MORAN, M. (1988), 'Review Article: Crises of the Welfare State', 18, *British Journal of Political Science*, 397–414.

MULLEN, T. (1989), 'The Social Fund—Cash-Limiting Social Security', 52, *Modern Law Review*, 64–92.

NELKEN, D. (1983), *The Limits of the Legal Process: A Study of Landlords, Law and Crime* (London: Academic Press).

OFFICE OF THE PRESIDENT OF SOCIAL SECURITY APPEAL TRIBUNALS (1988), *Social Security Appeal Tribunals: A Guide to Procedure* (2nd edn.) (London: HMSO).

OGUS, A, I. (1987), 'Bureaucrats as Institutional Heroes', 17, *Oxford Journal of Legal Studies*, 309–15.

—— BARENDT, E. (1988), *The Law of Social Security* (3rd edn.) (London: Butterworths).

OTTON, G. (1984), 'Managing Social Security: Government as Big Business', XXXVII *International Social Security Review*, 158–70.

PARTINGTON, M. (1986), 'The Restructuring of Social Security Appeal Tribunals', 163–81 in (ed.) HARLOW, C., *Public Law and Politics* (London: Sweet & Maxwell).

—— (1991), *Secretary of State's Powers of Adjudication in Social Security Law* (SAUS Working Paper No. 96) University of Bristol: School of Advanced Urban Studies.

PRESTATAIRE (1978), 'The Insurance Officer', 75, *Law Society Gazette*, 909.

PROSSER, T. (1977), 'Poverty, Ideology and Legality: Supplementary Benefit Appeal Tribunals and their Predecessors', 4, *British Journal of Law and Society*, 39–60.

—— (1981), 'The Politics of Discretion: Aspects of Discretionary Powers in the Supplementary Benefits Scheme', 148–70 in (eds.) ADLER, M., and ASQUITH, S., *Discretion and Welfare* (London: Heinemann).

RAWLINGS, R. (1986), *The Complaints Industry: A Review of sociolegal research on aspects of administrative justice* (ESRC).

REICH, C. (1964), 'The New Property', 73, *Yale Law Journal*, 733–87.

—— (1965), 'Individual Rights and Social Welfare: The Emerging Legal Issues', 74, *Yale Law Journal*, 1245–57.

RINGEN, S. (1987), *The Possibility of Politics; A Study in the Political Economy of the Welfare State* (Oxford: Clarendon Press).

ROSE, H. (1975), 'Who can de-label the Claimant?', 143–54 in (eds.) ADLER, M., and BRADLEY, A. (1975).

ROYAL COMMISSION ON LEGAL SERVICES (1979), *Final Report* (Cmnd. 7648) (London: HMSO).

ROWLAND, M. (1991), *Rights Guide to Non-Means Tested Benefits* (London: Child Poverty Action Group).

SAINSBURY, R. (1988), 'Deciding Social Security Claims: A Study in the Administrative Theory and Practice of Social Security', unpublished Ph.D. thesis (University of Edinburgh).

—— (1989), 'The Social Security Chief Adjudication Officer: The First Four Years', *Public Law*, 323–41.

—— EARDLEY, T. (1991), *Housing Benefit Reviews* (DSS Research Report Series No. 3) (London: HMSO).

SAMPFORD, C. J. G., and GALLIGAN, D. J. (eds.) (1986), *Law, Rights and the Welfare State* (London: Croom Helm).

SANDERS, A. (1987), 'Constructing the Case for the Prosecution' 14, *Journal of Law and Society*, 229–53.

SILBURN, R. (1991), 'Beveridge and the wartime consensus', 25, *Social Policy and Administration*, 80–6.

SKOLER, D. L., and ZEITZER, I. R. (1982), 'Social Security Appeals Systems: A nine-nation review', 35, *International Social Security Review*, 57–77.

SKOLNICK, J. H. (1966), *Justice Without Trial: Law Enforcement in Democratic Society* (New York: John Wiley).

SMITH, R. (1988), 'CPAG's Vantage Point on Group Actions', 85 *Law Society Gazette*, 29–30.

SWADLING, W. J. (1988), 'Liability for Negligent Refusal of Unemployment Benefit', *Public Law*, 328–39.

TOWNSEND, P. (1979), *Poverty in the United Kingdom* (London: Allen Lane).

—— GORDON, D. (1989), 'Memorandum', 45–74 in House of Commons Social Services Committee, *Minimum Income: Memoranda laid before the Committee* (HC 579, Session 1988–9).

WALKER, C. (1986), 'Reforming Supplementary Benefit: The Impact on Claimants', 20, *Social Policy and Administration*, 91–102.

—— (1987), 'Reforming Social Security—Despite the Claimant', 101–9 in WALKER, A., and WALKER, C. (eds.) *The Growing Divide: A Social Audit, 1979–1987* (London: Child Poverty Action Group).

WIKELEY, N. J. (1985), 'The Membership of Social Security Appeal Tribunals', 10, *Holdsworth Law Review*, 117–24.

—— (1986a), 'The Relationship between the DHSS and the DE: A Question of Agency', 15, *Industrial Law Journal*, 60–4.

—— (1986b), 'Housing Benefit Review Boards: the New Slum?', 5, *Civil Justice Quarterly*, 18–25.

—— (1988), 'R v. Secretary of State for Social Services, ex parte Child Poverty Action Group and Others', *Journal of Social Welfare Law*, 269–74.

—— (1989), 'Unemployment Benefit, the State and the Labour Market', 16, *Journal of Law and Society*, 291–309.

—— (1991), 'Reviewing Social Fund Decisions', 10, *Civil Justice Quarterly*, 15–20.

WILSON, E. (1977), *Women and the Welfare State* (London: Tavistock).

WRAITH, R. E., and HUTCHESSON, P. G. (1973), *Administrative Tribunals* (London: George Allen & Unwin).

YOUNG, R. (1990), 'The Effectiveness of Representation at Tribunals', 9, *Civil Justice Quarterly*, 16–23.

ZANDER, M. (1988), *Cases and Materials on the English Legal System* (London: Weidenfeld & Nicolson).

Index of Names

Index of Subjects